James Brooks

**A Seven Months' Run, Up, and Down, and Around the World**

Vol. 1

James Brooks

**A Seven Months' Run, Up, and Down, and Around the World**
*Vol. 1*

ISBN/EAN: 9783337427719

Printed in Europe, USA, Canada, Australia, Japan

Cover: Foto ©Andreas Hilbeck / pixelio.de

More available books at **www.hansebooks.com**

# [illegible] RUN,

[illegible] D I[illegible] AROUND
TH[illegible]

JAMES BR[illegible]

*[illegible]RITTEN IN LETTERS TO THE N. Y. EVENING EX[illegible]*

NEW YORK:
D. APPLETON & COMPANY,
549 & 551 BROADWAY.
1872.

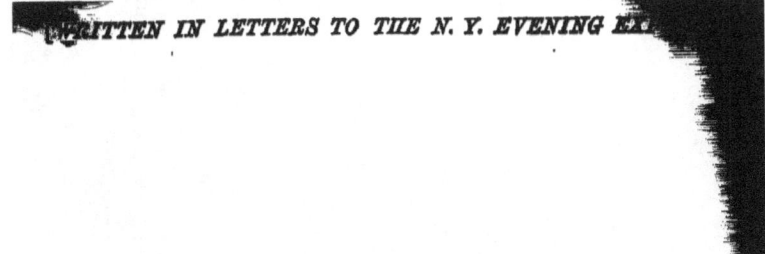

ENTERED, according to Act of Congress, in the year 1872, by
D. APPLETON & CO.,
In the Office of the Librarian of Congress, at Washington.

# TO THE PUBLIC.

When I left home, late in May, 1871, after an extraordinary session of Congress, it was for the sake of health, to free body and mind from work and excitement of all sorts, such as I had broken down under, in the hot, unhealthy air, and unnatural light of the House of Representatives and its Committee rooms. Then, it never entered my head "to scribble" (for that is the only proper word) the notes which are here embodied in a book, not altogether with my approbation, though of course, with my consent. A life-long habit of work compelled me to work (I could not help it), and hence, in disobedience of the orders of my physician, I took to scribbling, always in pencil, these notes or letters, which others would have kept in their trunks, but which I sent home, rude and rough, "and good enough for a newspaper," perhaps, which lives but a day, but not good enough for a book, especially for a book of travels.

All of them save one were in pencil on Japanese mulberry-paper, often pencilled on my hat, sometimes, on my knees, and oftener yet on decks, or, in the cabins of steamers, roughly rolling and jerking, and then quickly mailed without being read—from Yokohama and Yedo, in Japan, to Pekin and Canton, in China, or, from Sumatra or Ceylon, or, from India to Madras in the south, to Calcutta and Allahabad in the north, and Bombay in the west. These notes, thus scribbled and thus mailed, have no literary merit, of course—are not intended to have any, and if they are good for any thing, it is because they were pencilled and mailed "on the spot" fresh and photographic, thereby. To revise them now, I have neither time nor inclination, not even time carefully to read them, until I see them in book-proof, where, when irrevocable, I cannot, if dissatisfied, remould them, and thus extract for the sake of style whatever life or vitality there may be in the notes.

Japan, since July, when I was there, has "progressed" so rapidly, that, the then, great, mighty, sacred, and invisible Mikado has become as visible as any European monarch; and the one- or two-sworded retainers of the Daimios are putting off their swords as well as their costumes (pity for that), and becoming American- and European-ized so rapidly, that, in some respects, my notes, not a year old now, will soon become almost as antiquated as Sir Richard Alcock's book, published not ten years since, the very reading of which half affrighted me, when first thinking of entering Japan.

China, unchanged and unchangeable from the days of Marco Polo, will probably remain thus, until Americans or Englishmen tempt the Mandarins, by fat contracts, to build railroads and telegraphs, and thus to defy the "Fung-Shuey."

The American tourists, who have long been running over Europe and parts of Africa, will find in these notes, if not a guide-book, the outlines for one, and they will see, that they can now run over Japan, China, and India, as well as Egypt and parts of Italy, in less than a year.

To tempt my countrymen of the new World, with their wives and daughters, even to visit this very old world of the East, and thus to invite them to new fields of instruction and reflection, I have, not without reluctance, consented to this unprepared publication.

J. B.

WASHINGTON, D. C., *April* 12, 1872.

# CONTENTS.

### LETTER I.
#### ON, TO, AND OVER THE PACIFIC.

The Start from New York to go round the World.—Thinking out loud on Paper.—No fine Writing, Scribbling only.—Car Life on the Prairies and Rocky Mountains, but no Rocky Mountains.—The Way the Engineer dodges them.—The Holy Land of Mormondom, . . . . . . . . . . . 1

### LETTER II.
#### ON, TO, AND OVER THE PACIFIC.

The Mormon Holy Land.—Geographically like the Holy Land over the Sea.—How Irrigation has made the Desert a Garden.—The Apostles and Elders of Mormondom.—The Holy Temple.—Brigham Young in the Temple.—The Women and the Fashions in Salt Lake City.—Beelzebub stirring up Rebellion.—The Grasshoppers and the Gulls, . . . . . . . . . . . 10

### LETTER III.
#### ON AND FROM THE PACIFIC.

Around the World only a "Trip."—Snow on the Mountains and Alkali Plains.—Forty Miles of Snow-sheds.—Sudden Descent from Ice and Snow to Apricots and Strawberries.—Sacramento.—New Railroad and Steamboat Routes, . . . 18

### LETTER IV.
#### ON THE PACIFIC.

From the Golden Gate to Yokohama.—The "Japan," and the motley Crowd on board.—Is, or is not, the Pacific Ocean a Humbug?—The Amusements on board.—The Police of the Ship.—Spoke a Boston Ship.—Meeting a Steamer in Mid-ocean, exchanging Mails, etc., . . . . . . . . . 24

### LETTER V.
#### ON THE PACIFIC.

Life and Thoughts on Ship-board.—The Day Lost in *Rounding* the World.—"Down East" is out West.—A Puzzled Traveller.—Summer Life on this Ocean.—The Second Exchange of Letters—The Sixteenth Amendment.—Curious Congregation of Passengers, . . . . . . . . . 31

## CONTENTS.

### LETTER VI.

*FIRST IMPRESSIONS IN JAPAN.*

Arrival in Japan.—First Impressions on the Coast.—The Fishermen in "Georgia Costume."—Everything New, Everything Odd.—Bamboo Baskets for Hats.—Straw Overcoats.—Landing on the Hatoba.—The Cues of the Japanese.—The Brawny Coolies.—Travelling Restaurants.—Strange Street Spectacles.—The Tattooed Men.—The Horse Boy (Betto).—Hair Dressing.—Shocking Black Teeth of the Married Women, . . . . . . . . . . . 40

### LETTER VII.

*THE CITY OF YEDO.*

The First Day in Yedo.—The Ride on the "Tocaido."—Strange Sights there.—The Pretty Tea Girls.—The Tiny Tea Cups.—Rooms with Paper Partitions.—The Beggars.—The Gin-rick-a Sha.—Ride in State along the "Tocaido."—Hogs in Baskets.—No Tycoon, only a "Mikado."—How we Stare and how they Stare at us.—Great Fire in Yedo, . . . . . . . . . . . 52

### LETTER VIII.

*LIFE AND SIGHTS IN YEDO.*

Sintoo and Buddhist Temples.—The Priests.—The Sacred Cream-Colored Horses.—Theatres in the Temples.—The Opera in Yedo.—Funny Ride thereto in Gin-rick-a Shas, . . . . . . . . . . . 64

### LETTER IX.

*LIFE AND SIGHTS IN YEDO.*

Eyes only Useful Here.—Tongue and Ears Useless.—Shopping in Yedo.—Hotels in Japan.—Grand Hotel in Yedo.—Breakfast with the Ministry of Foreign Affairs at Hamagoten.—Dinner at a Beautiful Country-Seat.—Discussions, Political and Theological.—Why the Japanese don't like Christians.—The Schools of Japan.—Reading, Writing, and Arithmetic almost Universal, . . . . . 75

### LETTER X.

*TRAVELLER'S LIFE IN THE INTERIOR.*

The Great God of Kamakura.—"Statue of Dai-bootz."—Life in Japanese Tea-Houses.—Ride in a Cango Bamboo Basket.—The Temples around Kamakura.—Beautiful Scenery.—Fields cultivated like Gardens.—The Life and Rank of Japanese Farmers.—Visit to the Cave of Inosima.—Fish Life and Fish Dinners.—The "Mikado" and the "Tocaido."—Politeness and Amiability of the Japanese Farmers, . . . . . . . . . . . 87

### LETTER XI.

*RETURN TO YEDO.*

In Yedo a Second Time.—Now under a British Escort.—The English Dragoons and Japanese Yakonins.—The British Student Interpreters.—Only a Hundred Caucasians among a Million of Japs.—Paper Windows.—Uneasy Sleeping.—Two-Sworded Loafers.—A Thousand British Troops in Yokohama.—Cheap Shopping in Yedo.—Fashionable Riding, . . . . . . . . 98

## LETTER XII.

### *THINGS IN JAPAN.*

Women among the Japanese.—Their Position and Condition.—Promiscuous Bathing-houses.—The Theatre.—Ticketing Straw Shoes therein.—Jap Stump Orators.—Bamboo in Japan.—Japanese Art.—Shopping in "Curio" Street.—Can spend any Amount of Money.—The Steel of Japan.—The Government of Japan a Feudality.—Railroads, Telegraph, and Mint in Japan, . . . 104

## LETTER XIII.

### *ON THE JAPAN SEAS.*

Adieu to Yokohama.—The Foreigners and their Life there.—The All Sorts of Clothes of the East.—The Japanese Passengers on board the Costa Rica.—A Japanese Prince and his Retinue on board.—A Typhoon dodged.—Frightful Loss of Life and Property.— An Earthquake felt.— Curiosity satisfied.— Motley Cargo of the Costa Rica.—Butcher's Meat called Fowl, . . . . . . . 112

## LETTER XIV.

### *ON THE INLAND SEA OF JAPAN.*

The Beautiful Inland Sea of Japan.—Luxurious Travelling.—Prince Hizen.—Vampire Cat.—Bay of Nagasaki.—The Oldest European Settlement.—The Roman Catholic Priests.—Pappenburg Island.—Thousands of Christians thrown from the Precipice.—The Faith of Roman Catholic Missionaries.—Street Scenes in Nagasaki.—Needle Making.—Porcelain Painting.—Begging Buddhist Priest.—Street Actors.—Japanese Confectionery.—Japanese Woman's Toilet-Box.—Receipt for Blacking the Teeth.—Final Leave of Japan, . . . . . 120

## LETTER XV.

### *ON, AND OVER TO CHINA.*

On the Yellow Sea, bound to Shanghai.—The Great Yang-tze and its Yellow Water.—Up the Whang-poo.—Reflections on entering the Great Gates of China.—Thermometer in Shanghai.—Hot, Hotter, Hottest.—Air wanted, a Puff or a Typhoon.—Things In and About Shanghai.—The Summer Costume.—Innumerable Mounds or Graves in the Cotton-Fields.—American Flag in the Yang-tze.—We are taking the Coasting Trade of China, etc., . . . . . 129

## LETTER XVI.

### *THE HEALTH OF CHINA.*

Where's Chefoo?—A Watering-Place in China.—Amusements There.—The American and Other Fleets.—The Noisy Salutations of the Fleets.—Church Service on the Colorado.—The Corean Expedition.—The Race of the Rival American Barges.—Rain here.—Breakfast by the Russian Admiral.—The English (Universal) Language.—Entertainments given us by the Russians.—Affinity of Russians and Americans.—Admiral Rodgers's State Breakfast.—Divine Service on board the Russian Flag-Ship.—A Busy Week.—The Novel Assemblage at Chefoo about to disperse, . . . . . . . . . . . 140

## CONTENTS.

### LETTER XVII.

#### ON THE PEIHO RIVER.

Tremendous Flood on the River of Peiho.—Whole Villages washed away.—The People drowned out.—Widespread Desolation.—Living on the River on a Yankee Steamer.—The Grand Canal broken loose.—The Crooked Peiho River.—The Way we wound up the River.—The Year-ago Massacre of Europeans and Catholics in Tien-tsin.—The then Fright of all Missionaries.—Scare about going there.— Guns and Gunboats Commercial and Christian Guarantees.—An Exploration of the Old Under-water Tien-tsin, in a British Launch.—Innumerable Junks.—The Ruins of the Roman Catholic Cathedral.—The Tombs of the slain Sisters.—Terrors predicted for Tourists to Pekin.—Nevertheless, On, On to Pekin, . 149

### LETTER XVIII.

#### ON, TO PEKIN.

Arrival at Tung-Chow.—Lodged in a Temple.—Ice in Abundance now.—On to Pekin that Night.—The Gates of Pekin at Sunset.—The Infernal Road to the Celestial City, in a Mule Cart.—Bump, Thump.—No Getting Out, no Living In.—The Sights on the Tung-Chow and Pekin Road.—The Wheelbarrow Gentry.—Caravans.—First Sight of the Bactrian Camel.—The Great Walls of the City after Sunset.—What John Chinaman thinks of an American-dressed Woman entering his Capital in an Open Sedan-chair.—Difference of Opinion as to Pekin and New York Fashions.—Happy Welcome in the Russian Legation.—A Cossack Porter opens the Great Gates, . . . . . 157

### LETTER XIX.

#### THE JOURNEY TO PEKIN.

How he got to Pekin in a Springless Cart, over a Granite-Paved Imperial Road, Thirteen Miles long when first made, and passable, now thirty, or more, from the Holes in it, and the Crooks to dodge those Holes.—Bones all aching from Pounding, but Bone-Pounding Good Medicine at Times.—The Fit-Out for the River Peiho Journey in Sampans.—Hospitality of the Tien-tsiners.—Bad Water. —Must Liquor or Tea.—Dead Chinamen by millions, and Graves everywhere bad for Wells.—Catalogue of a Peiho Boat Outfit.—The Terrors of the Route all exaggerated.—The High Water a Help.—Cut across Lots.—The Supplies *en route*.—Beggars.—A not Disagreeable Journey.—All Sleeping Unprotected.— No Real Perils.—Coolie Comforts.—Sights on the River.—British Manufactures. —The Cock keeps Time for the Coolie in the Morning.—Life in a Junk.—Toilettes there.—The Countless Babies here, . . . . . . 164

### LETTER XX.

#### FROM PEKIN.

The Guide-Books of Pekin.—The "Ji-hia-kieu-wen-kau" and the "Chen-yuen-chi-lio."—Three Cities within Pekin, the Manchu or Tartar, Chinese, and Imperial.— Shopping in Pekin.—Great Fur Market.—Mongolia, Manchuria, Corea, and Siberia Sables, Ermine, etc., etc.—Precious Stones.—Jade.—Greek Chapel on the Grounds of the Russian Legation.—Life among Chinese Russians.— Catholic and Protestant Missionaries in Pekin.—Visit to the Roman Catholic Cathedral.— French Priests and Sisters of Charity.—School for Chinese Children.—Money and the Missionaries.—Conflicts between them. — Foreign and Anti-Foreign Party in China.—Chinese Efforts to create Prejudice against Christians, . 173

## CONTENTS.

### LETTER XXI.
#### *FROM PEKIN.*

Paradise in-doors, Tartarus out.—Pekin Holes, Mud, Dust, Dirt.—No Noses in Pekin.—Sights and Smells.—Wealthy Chinese.—Sumptuary Laws in China.—Sedan-chairs.—Marriages and Funerals.—Women of no Account.—Polygamy.—Women's Fashions in Pekin.—Dr. Williams, the Secretary, Bibliophilist, and Encyclopædist.—The Chinese retrograding.—Confucianism losing its Influence.—Christianity.—Roman Catholics, when starting here, teaching the Material as well as the Spiritual.—Conflict of Christ and Confucius.—The Chinese Classics, . . . . . . . . . . . 182

### LETTER XXII.
#### *THE TEMPLES IN PEKIN.*

The Temples in China.—Confucius and the Lama.—The Lessons of Confucius.—His Influence in the Government of the Chinese.—The Sages of China.—Tablets to the Disciples of Confucius.—The Competitive Students.—The Despotism and Democracy of China.—The Diagrams.—The Yang and the Yin.—Intelligence of the Chinese.—The Lama Buddhist Temple.—Mongolian Priests.—Contrast of the Lama and Confucius Temples.—A Chinese Mandarin's House.—Yang was his Name.—Sensation in the Streets.—The Interior of the Mandarin's House.—The Wife and Handmaids.—Description of the Wife's Dress.—Refreshments.—Walks on the Roof of the House, . . . . . . . 190

### LETTER XXIII.
#### *THE GOVERNMENT OF CHINA.*

The Great Wall of China.—The Overland Route to St. Petersburg.—Turned back by a Mohammedan *Émeute.*—Now too late or too early in the Season.—Can telegraph from here to New York in twelve or sixteen Days.—The Government of China.—Confucius a sort of Ben Franklin or Thomas Jefferson.—No Hereditary Aristocracy.—Public Sentiment governs here as in Great Britain and the United States.—Railroads and Telegraphs resisted by Superstitions, to be overcome.—China making Great Preparations for War.—Casting Cannon, etc.—China retrograding.—Corruption the Cause.—Mandarin Titles bought and sold.—The Literati Mandarins now dishonest.—The Boy Emperor, fifteen Years of Age.—His Future not promising.—The Dowager hunting a Wife for him.—The Pekin *Gazette,* . . . . . . . . 199

### LETTER XXIV.
#### *FROM THE GREAT WALL OF CHINA.*

On Top of the Great Wall of China.—Droves of Sheep, Hogs, Ponies, Donkeys.—Mongolians and Manchus.—Speech-making on Top of the Great Wall.—Speech of J. B. to the Great Wall.—Tartars, a Species of Yankees, leaping over all Walls.—Outfit for the Trip from Pekin to the Great Wall.—Brick Tea.—Sheep's-tail Soup.—Eggs in Abundance.—Mule Litters.—Description of the Craft.—The Muleteers.—Mingling Mire, Mud, and Dust.—Sounding for the Bottom of the Bogs.—Dodging into Farms and Gardens.—Roads in China are Ditches.—The Pass of Nan-Kow.—First Night's Experience in a Mongolian Inn.—A Brick Oven to sleep on.—Journey to the Wall over a Rough and Terrible Road.—A Series of Walls.—A Lunch amid Ruins of the Wall.—The Comfort of a Cup of Cold Water, . . . . . . . . . . . 208

## CONTENTS.

### LETTER XXV,
#### RETURN TO PEKIN.

The Ming Tombs.—The Grand Approach to them.—All going to ruin.—The Summer Palace of the Emperors.—"Yueng-Ming-Yuen-Ching," the man-of-all-work.—Letters of Credit no Service in Pekin.—No Coin or Currency in China.—Sycee.—The North of China.—The Emperor gives Audience at 5 A. M.—The Marble Bridge and the Lotus.—The Temple of Heaven.—The Temple of Earth.—The Sacrifices in these Temples by the Emperor, . . . . . . . . . 220

### LETTER XXVI.
#### RETURNING SOUTHWARD.

A Traveller retracing his Steps.—Tung Chow, on the Peiho River.—The Wheelbarrow Traffic.—Death to the Coolies.— Processions *en route*.—Of Funerals and Weddings.—A Good Story told of Gov. Seward.—Mistaking a Funeral Procession for an Ovation to Himself.—Expense of Travelling as a Grandee.—A Temple for a Hotel.—Running the Gauntlet of the Junks to Tien-tsin.—The Noisy Monosyllables of the Chinese.—Huge Pyramids of Salt.—Home, Sweet Home.—The Szechuen.—Under a Yankee Captain from Maine.— The Grapes of the Peiho.—The Rolling Screw Steamers of the Yellow Sea.—Rivalry of British and American Steamers.—Chinese Customs collected by Foreigners.—The American Flag driven off.—Manufactures driven off, . . . . . . . . 236

### LETTER XXVII.
#### THINGS IN SHANGHAI.

Shanghai.—Its Enterprises and Surroundings.—The Hot Sun of Shanghai.—Turning White Men Yellow.—The City Government of Shanghai.—Eastern Hours for Breakfast and Dinner.—The Great Commerce of Shanghai.—Much of it passing into Chinese Hands.—Tea Trade.—Tea-Tasters.—Telegraphs to, and from Shanghai.—Tea Steamers up the Yang-tze.—Foreign Schemes to dodge the Fung Shuey.—Hostility to Electricity.—The Telegraphs from Shanghai *via* Nagasaki and Vladivastock, in Russia, . . . . . . . . . . 247

### LETTER XXVIII.
#### FROM THE ENGLISH COLONY OF HONG KONG.

How Screw-Steamers roll.—Cabins, Hot, Hotter, Hottest.—Chow Chow excellent.—Sleep in a Stew Prison.—The Great English (P. & O.) and French Lines of Steamers in the East.—Hong Kong.—Typhoons here.—The City the Refuge of the Refuse Chinese.—Curious Intermixture of Population.—The Coolie Emigration here.—The Dialects of China.—Pidgen English.—Chinese Kitchens and Cooks, etc., etc., . . . . . . . . . . . 255

### LETTER XXIX.
#### THINGS IN CANTON.

What Canton is.—Its People, Streets, Sewers, etc., etc.—The Temples of Canton.—Sacred Hogs, Confucius and the Stalls.—Caging Students ambitious to be Mandarins.—Do Chinamen eat Cats, Dogs, and Rats?—The Manufactories of Canton.—The Silk Gauzes.—An Improvised Breakfast on a Pagoda.—No Beasts of Burthen in the City.—All Coolie Work.—A Sabbath in Canton.—Boat Life there.—Ducks and their Owners.—Gates and Police.—No Going Out Nights.—No Courting.—No Clubs, . . . . . . . . . . 265

### LETTER XXX.

#### THOUGHTS ON THE CHINA SEAS.

The Imitative Powers of the Chinese.—Their Love of Money.—Population of China over-estimated.—Pisciculture in Canton.—Chinese Dialects.—War Talk.—Superstitions of the Ignorant.—Singapore.—The Malay Divers.—Foreign Commerce.—The Census.—The Jungle.—Agriculture, etc., etc., . . . . 276

### LETTER XXXI.

#### FROM CEYLON AND THE BAY OF BENGAL.

England, Continuous England.—The Steamer Congregation in Ceylon.—A Grand Oriental Hotel.—Buddhism born here.—Sapphires, Rubies, and Pearls.—The Cingalese great Cheats.—A Monkey Story.—Curious Boats and Boatmen in Galle.—Men here mistaken for Women, and *vice versa*.—Madras, and Things there.—The Latin Races here crowded off by the Anglo-Saxon.—Englishmen here patronize the Shastra and the Veda, as well as the Bible.—Their Race kept distinct.—A Handful of Englishmen governing a World.—Juggling in Madras.—Golconda and Juggernaut.—Cyclones and the Church at Sea.—Hymns, etc. . . . 283

### LETTER XXXII.

#### BRITISH INDIA.

England Forever and Ever—200,000,000 British Subjects—Standing Army of 320,000 Soldiers.—Vast Imports and Exports.—East Indians.—Monkeys or Men.—Trade and Commerce of India.—The Holy Ganges.—English Water-Works on it.—Calcutta no longer the "Black Hole"—Hot, not Unhealthy.—The Punkah Fan the Great Institution of India.—The Punkah Everywhere.—Tudor and His Ice the Great Things of the East.—The Hancocks, the Websters, Nothing.—The Tudor Every Thing.—Wenham Something.—Boston Nothing.—The Hoogley River and the Cyclones.—Enchanting Approach to Calcutta.—The King of Oude.—A Seventeen Days' Hindoo Holiday in Calcutta.—Polygamy and Polyandry.—Hindooism, Buddhism, Brahminism and Mohammedanism.—The 320,-000 Standing Army Government of India not a Bad One, . . . . 292

### LETTER XXXIII.

#### THINGS AND THOUGHTS IN CALCUTTA.

The Impudent Crows of Calcutta.—How they chatter.—A Drove of Elephants embarking for War.—The "Central Park" and "Hyde Park" of Calcutta.—Funny Liveries.—The Trade of the Metropolis of India.—Exports, Cutch, Coir, Jute, Indigo, and so on.—The Cocoa-nut Tree.—American Trade.—Assam Tea.—The Opium Trade, a Government Monopoly.—The Flocks of Servants in Calcutta.—No Women Servants.—All Men.—Men as Washerwomen.—The Woman invisible.—English Women going to India.—The Chit and the Coolie.—The Ladies' Chit.—Charming Social Life in Calcutta, . . . . . . . . 303

## LETTER XXXIV.

### THE RUN ACROSS INDIA.

Things in India.—Rail from Calcutta to Bombay.—The Raging Sun of India.—The Parsees of Bombay.—Fire Worshippers.—Sunday Evening's Work in Calcutta.—India Railroad Cars.—How they are cooled, and how they are converting the Pagans.—The Telegraphs of India.—Journalism in India.—Coal in India.—The Way Coolies work.—Indian Muslins and Cashmere Shawls.—The Plains of the Ganges.—The Pagan Temples of India.—Hindoos more intelligent than Mohammedans.—Allahabad.—Jubbalpore.—The Passage of the Ghauts.—Entrance into Bombay, . . . . . . . . . 314

## LETTER XXXV.

### SIGHTS IN AND ABOUT BOMBAY.

Bombay.—What it is as a City.—Calcutta the Court; Bombay the Mart.—New Influences of the Suez Canal.—The Treasures of India here.—Cashmere Shawls.—The Bombay Fashionables on a Drive.—The Parsees.—The way they don't bury their Dead.—India Gods.—Where manufactured.—The Temples of India.—The Wonderful "Elephanta."—Dining Out in the East.—The Route to Persia and Aden.—The Census and Exports of Bombay.—Extent of Railroads in India.—Sound Banks and a good Currency, . . . . . . . 329

## LETTER XXXVI.

### ON THE ARABIAN AND RED SEAS.

Lascars, Africans, Chinese, Portuguese, and Englishmen, managing a Steamer.—The Infernal Sun of India.—The Reservoir of Surplus Englishmen.—How India exhausts European Life.—The British Soldier's Luxurious Life in Peace.—The Native Troops of India.—The Grip of England upon India.—Effect of Christianity upon Hindoos and Mohammedans.—The Hindoo Pantheon and 333,000,000 Gods.—The Brahmin Castes.—Bankers below Barbers.—Arabs and their Ocean Craft.—Railroad from London to Bombay.—Time, Five Days.—England encore, toujours, forever and ever.—The Red-Hot Red Sea.—This Unfinished Part of the Earth.—Aden the Fag End of Creation. — The Divers of Aden.— Strings of Camels Led by their Noses.—The Proper Time to Travel in the East.—Fares and Distances, . . . . . . . . . . . 340

## LETTER XXXVII.

### SUDDEN FLIGHT FROM ASIA AND AFRICA INTO EUROPE.

Among the Alps.—The Isthmus of Suez.—Suez Canal.—Will it pay?—Egypt and Alexandria.—Confederate Officers in the Pasha's Army.—Horrid (English) Railroad Cars.—Boreas and the Egyptian Sands.—Across the Mediterranean to Brindisi.—Things in Brindisi and Turin.—How cold it is.—Mt. Cenis and the Great Tunnel.—Glorious Scenery, . . . . . . . . 353

## LETTER XXXVIII.

### THINGS IN PARIS AND LONDON.

Things in Paris and in London.—Shopping in both Cities.—Paris sad just now.—An American almost Home in England.—Liverpool.—Rough Rocking on the Atlantic.—Put into Newfoundland for Coal.—St. John's.—Fishermen there.—Home again, Sweet Home, etc., . . . . . . . . 361

HOME FROM A FOREIGN SHORE, . . . . . . . . 371

# A SEVEN MONTHS' RUN,

## UP, AND DOWN, AND AROUND THE WORLD.

---

### LETTER I.

#### ON, TO, AND OVER THE PACIFIC.

The Start from New York to go round the World.—Thinking out loud on Paper.—No fine Writing, Scribbling only.—Car Life on the Prairies and Rocky Mountains, but no Rocky Mountains.—The Way the Engineer dodges them.—The Holy Land of Mormondom.

SALT LAKE CITY, *May* 26, 1871.

FIVE days' start from New York, only; left there Sunday night, May 21st (after Sunday was over), here, in the "Holy City," Friday, 7 P. M., trunks all right, ticketed from New York, with but one sight of them, no trouble, no fatigue, plenty of sleep, good enough living—the Tabernacle in view, and the Saints all about. The "Rail" could not do all this, not even the "Pacific" Rail; but the blessed invention of the sleeping-car rocks one so gently at night, and puts one so gently to sleep, that one is a little fresher, as the morning sun peeps through the windows, than if one slept at home, without the cradling and the motion.

I am ordered off by a doctor for a "trip," a trip only, *somewhere*, but where, there are no Congresses, no newspapers, no telegraphs, no rails, and I am going to obey, reserving the privilege only of thinking out loud on paper to you—nay, permitted to do nothing else—and I am going to obey that doctor, but just *how*, or just *where*, I can't see, though I am going over the Pacific into Asia to see. I should die, after my busy life, with nothing to do; but *this*—if your readers will expect nothing else save scribbling—pencil scratching, no fine writing, nothing but a traveller's thoughts out loud, will busy me, kill off idle hours, and, perhaps, amuse you.

Well, when one starts on a journey over, or "around the world," one naturally enough begins to count the first few miles in the twenty-four or twenty-five thousand (more or less, that depending upon deviations to come). The start from New York to Newark was the first count, seven great miles, which left some twenty-four thousand nine hundred and ninety-three to come. This species of arithmetic, however, soon tires one, and the blessed sleeping-car comes to relieve. I waked up among the mountains of Pennsylvania, in the winding gorges of the Alleghanies, near Altoona, where the Chinese gongs sound a terrible rattle for breakfast, and where scenery, as beautiful as cit should see, gladdens his eye, warms his heart, and makes him feel there is something on earth—even if it be Pennsylvania coal and coal-smoke—now and then, more cheering than miles of New York brown-stone or brick and mortar. We flew (a locomotive fly) over the crest of the Alleghanies, by such pretty mountain watering-places as

Cresson; and at 10.30 A. M. we were in that great inland workshop, Pittsburg, which all of us contribute more or less to build up in the taxes we universally pay. As a stream of freight cars met us, labelled "From Valparaiso to Batavia," I could not but think at first what a long journey that train is on, from South America to the East Indies, over sea; but when I reflected what hard work it is in this new country to find new names for its ever-springing-up cities and towns, the journey did not seem so long.

There was a dear little woman with us, and she had a dear little baby, and these dear little things were going somewhere West, to meet some dear big husband, who had rolled up dollars enough to roll them out from their Eastern home, but not dollars enough to spare to tempt him to go out and escort them on. The dear little woman *must* have air, and *would* have air, and, this being her first great journey, would look out of open windows. The consequence was, despite the ingenious inventions of the compartment-car, its upper windows, its ventilators, etc., etc., the dear little woman would, and did, cover us all over with dust and cinders. This led me to the reflection, that the car inventors, who are daily inventing all sorts of new things to cheat journeying out of its hardships, and to make it as pleasant as home, should invent a special compartment cage, to cage up dear little women, fresh and green in this journey of life, where they would be themselves all covered up with dirt and cinders, and catch great colds for themselves and their babies, to kill them, perhaps, soon after they reach their husbands.

But if I go on thus "thinking out loud," I shall never get to this, the Holy City, this Mecca, this Jerusalem. The 23d (evening) we crossed the Mississippi, at Davenport (Iowa), where great works and great doings of all kinds are going on. Think of an opera-house there, and big breweries, and two bridges here over the stern Father of Waters. The 24th (morning) we crossed the Missouri, rising and roaring now, and looking like mush. The classic Greeks called such yellow rivers "golden" (*vide*, the golden Pactolus); but "mush" is the proper Yankee word for this yellow, turbid, wild, mud-mixed torrent. The big piers of the Union Pacific Railroad bridge, sixty or eighty feet under water, to rock bottom, are fast going down, and the same car that takes us from Chicago over the broad prairies of Illinois and Iowa, can take us over a bridge, on to the Rocky Mountains of Wyoming and Utah.

We are crossing the prairies of Nebraska, and ascending the eastern slopes of the Rocky Mountains —in a compartment, with an organ in the centre, from which the musically inclined are grinding out their melodies—in native "Old Hundred" or "Bridgewater" notes, while a Frenchman, an artist, of course, bound on to San Francisco, rolls out his *fol-de-rols* in thunder squalls, that astound the Pawnee squaws, and scare up the prairie dogs and antelopes. Everybody that has not seen an Indian, pants to see one, and the first Pawnee that turns up receives many a mite—more especially the squaw and the papoose slung on her back, from all the romantically inclined young women. The classic barbarians here, contemptuously call the Indian, "Lo," from Pope's "Lo, the poor Indian, whose untutored mind sees God in clouds, and hears Him in the wind," while all the Eastern Popes think of him only as Cooper has painted him, and sympathize with him and his sufferings. Everybody, too, pants to see a prairie dog—miserable little squirrel-like wretches, that live in towns (in towns of holes), and pop up as the cars are coming, and pop down as the cars come,—or, an antelope (we are expecting, in vain, though, to breakfast and dine upon one) or deer, which we often see scampering in fright over the rocky hills and through the sage brush. We gather some prairie flowers; we buy more. All are very pretty; and thus car life and prairie life are charming to such as have not had too much of it.

Car life like ours is a new life, existing only in this country. The sleeping-car with beds and bed-clothes is known in no other land, and hence I will tarry by the wayside to think out loud about it. There were seventeen ladies and twenty-seven children in the car that preceded us yesterday, "the steward's" (that's the new name, I think, for the dark-colored young gentleman that "helps" in this craft, and makes up, and makes down, the beds)— but in this car of ours we have only seven little ones, not with mothers to match, though, for one mother owns five of the seven. The dark-colored young gentleman, when we order, drops down the upper beds, and pulls out the lower beds, and we tumble in behind the curtains, and strip off our gear as quickly as possible. Some go to bed at 8, and others at 12 P. M., and thus the eight-hour people can be regaled for hours by the stories, the adventures, the secrets, of the twelve-hour people, who have four mortal hours to tell all they know. Then, when the train stops to coal, or to water, we hear the gentle outgoing of some near neighbor's fairy breath, or the deep, sonorous snore of some hard sleeper, whom some nightmare is harassing. The hours of rising are not so irregular as the hours of retiring; for a sort of necessity compels everybody "to get up" at once, about six or seven. Then come scenes no mere scribling pencil of mine can exploit, only the light rays of the photographer. From some top-bed-chambers, hang out long tresses of hair; from others, projecting articles of dress; from others, the dangling, pantalooned legs of men—while all, to do all justice, laugh at the miseries and mysteries of the toilette, and make the most and the best of the universal huddle. We wash, as we best can; and when the gong rattles for breakfast, the most of us rush out, to give the dark-colored young master of the craft his opportunity to clean up, and clear off, the ruins of the night. Some, however, nay many, who cannot afford the dollar breakfast (for that is the price here of every meal), draw forth their lunch-baskets, and eat in the cars, and thus much disturb the master in making a day "palace" of his night sleeping hall. Night after night, this is the scene, from Omaha, on the Missouri, to Oaklands, on the Pacific waters.

Cheyenne—away up the hills, some thousands of feet above the level of the sea, no matter how many, but many enough at times to be very snowy, more windy, and very cold—is the Wyoming Territory Exchange of the Union Pacific Railroad. Near here we begin to see the snowy mountains; and near here we see, or think we see, the Rocky Mountains; but the Rocky Mountains on the line of the Union Pacific Railroad are grand humbugs. "There is not any Rocky Mountain," the traveller writes down in his note-book. "The geographer has been cheating us for a hundred years." "Lewis and Clarke, the first Pacific explorers, told lies." "Fremont wrote romances about Rocky Mountains, Rocky Mountain fastnesses, and Rocky Mountain peaks." "The United States Government engineers, in their great, big Pacific Railroad Government books, drew monstrous long yarns," etc. ! But there *are* Rocky Mountains, real, live, big, bouncing, frightful Rocky Mountains; but the Union Pacific Railroad has contrived so to get over, or through, and around them, that the traveller is cheated out of his eyes and seven senses, and there are no Rocky Mountains to him. We are going up, up, up; we all feel and know that. The vegetation indicates, we are going heavenward. Sherman, the tip-top, jumping-off railroad place, 8,242 feet above the level of the sea, demonstrates there are some Rocky Mountains; but we have only seen snowy peaks in the distance— Pike's Peak and Elk Mountain—and thus "going over the Rocky Mountains," on the Union Pacific Railroad, is all a joke to us.

Cheyenne, I was about to say, when led off on this Rocky Mountain Jack-o'-lantern digression, is an "Exchange" on the Union Pacific Railroad. The Denver (Colorado) Railroad comes in here, bringing passengers from St. Louis. The Western Union Pacific Railroad train meets the Eastern train here. We all gaze about to see whom we know. The United States Army rides in, from the forts all round, with its wives and children, to see "who is who, and what is what." Three trains, meeting 6,000 feet in the air, is the great event of the day. We eat, of course, thirty minutes (they give us fifty here). We stop to buy moss agate jewelry. We shake hands with everybody, from everywhere, or going everywhere. There is a daily evening newspaper here, and we devoured the telegrams, more especially to see how the madmen were carrying on, in Paris, the night before. In short, we know just as much, away up here in the air, of what the world is doing, as you know on Broadway, New York. There are two competing lines of telegraph all about us. We receive and send home messages. Indeed, we are at home, away up here in the Rocky Mountains, among the bears, the wildcats, and the rattlesnakes, if any are left, that have not run away with the buffaloes and the Indians.

From "Sherman," named after General Sherman, the tallest general in the army, we go down, down, down. Two engines pulled us up, but all the brakes are put on as we go down, down, down. Then we scour over the Laramie Plains, reach Laramie City, the hope, the haven, the heaven of the woman's righters, where sing the men—

> "Nice little baby, don't get in a fury,
> 'Cause mamma's gone to sit on the jury."

To Laramie succeeded darkness, and a night's ride; but the moon broke in upon us, with the magnificent scenery of the railroad. An observation-car, in early morning, was attached to the rear of the train, to give all the passengers an opportunity to see the Cañons, the Castle Rock, the Hanging Rock, the Pulpit Rock, the Devil's Slide, the Devil's Gate Station, etc. We wide opened our eyes and our ears, and took in all; but I am now so absorbed in the Holy Land, where I am, that scenery is nothing to me now. I tarry over the Sabbath to worship with the Saints in the Tabernacle; and, if I can get time, you shall hear more from me before I go into the outer darkness of the telegraph and mail, on the boundless Pacific Ocean.

## LETTER II.

### ON, TO, AND OVER THE PACIFIC.

The Mormon Holy Land.—Geographically like the Holy Land over the Sea.—How Irrigation has made the Desert a Garden.—The Apostles and Elders of Mormondom.—The Holy Temple.—Brigham Young in the Temple.—The Women and the Fashions in Salt Lake City.—Beelzebub stirring up Rebellion.—The Grasshoppers and the Gulls.

SALT LAKE, *May* 28, 1871.

WHAT to say of this extraordinary place, how to picture it, its industries, its progress, its great achievements, puzzle me. It is very like Jordan, and the Dead Sea, and that part of the Holy Land. The Salt Lake is the Dead Sea. There is a Jordan here pouring into this dead salt sea, where nothing can live, to which Dead Sea, here, there is no outlet, as in that near Jerusalem. The mountains are all about, but these are magnificent, snow-covered mountains, pouring down their rich waters to irrigate, awaken, develop, and enrich the soil—to drive the miserable sage brush off, and to substitute therefor all sorts of grain, and roots, and fruits that can make a people prosperous and happy. When Brigham, the Prophet, many years gone by, first led here his driven-off squadrons (so like the Israelites, driven off from Egypt to wander in the wilderness), this great valley, with its sage brush and its rough rocks, must have looked very like what the Dead Sea and Jordan now are; but Brigham and his tribes have made it teem with bread and honey, and to blossom like the rose. I cannot help, therefore, feeling a sort of admiration for these Illinois and Missouri, but Yankee led, banished prophets, apostles, and elders, and their hosts of followers from Scandinavia to Scotia—for these Celts, Britons, Germans, Danes, Norwegians, these representatives of the refuse of the world. The Lord, or the Devil (choose which), has here chosen the humblest, the most ignorant instruments, to do the greatest things. "And Love rules all," we are told, and we see it, or *seem* to see it, through the apostles and elders. Love brings the water harmoniously down from the mountains, and divides and subdivides the torrent into little streams, and brooks, and rivulets, and they flow over every man's field, by every man's door, and the patriarchs (most of them very unpromising-looking patriarchs, though), with their wives, and children, and flocks, drink it in, or see the earth drink it in, as Egypt drinks in the Nile waters. But there is no "report" from these high Courts of Love, that thus rule and regulate all. Reporters are not admitted to the Council of the apostles and elders. There are no general or special sessions, that we know of—no short-hand, nor long-hand reporters, no stenographers. But, in faith, we believe, or ought to believe, that Love rules all the land, and subjects all to its laws—for here, we are told, is the Millennium, nay,

Paradise, perhaps. Wonderful people! *La Allah*, as the Mussulman says. "Great is God, and Brigham is His prophet."

Everybody comes here now, of course, unless a body is in such a hurry that Mecca, or Jerusalem, is nothing to him. The curious can never happily pass over the great Pacific road without shooting off, on the Mormon tangent railroad, now thirty-six miles long, to see this Mecca of America. I shot off with a New York party on this railroad tangent. A Mr. Townsend, all the way from Maine, with only three wives (one of them just dead), keeps *the* hotel of the city, and a very fair and quite a large hotel it is, but very soon, with all its additions, it will not be half big enough, especially on a Sunday, when travellers most desire to be here, to worship in the Tabernacle, or Temple. Think what a day of rest a Sabbath is here! We breakfast on mountain trout, fresh from the icy streams. We march in the long trains of Saints and Saintesses to the holy Temple. A hundred or two, or more, of apostles and elders sit on an elevated platform, and we, the people, in mingled communion, sit below, and look up to the holy priesthood while they dispense the Old Testament of Abraham, Isaac, and Jacob, and the New Testament of Jesus Christ, as enlarged and expounded by Joe Smith, in his new Gospel of "glorious" Revelation. Our wives and progeny are all about. None of us have less than one child—some forty, or fifty, or sixty. The women are not fascinating, either in pretty faces (there are exceptions) or pretty fashions. The great Prophet Brigham discourages fashion, but the rascally innovation will come here, and is somewhat stronger than even the Prophet. A big hoop rustles around us now and then. Occasionally we see a coquettish cap, nicknamed a bonnet; silks, if not satins, also intrude; but the great mass of the women bring here their hats and robes, from their mothers and great-grandmothers, and the result is a head-gear representative here of Swede, of Scot, of Celt, of Yankee, the patterns, perhaps, of ten generations behind, with scoots of Quaker formation, and umbrellas of Italian conception. A photograph of Salt Lake fashions might suggest ideas to Eugenie, perhaps, if ever she recovers the fashionable dominion of the world.

We listened profoundly, for one hour and more, to a very clever discourse of an elder, or apostle, here, a Mr. Cannon, who does double duty—first, as daily editor of the *Deseret Journal*, and next, as preacher; but our great desire was to see Brigham, to hear Brigham, and to drink in the gospel of Joe Smith, the martyr, as dropped from the lips of Brigham. Heaven prospered our desires. Brigham arose —a good-looking man, now of seventy years, very like Tom Benton, the Missouri Senator, in his latter days—neatly and meekly dressed (by what wife? a wicked Gentile woman asked us), and he shrewdly, ably expounded his creed. There is no doubt of the all-sorts-of-ability of this remarkable man, whether he be preacher, prophet, governor, ruler, banker, farmer, railroad builder, miner, husband, or father. The Saints all look up, and marvel, and wonder, and even we sinners looked up, and marvelled, and wondered. He told us (and it was new to all of us) the City of Enoch was in the Gulf of Mexico, and the waters would one day recede northward, and the city come up again—while all the isles of the Gulf would be re-annexed to our continent, and become part and parcel of the United States (even St. Domingo, perhaps, without Grant's treaty of purchase and annexation).

Brigham, however, is not much longer to have undisputed religious dominion here, his worshippers tell us. Beelzebub is stirring up rebellion. The Episcopalians have planted a church here (wonder where the money comes from), costing forty or fifty thousand dollars. The Roman Catholics are already here. The Methodists are about to invade Utah with one of their prodigious camp-meetings, raking in Methodists, there, from the Missouri, at Omaha, to San Francisco, on the Pacific. They threaten to capture Brigham and all his hosts. Brigham, generously or tauntingly, offered them his huge new Tabernacle, holding 13,000 people, with its galleries, new, and the big organ, perhaps the biggest in the world, to be thrown in, for their great Love Feast; but they declined the taint, or the taunt, and they turn up in tents, in the open fields, under a cloudless sky. If any sect can capture Brigham and his hosts, it is the Methodists; but they cannot sing half as loud as his ten or twelve thousand congregation; they cannot cry "Amen" as loud, and they cannot pray louder. Their priesthood, close, and compact, and powerful as it is, is not half so close, compact, and powerful as his. I should like to be there to see the great battle of the hosts; but I am bound for the land of Confucius, and the heathen Chinee, and the Hindoo, and the Mussulman, and shall never see the great fight among the mountains of Utah.

The grasshoppers, not the Gentiles, are the greatest enemies of the Mormons. They eat up every thing, at times, and half-starve out the delving Saints. But Providence, Brigham told us, has come to the rescue of the Saints. The gulls, never before known here, were sent to eat the grasshoppers up. They came in swarms, devoured the grasshoppers in the fields, vomited them up in the deadly waters of Salt Lake, returned for more, re-did the like, and thus freed Mormondom from the pest. The Gentiles are coming in, in swarms, though, to work the mines. They find the money; Brigham finds the workmen, on hire. The Emma mine is a new silver mine, just sold to Californians and New-Yorkers for over a million, to be converted into a five million stock. The valley below here (south) is said to be full of mines on the mountain sides. Brigham has just concluded a contract with the Union Pacific Railroad directors to extend his thirty-sixth-mile road twenty miles further, that Company finding the iron, and Brigham doing the grading, for only eight hundred dollars per mile—for there is little or no grading or bridging to do. There is no doubt that all Southern Utah is more or less abounding in silver mines; and capitalists are here on hand looking after them. The Townsend Hotel is full of adventurers in mining. What effect all this invasion is to have upon Brigham and his Saints is not exactly to be foreseen; but when the Prophet has a new revelation, from Joe Smith or any other divine revelator, abolishing polygamy for the future (now that the country is settled, not at present, of course), then Brigham and his Saints have an organization that can and will successfully contend with Methodism or any other religious denomination. The double, triple, quadruple, if not centuple, wife system will not stand fire now. Its day was over with Abraham, Isaac, and Jacob, when the world was to be settled. I expect every day to hear some such new revelation from the great Temple, and Brigham, the great Knight Templar.

I visited every thing, or almost every thing, the two days I was here—the sulphur, natural, warm-baths in the city; the barracks (Camp Douglas), four miles off, where we station a general and several companies, to frighten the Saints to keep order, and the theatre, Saturday night—a first-class theatre, too, with a building as fine, and acting as good, as two-thirds of the theatres of New York—(the Prophet, like Beecher, allows his followers fun and frolic, and assists in it, now and then)—and last, not least of all, the house, the home, the sanctum of the great Prophet himself. Two of his daughters are stock actresses. But I must draw a veil over all that. It is not right for sinners to talk with saints, and then tell, is it?

# LETTER III.

### ON AND FROM THE PACIFIC.

Around the World only a "Trip."—Snow on the Mountains and Alkali Plains.—Forty Miles of Snow-sheds.—Sudden Descent from Ice and Snow to Apricots and Strawberries.—Sacramento.—New Railroad and Steamboat Routes.

SAN FRANCISCO, *June* 1, 1871.

I AM about leaving in the Pacific Mail Co.'s steamer, the Japan, for Yokohama, Yeddo, Shanghai, Hankow, Hong Kong, Canton, and ——, which is about as far as my geography goes, just now. Hence, I must scribble in pencil as fast as I can. The Pacific Mail steamers, all of them, are first-class, more abounding in sea comforts, I think, than any thing we have on the Atlantic; and therefore Japan, only twenty-two days from here, is not much of "a trip," so it seems to me now, though Japan once *did* seem a great way off—as far off as was California from Boston in the days of my youth—that is, the jumping-off place of the world. If the tropics do not threaten to burn us up in July and August, I shall "trip" it around the world. Every thing, you know, in this country is a "trip," even a journey around the world.

We left the snowy mountain surroundings of the Salt Lake Valley after "meeting," on Sunday, May

28, and in a short time reached Ogden, the end of the Union Pacific Railroad, owned mainly in Boston and New York, and the beginning of the Central Pacific Railroad, owned all in San Francisco and Sacramento. The sun was hot; but hot suns here are not like hot suns, East—the air is so dry and exhilarating. A long-troubling cough I brought with me from Washington is rapidly going, and when I reach the Alkali plains I am sure it will all be gone, This is the very land for consumption, bronchitis, or the like, if patients are not too far gone; though Brigham Young told us, in his discourse, his voice was about worn up, though his body was as vigorous as ever. But, May 29, strange to say—a phenomenon here now—a heavy rain met us, succeeded by a snow-storm, re-whitening all the mountains, covering even the Alkali plains, and making them whiter than the Alkali. But the rain and snow saved us from the trying dust of these plains. Our cars were as pleasant as ever, and we have been in them so long now, that they seem like home—sweet home, too, when contrasted with the rough cabins we often pass in the rough-looking towns and villages. The windmills increase, forcing up the water for the railroad tanks. There are three stations where water has to be brought in car-tanks to feed the locomotives. "Lots of Indians," dirty, filthy Piutes, are out begging whiskey, or money to buy whiskey with. "Backsheesh" squaws, in the West as well as in the East, sling papooses over their backs to touch the sympathies of ladies in the cars. The morning of the 29th we passed the Summit House of the Sierra Nevada, hid, however, in the midst of high snow-sheds; but the snow, as I should judge from peeps through the crevasses, was nearly a foot deep. Icicles were trickling down these snow-sheds. Sliding on the board walks of the restaurant places was the traveller's fun. These snow-sheds on these mountain sides are "cursed" by travellers, when panting to see the mountain tops. "Plague on them," was the universal cry for forty miles; but they save the traveller from all delays in the winter, and are here indispensably necessary to keep open the road. Two engines took up our long train of cars, lengthened the night before by an Uncle Sam's cavalry troop, bound from Fort McDermot, in Nevada, to Arizona (*via* Benicia), to fight the Camanches there. Soon, however, very soon (two hours and forty minutes), we were in the valley of the rich Sacramento—the hay harvest over, the wheat ready to cut, apricots and strawberries and cherries abundant, new potatoes on our table, every surrounding seeming like midsummer, the sun hot and high, and vegetation all parched up, save the ever-green grape-vines. Is this America? Is this in *our* country? Isn't it in Lombardy, from the Alpine descent, or, on the Po, or, further on southward, in Naples, say, near the lava of Vesuvius? Sometimes the cars come down from the Sierra all covered with snow, while the dust is blowing in the streets of Sacramento!

Sacramento is the ambitious capital of California, with a huge, costly dome on a State-house, now arising, and not yet done. I thought, two years ago, when here, I had dropped down from the Alps into Milan—such were the fruits, and such were the seeming luxuries of the climate. But we tarry here no more. "On," "*on*," ever "ON," is the law of the steam-car. "Fifteen minutes for dinner," never over twenty-five or thirty. The wonder is, we Americans do not all die, eating as we do; but we take on lunch baskets here and elsewhere, cherries, boxes of strawberries, apricots, California claret, Yankee doughnuts even, strayed thus far (crullers is the Middle States or California name for them); and thus, you see, we cannot starve. Sacramento is one hundred and thirty-five miles by rail from San Francisco, about sixty or seventy by the shortest rail and water route.

Speaking of railroads, I find here not a little excitement about a new rail route to run from San Francisco, not so much over, as around the Sierras, to Ogden, to connect with the Union Pacific there. Rich men and richer resources are in the new idea. The plan, substantially, is to use the existing Vallejo and Marysville Railroad, and from thence to fork off, connecting with Ben Holliday's Portland (Oregon) Road, through the Willamette Valley, and thence, from Klamath Lake down to Snake River. The Central Railroad people say this route will be two hundred or three hundred miles longer; the new railroad people say, forty miles shorter. Surveys alone can settle the question; but sooner or later, if for nothing else, for the Oregon trade, this road will be made; and the Union Pacific will have two forks, one, on to San Francisco (the Central), and the other, into Oregon and San Francisco. There is room here for all.

I have a thousand pleasant things to say of this rising city—this New York of the Pacific West, its Japan and Chinese gateway, and Australia's gateway, too, where steamers are now running, under the invigorating auspices of our Wm. H. Webb, who is here, looking after his line. I see on the wharves of the Pacific Mail Company, coffee, said to be as good as the Java, from Central America, and sugar, in quantities, in bags, and cassia, etc., all things indicating a fresh, growing commerce. But the big ship Japan has her steam up, threatening to cut me off, if I go on pencilling longer; and so you will not hear from me again till I am "down East," somewhere among the Antipodes, who are under our feet, just now. Am I going East, or West, to-day? What say geographers? Is Japan down East, or farther out West? Is this the end of "the great West," or, the beginning of that unknown land our starting point? My head is all agog with these extraordinary geographical and time calculations. My watch is not worth a sixpence, measured by New York time. While we breakfast, you dine, and while we dine, you go to bed. I telegraph, and you get my telegram before it starts. How will it be in the East, or the West, where I am going? I am losing a day of my life now by travelling. Shall I gain it by keeping on? We shall see. But—"All on board that's going!" and I close. "Adieu," "adieu."

## LETTER IV.

*ON THE PACIFIC.*

From the Golden Gate to Yokohama.—The "Japan," and the motley Crowd on board.—Is, or is not, the Pacific Ocean a Humbug?—The Amusements on board.—The Police of the Ship.—Spoke a Boston Ship.—Meeting a Steamer in Mid-ocean, exchanging Mails, etc.

*June* 1, 1871.

WE are passing the Golden Gate, and the broad Pacific is opening around us for a long, long voyage—four thousand seven hundred and eighty miles to Yokohama, in Japan, twenty-two days off, if not more, the rate we are to run. What a motley crowd we have just taken on board—the returning Japanese, Governor Ito & Co., who have just been making the tour of the United States, with Japanese women (not belonging to them, though), very much resembling our Indian squaws, but pretty well dressed, and with more intelligence; hundreds of Chinese, almost all men, but a few women, who have made "their fortune" in America, now returning home to enjoy it; and Englishmen, travelling for pleasure, and Germans, and Scotchmen, and the universal Yankee nation, of course. A Chinese " fortune "—happy people—is only three or four hundred dollars, not the New York three or four millions; and the "heathen Chinee" is happy in having earned enough to live hereafter magnificently at home. They scattered bits of paper on the water as we left the wharf, to appease their Joss (the God) of the Sea, and to bribe him to give us a prosperous voyage. We have three missionary women on board, from Albany and near by, going to Japan, to turn the Buddhists there into Christians—hopeless task, I fear. All these, with Chinese sailors, all, or nearly all, to manage the ship—Chinese servants, all—a Yankee captain, from Cape Cod, of course—a doctor, a purser, a steward, etc., make up our motley crowd, and are to be our companions over three weeks, on the way.

The sailing of a steamship from a Pacific port is an affair very different from that of the sailing of an Atlantic steamship from New York. All Chinadom and Japonicadom come down to see us off. The hard, harsh jangle of Chinadom on the wharf, screaming "adieux," was mingled with the softer, gentler, and more Tuscan-like notes of the Japanese; while English, and German, and French, and Italian, and Spanish, in our cabin, bade the politer adieu. We took on provisions enough to feed a city—bullocks, beasts of other kinds, sheep, henneries and duckeries, with tenants too full to count; vegetables, fresh from the Eden gardens of California; fruits of many kinds, with apricots and strawberries, luscious to look at now, however they may look, or taste, when Neptune exacts his tributes from us, a few hours hence. We shall live, I see, if we do not die of sea-sickness.

· · · · · ·

*June 3.*

The Pacific Ocean is a humbug. For twenty-four hours I have been tossed, and rocked, and turned inside out, just as I have been on that rough, boisterous, reckless bosom of waters they call the Atlantic, that never made any pretensions to gentleness or gentility. There is nothing Pacific on this ocean as yet. This is the second time I have tried it, northward, though, once before, as far up as Vancouver; but the captain promises better behavior from the winds and the waves, as soon as we get far enough off from the northerly winds of the California and Oregon coast.

· · · · · ·

*June 6.*

The Pacific Ocean is *not* a humbug; but the best-behaved, best-looking sea I ever was on. There has not been a ripple on the water for forty-eight hours. There is not a sea-sick victim on board. Sunday, June 4, the captain read the Episcopal service in "the Social Hall," the upper, frescoed, lookout deck of the ship, and all the Christians on board assembled to hear him—not the Buddhists, nor the devotees of Confucius, of course. Our missionary women sang their hymns, and the piano, acting as organ, accompanied them. We read, we write, we play shuffle-board on deck (not on Sunday, though), and pitch quoits, with cards and backgammon, and walk and talk. The Japanese are reading Japanese novels, with illustrative pictures all over them, quite equalling the genius of the New York publishers, or instructing us in words we deem it necessary to learn. "Ohio" means "good morning," and in the morning we "ohio" all we see. Thus we pass time, with the five meals per day, if we choose to eat so many, but with appetites that seem insatiable after our tributes to the sea.

The police of this ship is so admirable that I must give the captain, Freeman, a puff therefor. There is a cry of "Fire," "*Fire*,"—that terrible cry aboard ship, in mid-Pacific sea—but a *mock* cry here, to test the crew, and on the instant, every Chinaman is at his post, with streams of water flowing from hose all over the deck, and ready to rush anywhere he is sent. The life-boat is unrolled, and the India-rubber, canvas-covered raft is blown up in a very short time. The captain took some of us, last evening, all over his ship. The neatness of the *cuisine*, the pantry, and all the outworks indicate a husbandry, I must say—not housewivery, for men do all the work—not unsurpassed even by the Rotterdam or Amsterdam Dutch. The stores of the ship all pass through the purser's accounts, and double entry, or single entry, tell the owners of every thing in or out. The Chinese passengers on board, some of them, are going to their bunks; some are smoking opium in nearly an airtight cage set apart especially for them to indulge that vice in, and others reading, or telling tales, or playing on the banjo, we call it, with a chip. Happy they all seemed—the happiest of all, in seeming, the half-drunk opium-smokers, but all happy, in returning home to Hong-Kong, at fifty dollars only of cost, with rice enough to eat, mixed up with pork, and devoured with chop-sticks—a provender far better than any food they are likely to have hereafter at home. At 11 P. M., " Douse the glim " is the order of the night, and we all go to bed—Christians, Buddhists, Confuciusists, Europeans, men, women, children, all—when watchmen in every part of the ship watch over us and protect us during the night. I feel as safe—I hope I am not to be mistaken—as in my own bedroom at home, and the doors here are all unlocked, and the windows open to let in the refreshing air.

"*Ship ahoy!*" That's a refreshing sound, even on the Atlantic sea, where ships are crossing and recrossing all the time, and where you can see one almost every day. But here on the Pacific there are few or no ships, and little or no crossing and recrossing, so that "Ship ahoy!" startles us all up, and we all rush to our glasses to see. As the morn broke in upon us, a big ship, under full sail, was descried crossing our course, and soon we saw the American flag, and soon after a boat put out to meet us. The ship was a Boston ship, the Daniel Marcy, one hundred and sixty-three days from New York, having left before Christmas, and seen nothing since; passed Cape Horn, lost her longitude, and wanted to know where she was. There was a woman on board with four sick children, seen on deck—how many under, deponent cannot say—and for one hundred and sixty-three days no news, no newspapers, no telegraphs, no nothing on board that ship! Well, that's what I came here for—not exactly to get out of the world, but to be upon that part of the world where "no nothing" could get after me. Our captain gave his Yankee *confrère*, for the benefit of his wife and babies, two bags of new (California) potatoes, fresh beef, fresh mutton, and fresh newspapers; and, when all that had got on board the Daniel Marcy, there must have been happiness there, to say nothing of the "longitude."

Latitude 36° 50′, longitude 142° 10′. "*The Mail closes to-night at* 6 P. M.," is posted up on our ship. What meaneth this? Why, the steamer from Japan (left Yokohama on the 22d of May) is to meet us to-night, or to-morrow, and we must all have our letters ready to send home to our friends. Hence, everybody is writing home; the ladies with their desks on their knees (what a gift they have in being able to write anyhow, or everywhere!), and we gentlemen, in the cabin, or in our state-rooms, on our wash-stands. Pen, ink, paper, and pencil are in the greatest demand. The meeting of the steamers is to be another great event, and we are to give them news from Europe and America, and they are to give us news from Niphon, and the Tycoon, or the Mikado. There are "politics" in Japan, I am learning, as in the United States, and I am becoming as interested in Mikados and Tycoons as in General Grant or St. Domingo. What's the news from—not New York, but the Corea? Our little fleet, I hear, has gone up to open Corea, or Korea—a part of the Chinese appendage dominion not yet opened by gunpowder. "What is the value of an Itzebu (Japanese paper money), two New York shillings, or three?" "How are we to live or board in Yedo?" "Will the Daimio's retainers stab or cut up us, foreign devils?" as the Chinese call us. These are all most important questions; but the Japanese on board say we shall have no trouble, and shall travel as pleasantly as in New York or California. We shall see.

## LETTER V.

### ON THE PACIFIC.

Life and Thoughts on Ship-board.—The Day Lost in *Rounding* the World.—"Down East" is out West.—A Puzzled Traveller.—Summer Life on this Ocean.—The Second Exchange of Letters.—The Sixteenth Amendment.—Curious Congregation of Passengers.

*June*, 1871—Lat. 36° N., Lon. 180° E.

No date, you see. We have dropped out Friday, which ought to be June 16th, 1871, but we have dropped it out (a *dies non*), and it *is* Saturday now, June 17. We have not had any Friday, and never shall have any June 16. There are but six days to us this week—nay, only five, from Sunday to Sunday. I am puzzling over this in geography and on chart, and, though doubtless it is all clear enough to the navigator and astronomer, I have found it not so easy to store it away in my head. Watches, days and days ago, I found to be good for nothing to the traveller by steam, but the sudden loss of faith in almanacs and the calendar is confusing. London, I am told, is just under our feet, or Greenwich rather, the astronomer's headquarters, and we are 180° (of the 360°) around the world, that is, half around—from Greenwich, and we have, therefore, lost a day, by the chronometer time of Greenwich. I expect to have all this clear by the time I get to Greenwich, but nothing is very clear just now in my muddled mind, save that there is no "Friday, June 16," for us, as for the rest of mankind. We are not in Gibeon nor the Valley of Ajalon, with enemies to avenge, as Joshua had, when he ordered the sun and moon to stand still; but, the sun stands still to us, in this wild wilderness of waters, as we lose the day, and there is no Friday, June 16, 1871, to us, and there never will be!

But, as one approaches the portals of the rising sun, one must expect to be puzzled. Every thing ahead is beginning to be, or seems to be, topsy-turvy. We are going West, and have been going West some sixteen days, to get East. We are going to the setting of the sun to approach its rising! In my early days in Maine the more "down East" I went, the more I saw of the "Eastern stage," promising to take passengers further East. I then searched for that "East" at the head of the Bay of Fundy, but I gave it up, as there was then running an "Eastern stage!" In later days, Cincinnati was "West," Chicago, the "far West," and St. Paul's and St. Louis, the end of "the boundless West;" but here I am, some twenty-three days from New York, all the while going West, and that "Will o' the Wisp" is not reached, and never will be. As if all these things could not enough puzzle one, or seem enough topsy-turvy, I see the Japanese and Chinese on board reading upside down, from right to left, in perpendicular instead of horizontal lines, and their books begin where ours end—the preface, where our *finis* is. Their locks on their boxes and trunks are all made to lock by turning the key from the left to the right. Their carpenters use the plane by drawing it to them, and their tailors stitch *from* them. All this, perhaps, is not to be wondered at among people whose night is our day, and whose heads are under our heels, but they confuse one's senses, more especially when one sees a day dropped out from under one, and the sun, as it were, standing still without a miracle!

I have been hesitating for some days whether or not I shall give the Pacific Ocean a good character or a bad one; but, upon the whole, I have concluded it deserves a certificate, more especially in contrast with the Atlantic, the English Channel, the Bay of Fundy, the Mediterranean, Lake Ontario, or any other like rowdy seas. The *Pacific*, though, if a taking, is rather a cheating, Christian name, for it does kick up and flop over at times, and flutters often. It is not everlastingly pacific, *that* is certain; but, upon the whole, it is a pretty-well-behaved ocean— this part of it at least, where no typhoons or cyclones rage. In June, a big steamer like this, the Japan, with plenty of men on board, is a yacht that a New York commodore might envy, and such as Cleopatra, who led astray so many Romans in her galley, never dreamed of. And we carry with us a sort of miniature Newport or New London; we eat, we drink, we make merry, we dance, we sing; material pleasures only, but we read, we write, we think, we preach, we pray, we do every thing on board that people do at Newport or Long Branch in summer, besides having two Sundays now in one week. Sure, an ocean where all this can be done, deserves a certificate of good character, and it is hereby written—

That if, in summer, a man with his family would go a yachting, on a pleasure "trip" only, there is nothing like this on the Pacific, more especially if on one's way to Japan to see the drolleries and curiosities of the East, where something new must ever turn up, and something fresh must ever be seen.

There is a pleasure even in having one's senses muddled, as mine are, in the loss of a real live day, and in being among people who turn every thing inside out or upside down.

Besides the study of navigation on board ship, "horizon," "altitude," "parallax," etc., etc., we naturally study up and talk of a great many other things. The "Japs" are educating us on their recent revolutions, on the Tycoon, Mikado, and Daimio nobles, and telling us how to travel in Niphon, or relating the marvels of Yedo. We see them read their novels, and we beg for translations thereof. Japan already has become quite familiar with us. While America has our hearts, with all that is in it—that America, now so far away, and so rapidly running under our feet—we much discuss which is the nearest route to Japan and China, whether over Puget

Sound or by San Francisco. Longitude narrows, you know, as we reach the North Pole; hence, Puget Sound (north) is, on the great circle, nearer than San Francisco (south); but there is no sailing on that great circle. There are islands northward in the way, and the winds are not favorable. Yokohama, Japan, however, is 4,780 miles as we sail on the chart from San Francisco, but only 4,100 miles from Puget Sound, so that over 603 miles can be saved from the Sound over the North Pacific Railroad—say from New York to Yokohama, now the great seaport of Japan, and *en route* to Shanghai and Hong Kong. The San Francisco journalists, however, will not admit this—nay, will cipher it away, or try to; but I have measured it on the chart, and it seems truly so. Puget Sound, too, is the best internal sheet of water in the United States (*haud non expertus loquor*), navigable to the very shores, well timbered, and the climate by no means so cold as the latitude indicates. We discuss lines of telegraph, too. We Yankees now must reach the East. John Bull has just stretched his wiry arms out beyond Bombay and Calcutta, and his "tick" is now heard from London to Shanghai, and in the Yang-Tze-Kiang—the Amazon and Mississippi of the Chinese world. What can we do? How can we thus "tick?" We must bargain with the Russians, it seems to me, and stretch our wires through Alaska and the Aleutian Islands to Petropaulauski in Kamschatka, and thence down the Kurile Islands to

Japan, thence to Saghalin (now a long Russian island, stolen from the Japanese), and thence to the Amoor or Manchuria. The two great friendly Governments can thus encircle the world, and be independent of all Europe, save Russia in Europe. The real greatness of Russia is now for the first time bursting upon my vision—not Russia in Europe, for I comprehended all that, but Russia in Asia, which now commands the frontier of China, and, in commanding the sea of Japan, and the sea of Okhotsh, commands, also, more or less, the whole North Pacific Ocean. We ignorant politicians have much to learn from our whalers, even, I see; and I am hearing, on ship board, their voyages, their tales, and adventures, and no romances are more delightful reading just now.

Well, well; with no telegraph, no newspapers, no nothing about us but a whale or two, and seagulls, and white birds, and porpoises—politics, nor electricity, nor rails, ought ever to enter our brains; but bad habits of thinking follow one, even when sent off to rest. And sure, there is no rest like this on the Pacific. Eating is the great order of the day. We eat, if we please, at 6 A. M. (a sort of French breakfast, tea, coffee, and crust), really breakfast at 9 A. M., lunch at noon, dine at 6 P. M., and tea at $8\frac{1}{2}$. Next to eating, if not over, or above it, is sleeping. We sleep and we eat; we eat and we sleep. When Sancho Panza exclaimed, "Blessed be the man that invented sleep," he was thinking, doubtless, only of Castile and Arragon; but doubly blessed be the man that invented sleep for the Pacific Ocean. The days would be endless if we did not sleep, and the nights are endless, though we do sleep. We have not spoken or seen a ship since, days ago, we met by arrangement the steamer from China to San Francisco, with some one thousand two hundred Chinese on board, a sea of heads, bald and pig-tailed, going over to try their fortunes in America. We see nothing on the Pacific but birds, that follow us for our offal, or porpoises, or a whale or two. We seem far beyond the reach of commerce, or civilization, or any of their tracks. No "ship ahoy" greets us; no smoke from the pipe of some distant steamer. What an eternal waste of waters! Will it ever end? We shall see.

. . . . . . .

*June* 23.

Now over three weeks on board, and we are hoping to meet the outward-bound steamer from Yokohama, and send off letters to America by her. The fog is against us, however. We are in the Gulf Stream, the Kuro Siwo of Japan, and the warmer water is sending up fogs and rain. It is now the rainy season in Japan, and we shall be lucky if we see the coast before we are right on it.

. . . . . . .

The week we have passed since I began this sketching or scribbling, as you please to call it, has not been a week without incidents. We have three missionary ladies on board, intending to pass some years in Japan, instructing Japanese children, to convert them from their heathenism, if they can; but the Japs on board give them very little encouragement. These ladies are Mrs. Pruyn of Albany, Mrs. Pierson of Michigan, and Miss Crosby of Poughkeepsie. Mrs. Pruyn favored us with a discourse on Sunday. Discovering the capacity of these ladies, in a mock trial we had of a Teuton for stealing the sponge of a Scot, we put two of them on the jury and made the other the official reporter of the case. They discharged their duties so well that we all begin to think better of the 16th Amendment.

Among our Japs on board are two returning from Italy, where they have been with silk-worms' eggs, on cards, to sell. This has become a great speculation, and the Japs are going into it with zeal. The Japs almost always—always when they can—take cabin passages; the Chinese seldom, or never. We have several well-off, if not rich, Chinamen on board; but they have preferred herding with their countrymen and living on rice and pork to living with us, or with the Japanese, in the cabins. The Chinese are intensely economical, it seems; the Japanese far less calculating. We have also on board four or five Americans going out to offer their services to the Emperor of China, as sailors, officers, or engineers, for their navy. One of them already has had command of a Chinese gunboat, and fought the rebels and pirates. Another was shipwrecked in Corea, where Admiral Rogers has gone with our fleet to admonish the Coreans, and he tells a terrible tale of suffering, inflicted by them and by the Chinese Tartars, to whom the Coreans handed him over.

Thus, in our motley company of the world's representatives, we hear and tell tales, exchange or "swap" experiences, and a log might be made up of our mutual narratives, more interesting, probably, than any of the books in our ship's library. But, if we are to meet the California-bound steamer off the Japan coast, this yarn must be spun no longer, and so I bite off, and notch up the thread.

## LETTER VI.

### *FIRST IMPRESSIONS IN JAPAN.*

Arrival in Japan.—First Impressions on the Coast.—The Fishermen in "Georgia Costume."—Everything New, Everything Odd.—Bamboo Baskets for Hats.—Straw Overcoats.—Landing on the Hatoba.—The Cues of the Japanese.—The Brawny Coolies.—Travelling Restaurants.—Strange Street Spectacles.—The Tattooed Men.—The Horse Boy (Betto).—Hair Dressing.—Shocking Black Teeth of the Married Women.

YOKOHAMA, *June* 26, 1871.

SOMETHING new! Every thing new, at last! Under your world now, how every thing in this world seems up-side down, and down-side up! I feel very like, nay, just like, the Boston Yankee, who first saw Boston, and felt his rural ideas revolving within his head, and I act more like Ben Franklin, the printer, when he first turned up in Philadelphia, with both eyes as open as saucers, munching his roll, staring at, and astounded by every thing. Long and long ago, after travelling over many lands, I was sure I had reached the Horatian *nil admirari*—but I am mistaken, for I am wondering over every thing to-day.

At daybreak on the Sabbath morning our good ship bade good-bye to the pretty-well-behaved Pacific, and turned a cape and the light-houses that opened on us the bay of Yedo. Up early, to see and to study, the first living things to refresh our long ocean-wearied eyes were the fishermen of the island of Niphon. Report says (I have not tried its truth) that Japan is about the best fishing ground of the universe. You know (or if you don't, you ought), that in the Boston State House, over the Speaker's chair, is a codfish, the emblem of Massachusetts' rise, progress, and prosperity before the days of East India ships and the spinning jenny. The fish, in like manner, is reverenced here in Japan. It is a basis of Japan life and prosperity. Hence, I levelled eyes and glasses, as naturally man will, on the first life seen—that is, on the fishermen. What queer boats! What queer oars, or sculls! What queer-looking sails, of mats! Boreas can hardly blow over such broad-cast boats. Nobody rows—everybody sculls; and they scull with one oar, two, three, four, five, six—as many as need be for the boat or junk— and they scull as fast as they could row, in such heavy and clumsy boats. History says—wharf-history, I never read it in books, but it may be true— that when the Tycoons and Daimios found the Japanese sculling off, or sailing off, from Japan, they ordered the better class of Chinese junks, that the Japanese had been imitating, to be so constructed that they could never well get over to China—aye, to be so heavy, so clumsy, that Neptune, in his roaring moods, would tip them over, or roll them under, if ever they ventured out of sight of land. Hence the ugliness of these junks, and ocean-uselessness. The June California steamer, out from here, picked up the crew of one, three-fourths of them starved to death, because they could not find their way only from Hiogo to Yokohama, having been blown outside of land. The fishermen we met, such of them as had seines, were scaring the fish into them by pounding furiously on the bottom of the boats! Can this be done? I charge nothing to the Cape Codders for letting them into the Japanese secret of catching fish. But what most astonished us new comers was the Georgia costume, *minus* the spurs, of these interesting fishermen! The fishermen were as naked as the fish—that is, the most of these fishermen! Some of them had something on, but nothing to speak of. Anatomy could be studied practically, as well as phrenology, and physiognomy, and physiology—that is, muscular and venous anatomy. Some of our passengers, at first, were a little confused and confounded over this new development of life, and dropped their lorgnettes; but I see the same passengers now in Yokohama streets, and they are done blushing already.

The first day an American spends in Europe, say in England (I speak now for myself), is a great day, if not the greatest, of his life. The beautifully green fields, the hedges, the cottages, etc., bewitch him; but this first day in this Eastern Asia does not exactly bewitch so much as it bedevils a traveller. The livery of a trading company's boatman, sent out to escort home a passenger by the steamer—what was it, think you? A little turban on the head, with nakedness to the hips, and then a yellow sash girdle, over blue nankin trowsers, running into straw shoes! Was not this a novel livery? Can any of the grandees of Hyde Park, or of the Central Park, come quite up to this great swell? Then numerous police, or custom-house boats, crowded around us, the most of the boatmen with respectable clothes on (not all), some with one sword, others, with two. Some of them had on baskets for bonnets, or hats, made of straw or bamboo; others, with heads wrapped up in handkerchiefs; others, with nothing on their heads but their cues, not pig-tails of Chinese magnificence, but short pipe-stem cues, on the top of the crown. A hundred boats, as usual, were clamorous and greedy for one passenger, and hundreds of hands were ready to grab every trunk and carpet-bag— New York, as well as Yokohama life, you will add. The arrival of a Pacific Mail steamer from California is a great event in Yokohama, and soon the ship was full of Europeans, to see and to study what was going on. One thing strange—but that must be noted—was a large delegation of California women to welcome their forlorn sisters, ever coming over here upon desperate sinful speculation. The men of the East—the European men, I mean—far outnumber the women, and hence such scenes as this I describe. As we landed our missionary sisters, and took in these frail ones, what a pity, it seemed to me, that Christian San Francisco could not be purified before this embassy was made to the Buddhists and Sintoos of Yokohama!

The Japan custom-house officers are not very particular as to baggage, not even looking into it, though very peculiar. They have ears, but our lingo is not theirs, and hence they profit in nothing therefrom; and they have eyes, but they see nothing custom-house-ward thereby. Hence, we slip and slide in, without the least trouble—but their five per cent. *ad valorem* is not the forty, and fifty, and one hundred per cent. in *our* American civilization; and, therefore, there is not so much need of our American spying or searching. Soldiers with not very alarming-looking muskets, save in their sword bayonets, watch over "the Bund," as they call it here—a sort of pier or wharf. In custom-house tongue it might be called a gate or portcullis. We pass them, and then began a series of cryings or yellings that scare fresh-come European or American horses half to death, and even frighten our passenger dogs, and would frighten us, if we were not now expecting any thing and every thing new. "Yeow," "yeow," or "yow," "yow," or "yew," "yew," or something like it in the cat-mewing line, are screaming whole battalions of porters, and carriers; and men-horses are dragging, on miserable round plank wheels, granite, and timber, or lumber. "Yeow," "yeow," goes up to heaven, and rolls over all the earth. It is "yeow," "yeow," at daybreak in the morning, and "yeow," all night, among the coolie Japs, loading and unloading the ships in the harbor. There is no need of horses (I have already come to that conclusion), or elephants, where men can carry such loads. When, years ago, off Constantinople, I first saw men turned into horses, I thought that was something wonderful; but these one-horse Japs, with their enormous loads, shame the Turks, the Grand Turks, even. What glorious muscular legs they have, so admirably developed! I wish I had a pair of them to trot over the world with. What brawny arms, pointed off, though, with little hands! Gymnast or boxer would have to stand back in " a primary," where a fellow had such props, or such pointers. There, comes a travelling restaurant! That's the way to live, where your dinner comes on a fellow's shoulders to you, a whole score of you, and where you do not have to go to the dinner—where rice and chop-sticks, and fish, raw fish, too, are all ready for you—where you can squat down on a mat, and have a Delmonico treat for only a few " cash," that is two, or three, or four " Tempos "—not five cents, even—none of your five-dollar " Delmonico's ! " There's life, there's happiness, there's economy. True, it rains; but has not the fellow a basket-hat on, that sheds all rain as well as all sun ?—not a mere *parapluie*, a rain-shedder, as the French call it, but an umbrella, or ombrella, too, in Latina lingua. And has he not brought out, too, to shed the rain, a great straw cloak, or mantilla, that covers all but his legs, and his one-story mounted shoes, or pattens, tied on by a rope of braided straw? If it were not for the looks of the thing, among the Yankee and English aristocracy of Yokohama, I would squat down and try the rice (not the raw fish) of that dinner. If one could only learn to squat like a Jap, one never would again use a chair, or a sofa. The fact is, in many things, "civilization," as it is called, is a humbug. Squatting on a clean mat, if you have only been brought up to do it, I am sure, from what I see here, is easier and preferable to sitting in a chair. The muscles of the legs have only to be trained from babyhood up, and a chair becomes as much of a nuisance as now is to us this mat. See how nicely our children squat, or young ladies, even, who will sew or write in bed, or on the floor, and by hours, too, without a groan. Hence, I reason, some of our civilization may be a humbug, if not much of it. There, are a lot of tumble boys, funny fellows, with caps on their heads, stuck with red and black feathers, looking like roosters' combs, who roll up, and roll over, like balls of dirt, and then roll all together. . . They want only " a cash," a tenth part of a cent, thus to tumble, over and over. "All-Right," in the American-Japanese jugglers' corps, was thus trained in a Japan street, and graduated in that school. There, is a mother with a baby on her back, slung *à la* American Indian papoose, and the poor baby is fast asleep, with its head toppling all about. The mother, perhaps, would not have much, if any, clothes on, if it had not been necessary for her to throw over her the sack for the baby to sleep or live in. There, is a carpenter, pulling his foreplane toward him, not pushing from him, beautifully clad—exquisitely, I may add. No French *modiste* even could have clothed him richer, with a livery on, that no French high chamberlain could devise better; but the poor devil's only clothes, save a cotton scroll about his loins, and his straw shoes, were his skin, tattooed with all sorts of tortoises, storks, and other Jap divinities. It cost only three and a half dollars, *that* livery, they tell me, and it is the pride and glory of a true Jap to have it. You could not buy a hat in New York for that, you know. But to earn the three dollars and a half to get the livery, that's the difficulty. That surplus is a year's saving; and if it were not so, all Japanese of the working classes would have on the livery. There, is a wrestler, a big, burly fellow, the picked man of his clan, who was big enough to pass for a European. Wrestling here is of a *quasi* noble profession . . . It entitles a man to have two swords on, and to look down on common fellows. An actor in Japan is nothing—nobody—ranking only with beggars, while the wrestler is a grand *cockalorum*. An actor has no rank, no honors, and everybody looks down upon his (with us) great profession, and the only social difference between him and the beggar is, that he may rise— the beggar never. The beggar, by the way, bequeaths the profession from sire to son. The boy *must* follow the trade of the father. There is no hope, no future for him. Not even the coolie will work in the same gang with him. Put a beggar to work in a coolie gang, and every coolie "strikes" at once, refusing thus to associate with a beggar. When the beggar sees you coming, he prostrates himself on his knees, then falls upon the ground, and holds up his hand only for "cash." He utters a most woebegone cry to touch your heart, and to win your sympathies. There, comes something with two swords on, pony-mounted, and his Betto. The betto is a boy who follows his lordship's pony, and the pony races, and the betto races. Which will beat, ask you? The pony never. The betto has on his tattoo liverystraw shoes, it may be,—no shoes, perhaps. The betto will keep up with that pony day after day, thirty miles a day, and no pony can overdo that on a journey. This betto takes care of the pony, watches over and feeds him, and helps to take care of his master, too. There, is hair-dressing going on—public hair-dressing—on the front steps of the shop or house—one man dressing another man's hair, and doing up his cue. The women dress their hair in our old mothers' fashion of gone-by times (none of your long tails of false hair, said I, dangling behind, with a skewer to hold it up on top of the head), beautiful, glossy, black hair. "Thank the Lord," said I, to a Yokohama American lady, "we have reached a country at last, where the women wear only their own hair." "You are much mistaken," said she, "all that hair on top of Madame Jap's head is false hair." Madame shaves off, or cuts off, the original crown, and piles on the false hair. Once a week, only, is the hair done up, skewered, and glued, Spanish (Cadiz) style, thus defying the winds and the fogs for a whole week, and kept in place, nights, while sleeping on the mat-bed, with a wooden pillow under the nape of the neck. Woman, thus, you see, is woman everywhere. There is nothing true outside of their heads, though all so true and sweet, inside. These black teeth, too, of these Japanese Madames, are they not terrible? How can husbands ever kiss such black-teethed wives? When a woman is married here, she blackens her teeth, while our wives and daughters, when married, put on, not only a marriage ring, but all the other rings they can get. Such is fashion. But what more sense in the rings, and ear-rings and bracelets, these emblems of vassalage—I dare not write handcuffs—than in these black teeth? Nevertheless, the black teeth are beautiful black teeth, molars, and eye-teeth of the first chop. They put on some white preparation that turns them black, and they renew the operation about every week. These Jap women only miss, many of them, being very, very pretty. When their copper color is whitened up, they would pass for brunettes, even in America. But—if they are married—these abominable black teeth! this *boca negra*! But fashion is every thing. The hoops of our ladies (although not of half the amplitude they once were), their long *queues*, the substitutes for what ought to be bonnets, their flowing ringlets (whence come, or how once worn, *quien sabe ?*)—their corsets, their shoes, their heels, etc., astound the poor natives as much as these black teeth astound us. The young Japs, however, see in the mouths of their fair ones, the most tempting teeth—and no mouths are prettier.

But hold up. I am scribbling of fashion, and running into the moralities thereon, and revelling in my first day's frolic in Japland. My head is so running over with novelties and curiosities that, unless I retrace here, and write of the past, all THAT will be forgotten in the exciting present and the teeming future.

Was it not wonderful, meeting in mid-ocean two big steamers, at the exact place, and about the exact time appointed? You have, or ought to have had, two letters from me, both written *on*, and mailed *on*, the broad Pacific! The Pacific Mail Steamship Co. try so to arrange time and place that their steamers meet twice on the sea, and exchange letters, and news, and compliments. Pity there are not some islands in the way, for coal, for provisions, etc., as well as for letters, but there are not, and so we have to make islands of the floating ships, and make exchanges on board of them. No spectacle can be more striking, more impressive of the power of man over the elements, than these mid-ocean meetings. The sea of heads, shaven Chinese heads, one thousand two hundred of them in one steamer, filling the whole fore-deck, I have already noticed. We find out what passengers are going to America, and they who are coming from. We bring them news from America, and they, thus for the first time, on June 20th, brought us news from Paris to June 9th, by telegraph from Paris to Shanghae, and thence by steam. This exciting news, nine days later than we had at San Francisco, was devoured with zeal. So you see I have not quite realized one great aim of my visit—that of a repose beyond all the reach of steam or telegraph.

Nor have I dwelt upon the beautiful and extraordinary scenery that first met our eyes when entering the Bay of Yedo, the ever-green fields, the evergreen hills, with vegetation all alive from summit to base, often terraced, and ever beautiful. This Niphon (Japan) island is the Isle of Wight of this land of the rising sun. Daimios, richer than English nobles, with hundreds and hundreds, nay thousands, of retainers, preside and rule over this wonderful land.

There are no people, only millions and millions of human beings that we at home call people. No Maine Yankee, on first entering into the Hub of the Universe (Boston), ever stared more than I do, "pumped" more than I do, or is learning more than I am. If you think these rapid, racing, fly-on, fly-away scribblings of mine worth print, print away. I have not a moment for revision, nor book-making, not even for corresponding. I am jotting down only in my note-book, and sending it to you, hereafter to read it myself.

## LETTER VII.

### *THE CITY OF YEDO.*

The First Day in Yedo.—The Ride on the "Tocaido."—Strange Sights there.—The Pretty Tea Girls.—The Tiny Tea Cups.—Rooms with Paper Partitions.—The Beggars.—The Gin-rick-a Sha.—Ride in State along the "Tocaido."—Hogs in Baskets.—No Tycoon, only a "Mikado."—How we Stare and how they Stare at us.—Great Fire in Yedo.

YEDO, *June* 29, 1871.

I NEVER in my life worked so hard in one day, saw half as much, or learned half as much. Well, in this wilderness of men and things where shall I begin, or rather where shall I end? Don't talk to me any more of Broadway and its people, of the Strand in London, or the Boulevards of Paris! There is one long eternal street from Yokohama to Yedo, twenty-four miles long; not lit by gas, to be sure; not filled with palaces, certainly; not a hundred houses on it being two stories high, for fear earthquakes will topple them over; not paved with cobblestones or wood, but admirably *macadamized*—the Tocaido they call this long street, the Broadway of Japan, but not broader than Pine street, New York; rather the Appian Way of the Romans, for it runs the whole length of the island of Niphon, and is the royal road for every Jap to go from, and over, in the empire. The American Minister, Mr. De Long, honored my party by his presence, in his own carriage, over this Tocaido. Guards of the empire, to save us from saki (the whiskey of Japan), and the two-sworded rascals that get drunk on that saki, and whip off a head in a twinkle, escorted us on horseback, with stick and lantern, and yelled "*hi!*" "*hi!*" "*hi!*" to every poor Jap that did not scatter as the American lightning was coming. I had been reading and re-reading the two volumes of Sir Rutherford Alcock, the first British minister here (then with Townsend Harris, Esq., now of New York), and Sir Rutherford had so filled my head with bloody visions of Yedo, that I began to consider myself lucky if I could only get to, and from Yedo, and back, with my head *under* my arm. That "hi," "hi," "hi," and the consequent scattering—*that* "hi," "hi," "hi," I say, from Yaconin guardsmen and screaming "betto" (the boy that ran on foot by the carriage) has done the business for us, and my head is in its usual place, and likely to be, for all I can yet see in Yedo.

All Yedo seems to be moving down the Tocaido to Yokohama, and hence the long populousness of that Tocaido. Where gold glitters, there goes Jap, and though gold does not exactly glitter in Yokohama—only paper—paper *itzibus* (boos we shorten the word into), paper oriental English bank notes, and paper Japan rios (the dollar)—yet the paper is glittering enough to tempt the trading Jap down from Yedo to the foreign capital of Yokohama. A swamp there only ten or twelve years ago is now a city of over seventy thousand people, and it is growing (in Japs) so fast that even Jap houses, which don't cost much, cannot be built up fast enough to hold Japs needing them. We Americans, or Englishmen, rather, have sacked Japan of its golden kobans (coin) and golden itzibus, and we have compelled the Government to substitute paper therefor. When Com. Perry first landed here, in 1853, all was gold, gold, gold; now all is paper, paper, paper, save a stray Mexican dollar, which has a running value of about eight cents beyond the paper. Business stretches out from Yedo to run where commerce is, and where teas, silks, and bronzed copper, and lacquer ware go—and in twenty years more a fourth of Yedo will be on the swamps of Kanagawa and Yokohama.

What I saw on this Tocaido a good New York fancy reporter could make a thousand columns of, with pictures added on to make a thousand more; but a man does not see much when riding backward in an American Minister's carriage, in the hi, hi, hi style we were going, with guardsmen and betto. All the way, more or less, are planted pleasant teahouses. . . . . We "*tea*" here, when we must stop by the wayside, and in such little bits of cups that I could drink the content of twenty of them and then want more. Pretty tea girls stand by the entrance, and (their teeth not yet blackened) with ways so pretty, and courtesies so fascinating that tea, even without sugar or milk, becomes agreeable. Tea-houses are the grogshops of Japan. Our pretty lacquered waiters, the tea girls, hand you little tiny cups, with a mouthful in them, and you squat down on the nice, clean mats, if squat you can (I have to stretch out at length, and fill up half a tea room), and you sip, and sip, and sip, this mouthful of hot tea, as if the gods' nectar was going down your throat in infinitesimal drops of microscopic invisibility. Tea, like sleep, is a great invention. There's Bass' beer, all the way from London, stuck up in the corner of the tea-house shop, for beer-drinking, travelling Englishmen; but what's Bass' beer to tea, if you only can get enough of it, this hot weather with the thermometer over ninety? A Japan tea-house keeper picks out as pretty a place for the tea-house as he or she (the keeper) can get. The keeper covets, if possible, a view of, and the air of, the Bay of Yedo, along which, most of the way here, runs the Tocaido. The grand tea-house is cut up into numerous little rooms, with paper partitions between to part them, running on slides, but all removable at will, to restore the whole to one grand room. Cakes, sweetmeats, and candies are brought in with the tea, all put on the clean-matted floor (there are no seats), and we all squat or stretch out on that floor. It is stifling hot in these tea-houses just now, and a stretch out is a great relief to the traveler.

There is a river (the Logo) half-way up to Yedo, which we "pole" over on a flat-boat—horses on one boat, and we and the carriage on another. Beggars by the score beset us there. "Give us a Tempo" (one cent only), all pray, in the politest tones imaginable, with bows as graceful as if court-trained therefor. The lame, the halt, the blind, the idiotic, are there, and not only they, but people well enough looking to work. Beggars in Yedo proper have not yet met my eyes. The Government, I am told, particularly discourages begging there, and sends off the beggars that can work to work in the mines. One reason, probably, why the Government has put the ban on the beggars, I have written of before, is, that it wishes to discourage and break up the trade; but how can it be broken up, if even the poverty-stricken coolies, with no clothes on, will not work with the beggars? These beggars are the seventh class in Japan, ranking with actors, as I have written you; but there is a class below even these, the eighth and lowest (save one, the prostitutes), viz., the tanners, shoemakers, leather workers, skinners, etc. The Japs have no mutton (sheep die if they eat the grass here), but little beef, and that, before Perry came, not for food; and there is such a prejudice against those whose trade is to take life, or who are connected therewith, that it thus breaks out even against the shoemakers and leather workers. The prejudice, however, is so unnatural and unreasonable, that the tanners and their clan are petitioning hard to be relieved from the ban, and the Government will put them on an equality with other people as soon as the *vox populi*, that is, Tom, Dick, and Harry, will permit.

But, stop essaying. Get on to Yedo, the great city of the now extinct Tycoon—the city said to have two million human beings in it. On! on! But the *Gin-rick-a Shas* are in the way. What do you suppose is a *Gin-rick-a Sha?* Most people that ride here, ride, first, on Japanese ponies—a vicious, wicked little rascal (so say the Yankees here), that bites, and kicks, and flares up; next, they are carried in norimons (quality riding this is) by two coolies, in a sedan-covered chair; and next, in a cango, also carried by two coolies, on a pole over the coolies' shoulders—Satan's own invention for crooking up and cramping your legs, and making you miserable as you ride. Some Yedo genius lately, with no reverence for the customs of his great ancestors, has invented a *Gin-rick-a Sha,* which is a one-horse coolie carriage, a covered cart on springs, that one coolie can easily pull, and, therefore, infinitely better than the norimon, or cango, that two coolies must work. Thanks to that Yedo genius, you can go through the streets of Yedo now without being hived up in a norimon, or crooked and cramped in a cango. The progress of the age has got up, and got into Yedo, and I have hopes of a country that can invent a Gin-rick-a Sha. During the past year, in Yedo alone, they have made, numbered, and registered twenty-five thousand of these Gin-rick-a Shas, and each one pays an annual tax of three dollars.

4

On, on, on to Yedo! Well, as fast as possible. There's a team of coolies that block the way with a stick of timber two feet wide, or more, and twenty or thirty feet long, perhaps more. The coolies are stuck, but we raised our "hi," "hi," "hi," and the stick of timber cleared out for us. Coolies are both bullocks and horses here, and cheaper, too, for they only eat rice and fish, and not much of these, whereas horses and bullocks want ten times as much provender. Now, there, just as I am going on, is a drove of hogs in the way. A speculation in hogs is going on, just now, among the Japs who have seen China. The live hog market has been going up and down, just like stocks in the Wall Street market, and hogs here have their "bears" and "bulls," just as other stock, or stocks, have them. A sow and a litter of pigs, a little while gone by, sold as high as one thousand five hundred dollars, but now the bears have their way, and they have ruined the bulls in hogs. But they don't drive hogs here, on the Tocaido, as we do in America. When hogs are recalcitrant, as in America, they do not here turn tail where head ought to be, and drive them backward, but in mercy for the dear hog, they tenderly put him in a basket, and sling the basket on a pole over two coolies' shoulders, and in this way Japs drive hogs to the Yedo market, the hogs are cleared, and I am in Yedo!

And *this* is Yedo, and I am in Yedo; but alas, there is no Tycoon. The Tycoon has been tipped over, and tipped off his throne, since Commodore Perry's awful interview with his understrappers, and since Townsend Harris's great treaty. Kings, emperors, czars, kaisers, shahs, and others of the various big guns, are something; but the great Tycoon, and the city of the great Tycoon, have been my embodiments of grandeur and glory ever since I heard of Marco Polo, the first great Eastern traveller, and read the wonderful narratives of the great Dutchmen, from Holland, who made their first lodgment here, centuries ago. And there is no Tycoon now! There, are only the tombs of the great Tycoons—the Westminster Abbey of Japan—and that is all I can see! The Mikado has upset the Tycoon! There was a rebellion here, two or three years ago, and the spiritual, heaven-born, but hitherto powerless, Mikado turned up king, or emperor, and the poor Tycoon, and the old government of Tycoon, went under. They chopped off many heads, hung many up to dry, before all this happened; but the now unwarlike Tycoon, unlike his great ancestors, who robbed power from the Mikado by the sword in years gone by, gave up, disinclined longer to fight the gods' anointed, the spirit-born Mikado, and hence, while the Mikado lives in Yedo, the Tycoon has gone home to his estate in the country, to raise rice, catch fish, hunt falcons, or to enjoy other like rural and peaceful sports in his own castle, on the estates born to him. The Mikado is not visible to mortals, unless they wear straps. The American Minister has coaxed the Ministry up to letting him be seen by soldiers and sailors in straps, and by officials in the ambassadorial retinue; but alas, I have no straps, and these eyes of mine will never light upon the divine Mikado. I shall never see him, unless both he and I go to heaven together, and then he will be so high on the upper seats that mortal-born can never get near him. "In heaven there is one sun, on earth there is one Mikado," is a Confucian saying, in accordance with the idea of the country. But, nevertheless, say the middies, who have seen him, he is a big, fat boy, only wonderful for being a Mikado.

Yedo is, say, a fresh-born city in Montana or Wyoming, on the Pacific Railroad, say a city of pine boards, bamboo, thatched huts, one story high, seldom over that, though occasionally with two stories on—the upper mounted sometimes by a ladder, and sometimes by steps almost perpendicular, kept so clean and well polished as to be almost as slippery as ice. But don't misunderstand me. Yedo is at least two thousand years old. The pine boards are beautifully planed by some of the best carpenters in the world. The bamboos are the slide doors with paper windows, and the roofs are prettily thatched, if not covered, as most of them are, with tiles. The floors are all covered with beautiful mats. The walls are often lined with artistic drawings, and paintings, and sketches, that indicate a high degree of refinement. The windows are of paper; the outer shutters and doors of bamboo. They are lit at night by tapers of vegetable wax, with paper wicks, to flare well when the wind blows. Hence the universal use of lanterns to protect them from the winds. There is no neatness in the world like that in these wooden houses, not even among the Dutch in Amsterdam, or Rotterdam, or Schiedam, or any other Dutch dam. They shiver all over when foreigners' rough shoes tramp on their nice, spotless mats. They never thus tread on them, themselves, never; they always take off their shoes and leave them at the door, while we ramble and scamper, to their terror, over mats they sleep on—soft and nice beds they are, but plague on the wooden pillow. We look, peep, and spy into, and feel of, every thing, and they laugh at our curiosity; while they look, peep, and spy into every thing of ours, more especially into our ladies' habiliments. Long ringlets astonish them more than their skewered-up, sticky, waxed hair does us. They peep into our carpet-bags, as we peep into their closets, and they dance about, and jump, and wriggle before a mirror they take out, as we do before their curiosities. Hoop-petticoats astound them more than straw shoes and naked ankles do us. Every fashion, you thus see, that is not our fashion, is funny to us, and *vice versa*.

And, by the way, shoes are of many, many fashions here, as well as hats. The horse, the pony, the working bullock are straw shod. The working man and woman are straw shod. Nor are straw shoes so very ridiculous as the word straw would seem to import. A straw-bottomed shoe, fastened over the big toe, with straw straps around the ankle, is not a shoe to be laughed at in hot weather. I wish I could wear a pair, in lieu of my leather boots, this hot day. The straw shoes of the horses and bullocks seem stronger—but they are cheap, cost only a cent, everywhere to be had; and when worn out can be refurnished. They wear, however, a good while. The swell Japs are imitating the foreigners, and putting iron shoes on their horses; but the great body of the people stick to the straw. There are other men and women's shoes, some cost three cents, some six; the high officials wearing blue cloth or silk as a cover to the foot, and the shoe of the country underneath. There is a very nice shoe made all of wood—two-story shoes, I may call them, on two props, which go clatter, clatter, clatter, but keep the feet nice and clean. All shoes are put off as the house is entered, and thus everywhere, are clean mats and clean rooms.

They burnt down three hundred houses last night (in honor of our arrival? I don't write that)—only three hundred! But three hundred houses on fire is not much of a fire for Yedo. The houses do not cost much—only one hundred, two hundred, or three hundred dollars (this is my guess, only)—and all the fittings and furniture can be carried off, with screens, and mats, and paper sliding partitions, and pots and kettles, by two coolies, as the fire comes along. I *gin-rick-a sha'd* by the ruins this morning, and while in one place the firemen (they have them here) were sputtering water from a poor steam-engine (they have them too, now, poor ones) in other places the workmen were carrying off the ruins, preparatory to the erection of new dwellings, which, I am told, will all be up in a week. Houses that have to stand earthquakes are quickly *morticed*, not nailed up. Nothing is so fastened as not to stand an earthquake shake without toppling down. When the steam-engine and the fire are having a fight to see which beats, it is not uncommon, I am told, to see some poor believer offering up bits of paper scrolls to the god of fire, as a sacrifice to tempt the wicked demon to stop his flame spoutings.

## LETTER VIII.

*LIFE AND SIGHTS IN YEDO.*

Sintoo and Buddhist Temples.—The Priests.—The Sacred Cream-Colored Horses.—Theatres in the Temples.—The Opera in Yedo.—Funny Ride thereto in Gin-rick-a Shas.

YEDO, *June* 29, 1871.

LONG ago, I started to tell you what my hard day's work had been—the hardest of my life—but I ran off the track. Now, once more, I will try to get on. First, we went early to a Sintoo temple. They have two religions only in Japan—none other allowed (not even ours, the Christian, except to us outsiders)—the one, Sintoo, now the court (Mikado) religion, *up;* and the other, the Buddhist (the Tycoon), *down*, way down, and only propped up by Buddhist money at court. We first began "to do" the temple of Asaxa, some five or six miles from our hotel. Shops, shops, innumerable shops were on our way—shops for shoes, shops for clothes of all sorts, shops for fish, shops for rice, shops for tea, shops for silks and satins—nothing but five or six miles of shops. Temples and churches look very much alike the world over. Images, bells, lights, gold, glitter, etc., just the same; but the novelty here is a Pagoda, a grand Pagoda. The earthquakes do not tumble it over, only because it is built on some scientific foundation, in some scientific architecture, so as to be made earthquake-proof. The great novelties are —if not Barnum's old museum, something like it— a labyrinth called in our tongue a theatre, where you can go round and round, on a small space, half the day, and see life-size images of devils, saints, belles, beauties, beaux, dragons, mermaids, etc., "cutting up" in all sorts of ways. Bands of music play like thunder; and up hop, and down go, dragon and devil, and you see hell and heaven—our names for unknown Sintoo-Buddhist things. They expect only a tempo (a cent, from a Jap to see these wonders and monstrosities; they expect all they can get from the white barbarians,)—and the other great novelty is a pair of beautiful, sacred, cream-colored horses, ever saddled, if not ever bridled, with spirits invisible on their backs, that, every now and then, the priests trot about town, to scare off evil spirits from citizens' houses, and to purify and bless the air of Yedo. When these horses are trotted out, guards are sent ahead to announce their coming, and the Japanese are expected to prostrate themselves on the earth before them, so as not to see the gods on their backs. I would have given at least two tempos, if not more, to lay my hands upon the sacred beasts, but the spirits on their backs, alas! forbade any such heathen desecration. Asaxa, outside the temple, that is, on the temple grounds, is a sort of arcade or bazaar, in which toys, candies, rice-cakes, and all sorts of arcade things are sold. It is a place, too, where the people, by the thousands, when at leisure, or on holidays, go, if not to worship, to have fun, frolic, and a good time generally. The tumble-over boys, with their real rooster garniture, would entertain us for any length of time for a cent or two. The women Japs, by the hundreds, with babies slung over their backs, whose heads were roasting in the sun (fire-proof heads babies must have here, *mem.* for my note-book), flocked around us, and made the air so hot and stifling that, precious as woman is, her room here was better than her company. Some two-sworded fellows looked cross and scowled, but, in the main, the curious crowds were sociable, kind, very agreeable, though ever curious, especially to see what sort of stuff our ladies were made of.

The next temple we visited—rather, only the ruins of a temple—was Owina. When the Mikadoites rebelled against the Tycoonites, two or three years ago, this Owina temple, a stronghold of the Tycoon, was taken by assault. The Tycoon had for years kept there a Jap of the pure blood-royal, the sacred *azul* running in his veins, with intent to play him off against the real Mikado, if ever this real Mikado should become saucy, and attempt to get the better of the Tycoon. Owina was the home of this mock Mikado; and when the Tycoon thus went down, down went Owina in blood and in sorrow. We have only ruins, ruins, therefore, to see. Beautiful groves yet exist, magnificent trees, tea-gardens for the entertainment of visitors, singing and dancing girls—but no priest, no Buddhist, no Sintoo, no any thing but ruins, for acres and acres. Here, on the overhanging hills, was the only grand, that is, tip-top, re-view we had of Yedo. For thousands of acres there is nothing in sight but the houses, the parks, the castles, the streets, the river, the canals of Yedo. How big *is* Yedo? That is the great question of the day. I have tried hard to find out, officially and unofficially, but—*quien sabe?* Who knows? The officials won't tell, and they do know now, for the census has just been taken. Some foreigners say two millions; some one million; some only eight hundred thousand. If I were to *guess* from the great city, under my (Owina) eyes, I should say "the two millions;" but when I look at the vast parks of the Daimios (the nobles), with their retainers in the city, and the parks and castle of the awful, almighty Mikado (all the area of this city, including thirty-six square miles), I am ready to come down to "the one million." This difference of opinion arises from the floating character of the population. There are eighteen great Daimios, nine of whom once *had* to be in the capital, and they brought with them from six thousand to ten thousand retainers, each. There are three hundred and forty-two lesser-light Daimios, and they all had their retainers. Three hundred and forty-two thousand, it has been estimated, followers are in the trains of these, what the English call princes, dukes, earls, lords, knights, etc. This ebbing and flowing of a court city with imperial officials, priests, etc., make men differ on the population of Yedo.

The circumference of this Yedo view or city is estimated at twenty-five miles. The temples are legion. The god of war, and innumerable other gods, big and little, have their temples. Priests are as thick as grasshoppers in Utah. The Siro (Djiro), or the Imperial castle, covers nearly five miles within this circumference. My profane eyes can only get up high, and look down. High walls and many canals shut out the profane crowd from the pretty walks, bowers, flowers, dwarfed-trees and aquatic birds, that sing for and regale the lofty Mikado. Only ex-Secretary Seward, some middies, lieutenants, captains, admirals, ministers plenipotentiary, and like officials, have ever been blinded by the dazzling rays from the imperial person, or ever entered on the mats, or within the saloons of his palace or castle. Our great Tycoon was slipped in diplomatically, as a dazzling American beam from the setting sun. No ladies' eyes—that is, barbarian ladies' eyes—were ever permitted to be even downcast before his celestial splendor. The best I can do, then, is to look about and look down here from Owina.

The third temple " done " this day was Sheba (not the Queen of), a great Buddhist (Tycoon) temple, with a monstrous big bell, twelve feet high, and with room for four or more persons inside—an oblong bell, all of one diameter, the clapper of which, outside, is a great big wooden log, some fifteen feet long, which rough machinery *pounds* the bell with. The priests would not *pound* it for us, for love or money, in fear of frightening the town. Bell-metal, by the way, is much better and sweeter-toned here in Japan than in the United States. Tell Meneely and all his bell-men of that, and advise them to come here and learn how to make church-bells (not the clappers). Sheba looks so like a Catholic temple, a beautiful, costly one, that I could easily fancy myself in Rome, or Milan, or Venice—not exactly in the Roman St. Peter's, whose architecture is so superb, or in the Duomo of Milan, but in secondary cathedrals, with magnificent altar-work. The temple of Sheba is in the shade, just now, among the Sintoos, and at the Sintoo court, for it is the burial-place of some of the Tycoons, costly memorial monuments of whom fill an oblong, commemorating their grandeur. Their Sheba is their sanctuary, and hence, in all parts, rich and highly ornate, while incense is kept burning—it may be for the Tycoons. Beyond one of the temples, in a court, is a large bronze monument, entered by two heavy bronze gates, all presented by the king or emperor of Corea, hundreds of years ago, in honor of the sixth Tycoon.

Weary of temples and priests, monuments and the dead, we now, this same day, looked up the living, and visited the Foreign Office. The ladies with us had intense curiosity to see the Foreign Office, and the foreign ministers, etc.—for what is seen in the street and at the tea-houses is not "style;" and hence their curiosity was great to see the stylish high officers of state. It required some negotiations and much diplomacy to have ladies admitted to a foreign office and to a court; but the American Minister, highly esteemed by the Japanese here, and beloved, I may say, by all, was gratified in his request to have the ladies accompany us. The fact is, ladies are not much thought of in Japan. Woman is of no account, except to be useful. If poor, she works the farm, whirls the spinning-wheel, keeps the house, makes up the clothes (when people wear any), keeps the tea-houses, etc.; and if rich, she embroiders, paints, etc., as did the old Greek princesses, Penelope & Co.; but she is, nevertheless, of no account. The greater the wonder, therefore, that this low grade of creatures could ever be got into court! Only two foreign ladies ever before had the honor. But ours were admitted with us, drank tea and drank champagne, but did not smoke! and what was worse, kept the ministers from smoking, as they are too polite to smoke when others do not smoke, especially foreign women, whom, as they see us thinking much of, they think they must think something of, too, more especially when with foreigners. (*Mem.*—All foreign ministers should smoke; alas, I don't.) The prime-minister, Swakara, received us in state and in style, and five others, all in rich silk robes, and Ishibasha, a very clever man, who speaks English well, was the translator. What we all said—no matter. What we did only can interest anybody; but that would be too long to tell. The reception-room was fitted up in European style as to tables and chairs only, but every thing else was Japanese — mats (European carpets were laid over some of them, that our feet should not soil the mats), screens, hanging pictures, representing Japanese scenes, officials of rank, etc., and when once inside, and these screens were removed, a view was opened to us of a beautiful garden.

The next visit we made this day (after a drive in the park of the foreign ministers' quarter, a choice spot allowed the English mission to erect a palace upon, and to the gate "where the elephant could not go through," the Japanese name of a gate, where an elephant presented to the court once got squeezed)— was to Hamagoten, a bewitching spot, both near and on the sea, where the foreign Japanese ministers entertain the foreign ministers of Europe. Hamagoten is the fishing country residence of the old Tycoon. It looks out on the Bay of Yedo, takes in the cool sea breezes, and yet has all the charms and witcheries of country life — bowers, groves, tea-houses, flowers, plants, great trees and little dwarfed trees, artificial shrubbery that makes you laugh to look at its fantasies, lakes, gold fishes, etc. The Japanese grandees well know how to enjoy country life. They are lords of creation here. Duke, lord, nor knight, nor banker, in England, does not surpass, if equal, a right royal

Daimio in country sports and luxuries. But more, by-and-by, of Hamagoten.

Would you not think the doings of this day in Yedo were enough for a traveller? But we had the night before us, and if *all* Yedo was not startled by our doings, it was because all Yedo did not see us. A young American from New York, now in Yedo instructing Japanese in English and French, told us of a tea-house where was, in some sort, the Yedo opera, and where music was "done," and dancing was done, and the ballet corps, if not numerous, was striking and strange. Travellers must see all sights, you know. It would not do to go to Yedo without patronizing music and dancing, etc. We engaged six *gin-rick-a shas*. What sort of a *sha* this *gin* is, look back and see. Our party was six—six only, except the coolies that pulled the *gins*—and our out-riders on horseback were six in number. The coolies had mantles on when they started—that is all I need say of them now, for the weather was hot; and pulling a man or woman in a *gin-rick-a sha* is a perspiring action in hot weather. The coolies ran and raced, and the horses' feet clattered over the streets and stones of Yedo, and the swords of the guardsmen (Yakonins) rattled as the horses galloped to keep up with the "*gin*" and the coolies. We made a grand procession through many of the important streets of Yedo. Each coolie carried a lantern, and each horseman, too, though the moon was shining bright. Such a procession seldom, if ever before, waked up the Yedoites. Crowds collected to stare at us. Jap yelp upon yelp here announced our coming. John Gilpin's ride could not have equalled ours in the curiosity excited, though we fared far better than poor John.

The opera-house we visited, if I may dignify the tea-house we halted at with that high-sounding name, was not quite equal to the La Scala of Milan, or the Academy of Music. No boxes, no pit, no stage, only a mat floor, second story, in a low-roofed room. The orchestra or music—what shall I say of it?—was in the shape of six or seven guitar-looking things, with some strings on them, not pulled by the fingers, but hit by a piece of board. The ballet corps did double duty—acted, as well as chanted, pantomimed and danced. A New York opera-house critic could turn out, in the morning journal, a column of mysterious criticism upon the music and ballet I heard and saw, but I have no genius in that line, and so must stop. All I can say is, I stretched out on the mat and went to sleep, worn out with the day's doings—while others *chow-chowed* (ate) cakes and candies, sipped saki (Japanese whiskey), tea, and Bass' English beer. Happy was I to *gin-rick-a sha* it home, and sleep, sleep, as man never before slept, until he takes the sleep forever.

All now that can interest you of this hard day's work is the opera bill—thus made out on Japanese tea-paper, two feet long, which, being translated, reads thus·

TOKEI, 5 month, 13 day (*June* 29), 1871.

| | | |
|---|---|---|
| Six gin-rick-a shas (carriage riding for six)............ | 6 boos | $1 50 |
| Singing girls............... | 1 rio and 3 boos | 1 75 |
| Dancing girls.............. | 3 rio and 1 boo | 3 25 |
| Beer...................... | 1 boo | 25 |
| Fish (for coolies) and saki... | 2 rio and 1 boo | 2 25 |
| | | $9 00 |

All the cost for six United States Yankees, six Yakonins (guards), and six coolies, including the horses and carriage riding.

Something cheaper, you see, than the grand opera of Paris, London, and New York, to say nothing of the fish for the coolies and the Yakonins!

If I can ever get time to go to a theatre, I will send you a theatre bill of fare; but Jap plays, like Chinese plays, are eternal, often beginning in the morning and running through a week or two.

# LETTER IX.

### *LIFE AND SIGHTS IN YEDO.*

Eyes only Useful Here.—Tongue and Ears Useless.—Shopping in Yedo.—Hotels in Japan.—Grand Hotel in Yedo.—Breakfast with the Ministry of Foreign Affairs at Hamagoten.—Dinner at a Beautiful Country-Seat.—Discussions, Political and Theological.—Why the Japanese don't like Christians.—The Schools of Japan.—Reading, Writing, and Arithmetic almost Universal.

YEDO, *June* 30, 1871.

WHAT a miserable life it is to be in a country where you can understand nothing through your ears, except the yelling and mewing of cats, the barking of dogs, and the crying of babies, strapped on their mothers' or little sisters' backs! Even dogs bark, not in English, but in a Japanese way. The baby-crying is the only real familiar sound to greet my ears. The cocks have a new way of crowing, and the hens of cackling. None of the birds sing as our birds sing, if any of them sing at all, though they make an infernal noise for birds. There are no sheep to bleat and make you happy, and the cows, if there are any, and the bulls, but very few, are so well drilled they never low or roar. The temple bells, even, are not our bells. They do not speak English, or French, or German, or any other European language, but utter notes of their own. I should, therefore, have the blues in such a deaf and dumb land, if American and English friends had not sprung up in all directions. The fish, all, are new fish, as well as the birds; the trees, most of them, new trees; the flowers all new, if we had not imported many of them into America. I cannot even go a-shopping alone, where there is any thing wonderful to buy. I cannot tell what I want; and when I do, I cannot get at the price of it, especially in measures and weights, all new to us, and worse, by far, than the kilometres and kilogrammes of our French and Continental neighbors. If the rascals that went to work at that Tower of Babel had had any idea of what a confusion in the world they were making, do you think they would have tried to build it? Here I am in a Yedo street, staring and stared at, knowing nothing, and profiting nothing from Greek, Latin, or some considerable smattering in several European tongues. I would (perhaps?) give up all my five or six years of Greek and Latin, if I could only speak five or six words of Japanese, such as, "What's the price of this or that?" or, "Show me some silks, or crapes, or satins, or fans, or lacquer, or copper engraving." Here are thirty-five millions of living Japanese, and I have spent years of my life studying *dead* Latin, and *deader* Greek (I would do it over again, though); and I can't read the names of the streets, or the numbers of the street! I do not know even my letters! I want to ask a million of questions, such as "How do you weave or spin *that?*" or "carve this?" or, "Why do you stable your horses' heads where we put the horses' tails?" "Why do you mount your beasts on the wrong side?" "Why don't you use wheelbarrows in lieu of bamboo baskets, when digging canals in Yedo?" "Why do you saw backward?" "Why do you plane backward?" But I cannot talk; I am deaf; I am dumb; I might as well be a horse in Yedo, when alone, as a man in the streets all alone!

Shopping is the chief business of foreigners in Japan, and hence we all go a-shopping. There is a Curio Street in both Yokohama and Japan—that is, a street of curiosities. The lacquer ware is wonderful, both dear and cheap—dear, if very old and very artistic, and cheap as dirt, if fresh and poorly wrought on. The bronzes are astonishing. Where did the Japanese pick up their wonderful art in this? Their work in silk and crape, too, is wonderful, and very, very cheap for some things. Mantillas—if one may so call them—*obies*, that is, curiously-worked sashes to go round the waist, are often in the very highest art. A silk man in Yokohama is imitating European dressing-gowns, and he will fit you out in crape work for about five dollars, so that you would not be known from a peacock. Rock crystal is curiously wrought, and very precious to the Japanese. I have just been buying a suit of armor, once belonging to some stately Daimio, which cost him, four or five hundred years ago, if the official certificates do not lie, some five hundred dollars

—gold wrought, and embossed, and with terrible-looking gold dragons; but the days of armor are over now, and coats of mail being worth nothing to the owner—what I gave for it—no matter; but dog cheap, if the certificates do not lie. Sixty or seventy tons of Japanese *curios* went out on the last steamer for San Francisco, and they will make, if I am not misinformed, all the Yankee sight-seers there stare. I am negotiating for temples and pagodas, but the state "religion" is not down enough here yet to buy gods and temples cheap. What a pity they are not as cheap as armor! Oh, if I could only talk, talk, talk, how I would shop here in Yedo! And what is the use of the American great "gift of the gab" in such a deaf and dumb place as this?

I had got it into my head that there were no hotels in Japan—nothing but tea-houses and mats for foreigners to live in, or sleep on; but I am mistaken. There is a European hotel here in Yedo—an American hotel, I had better say—run now by an American, as big as the old burnt-down Congress Hall or United States, of Saratoga—nay, as big as the Ocean House, at Newport. The Japanese built it, under English inspiration, to meet the wants of foreigners expected at Yedo, but they have never come, and the hotel has never paid a cent in return to the builders. Some five hundred people could be crowded into it, but now it has not thirty guests, and the most of them boarders in official position, or teachers. There is a Yankee captain here, from New

York, who has been running steamships for some time, between port and port in Japan, mainly for the Japanese Government. We have no consul now at Yedo, but a vice-consul acts by ambassadorial appointment, and boards at the hotel, with the United States flag up over him. The Minister resides in Yokohama, and has not a place in Yedo to put his head in, save this hotel. And there, is the "Grand Hotel" in Yokohama, and the "International Hotel," and there are lots of other hotels for Tom, Dick, and Harry. There will be rest for you, you see, future traveller to Japan, and very, very fair fare, if not the best of fare, such as in America. You *can* have chairs to sit on at table, and not be compelled to squat on mats, and eat with chop-sticks on the floor. Civilization has got here, and is teaching all sorts of its novelties to the wonder-stricken Japs, who think we are fools to fill up our rooms with tables, and sofas, and chairs, and bedsteads. They hang out beautiful screens, some of them high works of art, and when you open your eyes in the morning, you see, not graceless chairs and crooked-legged tables, but works of art all over and around you. Away with the screens, and lo, presto! every room in your house, on the same floor, is turned into one grand room. I have thought this great Yedo hotel might be converted into a grand watering-place on the Bay of Yedo—for it is all alone by itself, wall-surrounded, set apart and consecrated to foreign residents only. Bathing and boating are here close at hand. Some day hence, it may be, Americans will come over to Yedo as to Long Branch, or Cape May; for, with the exception of the mosquitoes, that we shut off with nets, and the fleas, which we can scare off with flea-powder, it is a paradise of a place. The climate in summer is very like that of Cape May, or Old Point Comfort. The Japs are so impressed by the grandeur of this two-storied hotel, with a tower, that shakes well when an earthquake comes along, or a typhoon, that they pay twelve and a half cents of our money to come in and look at it, and the keeper lets out the privilege or monopoly at seventy dollars per month.

I have had two distinguished invitations to go out in Yedo, both from Japanese—one to breakfast, the other to dine—and I accepted them with pleasure, without knowing, though somewhat fearing, the strange things I might have to eat. (At the Chinese meals, it is (not Japanese) where one may have rats, cats, or dogs, and birds' nests, as well as fish and rice.) The service, I am sorry to say, both at the breakfast and dinner, was European. We all sat upright, all ate with knives and forks, all drank European wines, as well as tea, with no saki; all smoked, though with pipes of very different organizations.

The breakfast was given to the American Minister and myself by the Prime-Minister of the Board of Foreign Affairs, and was in the beautiful garden of Hamagoten. Invited at eleven A. M., we breakfasted till four P. M.! One poor, hard-working fellow, the very clever interpreter, Ishibashi, did all the talking for us (double-talked), and we gave him no time for eating, only for talk, talk, talk. Five hours of talk, only think of it, for an interpreter! The talk was about almost every thing on the earth, over the earth, and under the earth, more particularly, though, on affairs of government, and the science of government, in which these Japanese gentleman seem to be deeply interested. Their conversation exhibited skill, learning, and ability, and showed they had been well educated, not only in their own books, but were pretty well acquainted with American and European affairs. They puzzled much over the fact that the American Minister and myself were friends though far apart in politics. They fight and kill in party politics, while we only vote. They could not well understand why Nevada, *his* State, should have as much influence in Congress (the Senate) as *mine*, New York (nor can I). They could not understand our tariffs, nor can I. Their history they hold to be good for two thousand two hundred years, and pretty accurate for two thousand five hundred years. They have records they rely on so far back. Their letters, they own, they get from China, and the classics of Confucius and Mencius are their classics. They think they are Mongolian, not of Chinese origin, and probably they came down from Corea. The costumes of these gentlemen were robes of a peculiar silk, one of them white (flowered), with Turkish trowsers and sandals. The chief had on an extraordinary hat, the tissue of which I cannot describe—a hat uplifted like a tower, and only to cover the queue. This hat was put on in deference to the guests, whereas we take off hats in deference; and when the hat wearied him from its weight he begged permission to take it off, and we cheerfully relieved him from the burden, of course. The servants waited upon us in the most deferential silence. Not a look or emotion ever escaped them. From behind screens they peeped in to imagine our wants, and instantly heeded them. A small boy did the table-bell business, and when any thing extra was needed, the *boy-bell* ran in, and on hands and knees tumbled on the floor, to hear the whisper of the high personage commanding him.

The dinner was given us with our ladies, though ladies seem of no account in Japan, woman's rights never having reached here; but our Japanese host had been in America, spoke English, and knew American habits well. We went to the place of the dinner—a magnificent country-seat, though in the city, by the water's edge—in a Japanese pleasure boat, sculled, not rowed, by Japs, and the seats were pretty mats, and the sides of our cabins were paper slides with pictures upon them. On, on, on, we were "sculled," on the Bay of Yedo not far from its port, and up a river, under many bridges and through canals—how far I do not know, only regretting, so much of novelty was to be seen by the way, that the distance was not longer. Junks, heavily laden with the produce of the country, were passed; fishermen's nets were glided over; manufactories were seen, etc. Yedo seen by land I have tried to sketch, but this was Yedo by water. Our Japanese entertainers were very gallant to our ladies. Two of them spoke English, were well educated in New Brunswick, N. J., and in New England. They showed us all over the delightful pleasure-grounds. We sailed on little artificial lakes in pleasure-boats. We saw for the first time the tea-plant growing. We had explained to us the wonderful process of grafting and dwarfing trees by which gate-ways are made of them, and how they are turned into junks, castles, temples, beasts, lions, dragons—any thing you want. Some of them, years old, were scarcely a foot high, and yet perfect as trees, otherwise, in all their trunks, branches or limbs, and leaves. The flowers, too, are thus dwarfed—many of them not an inch high, in flower-pots, but perfect as flowers. I know nothing of botany or horticulture, or I would expand on this wonderful art. It fills me with amazement, for I do not recollect of ever reading of the like before my coming here. The summer-houses (tea-houses) were numerous in this place. The walks were shady and pretty. Little fountains gurgle out their tiny waters. We Americans, that build up hundred-thousand dollar country seats, think we know something; but in this line we are behind the age. Such a "seat" as I am dining in would cost, near New York, half a million of dollars.

As we were dining—and we had European luxuries in European style—the Japanese women would peep round the screens to peep at our ladies. Curiosity is the same with the sex the world over. We discussed many things; theology not a little. The Japs have an idea like ours of the creation of the human race, but as I understood our table expounder of Japanese theology, they believe woman (our Eve) was made before our man (Adam). This exposition delighted our ladies, and I send it especially to gladden the hearts of Mrs. Stanton and others. It is hard to put up, even at a Pagan's hospitable table, with Pagan gods, and goddesses, and spirits, and to be compelled to listen to the divinity of them (ugly-looking blocks and images as they are), but it is harder yet to hear our Old Testament and New Testament all overthrown, and to be told Christ, like Mahomet, Confucius and Mencius, or Brigham Young, was only a very clever man—as good and as wise as Confucius, perhaps, but no wiser nor better. I asked, "Why they fought Christianity so in Japan?" "Because," they replied, "it interferes with the Government." "Its ministers are often impertinent." "They interfere with what they have no concern." "The Roman Catholics, you know, once were allowed full swing here; had missions and followers everywhere; and they turned into politicians, such politicians that we had to clear out the whole of them." Nevertheless, the medical missionaries are well received in Japan. One of them, Dr.

Hepburne, is dearly beloved by them, and has made an Anglo-Jap dictionary, the only one, and which all, more or less, are studying.

I have had long talks, here and elsewhere, on the schools of Japan—on reading and writing, arithmetic, etc. The Japanese tell me not everybody reads and writes, but almost everybody, more or less. Everybody keeps accounts, or seems to—not reckoning as we do with Arabic figures, but on boxes with pegs for our numbers. The dialects of the thirty-five millions of people in Japan are numerous, and as puzzling, even to the natives, as are the dialects of Yorkshire and Lancashire in England, or the Welsh or the Celtic to the English. The Court has one tongue, the coolies another, and the provinces all have their dialects. "Education," however, as we call it, is pretty well diffused in Japan—that is, reading, writing, and arithmetic, or the three "R's," as some call it. But is reading, writing, and arithmetic "education?" I do not think it is. Are common schools that teach only the "R's" good for much? Certainly not in Japan, as I see things here (if in America). The three "R's" are only tools to work with, and if that is all a man knows, his tools are more likely to be used by others against than for him. Here all, more or less, are the creatures, instruments, tools of the Princes, the Daimios, the nobility, the two-sworded men, who ride rough-shod over the many, and keep them poor while they hold all the wealth. Some one and a half millions thus quarter upon the other thirty-three and a half millions, though all, or nearly all, can read, write, and cipher as well as we do in the United States.

Our dinner over, we glided back in our luxurious gondola—shall I call it?—to the Hotel of Yedo. Our party spent the evening on the cool waters of the bay among the fishermen, listening to their "yeow," "yeow," or singing, or chanting, or studying the stars to see if the same luminaries were over our heads as over our dear, dear friends now under our feet at home. It relieves one of one's homesickness to see the same bright lights over one's head that one sees at home, and thus to feel in this deaf and dumb life here, the world is the same for Jap, and John, and Jerry, no matter where born.

# LETTER X.

### *TRAVELLER'S LIFE IN THE INTERIOR.*

The Great God of Kamakura.—"Statue of Dai-bootz."—Life in Japanese Tea-Houses.—Ride in a Cango Bamboo Basket.—The Temples around Kamakura.—Beautiful Scenery.—Fields cultivated like Gardens.—The Life and Rank of Japanese Farmers.—Visit to the Cave of Inosima.—Fish Life and Fish Dinners.—The "Mikado" and the "Tocaido."—Politeness and Amiability of the Japanese Farmers.

FUJISAWA, *July* 3, 1871.

HAPPY times we are having in a tea-house tavern —hotel we should call it—but there are no beds to sleep on, no tables to eat on, no chairs to sit on! There is a jolly party of us, and we are doing our own cooking, with maidens all around to stare at us, the mother of them all to admire us, and a whole village about to help us. We should not cook if we could trust the maidens to cook the fish for us; but there is no foretelling what they might put into the fish for sauce, and the copper sauce-pans they fry fish in, and the matters they fry it with, are thought to be rather suspicious. We brought our own bread and butter—both are unknown in Japan as native-used articles of food—and with this, and sardines, and plenty of excellent fish and tea, we made a first-rate dinner.

We are on our way to see a great god, if not *the* great god, of Kamakura (once a great city, a capital, but now all run down), and the great god is "*Daibootz*," or "Great Buddha"—but we tarry in this teahouse over-night. I do not think much of sleeping on mats all night. They are full of fleas, big ones, and they bite, too. They are full of mosquitoes, but we don't care for them, if our net bars are strong enough to stand their twisting and wriggling to break in, but they are not. "Buzz," "buzz," "whizz," "whizz." You know all about that, even in New York city, and all over Jersey. Then we had Japan guitar music nearly all night, from the damsels below, which is no better than mosquito music, I being judge. Then we had cat music. The cats of Japan seem to me to have extraordinary lung strength, and when they utter their love notes, and purr, and squall here, they make the welkin ring. One of our man party jumped about all night, flea-bitten; the ladies averred they had not closed their eyes, but who believed them? As for myself, I am flea-proof, mosquito-bomb-proof. I snored, they say —the only sign I was not sleeping well, just as well as usual. You would not understand Japan-travelling if I did not enter into all these *minutiæ*, and therefore you must excuse the personality.

We had a whole floor to ourselves, and on that floor perhaps a dozen rooms—all one, though, when the paper screens were removed. Such tenements as these, you see, are not very favorable for private life, or secrecy, or domesticity. One cannot whisper at night without being heard all over the domicil. A husband can not scold a wife, or, a wife "Caudle" a husband, without everybody's hearing. Flirting is impossible, and courting would be, if courting were ever heard of in Japan. Wives are not won by courting here, but put in the market by father and mother to the best or most fitting bidder. They know little or nothing of their future husbands till their teeth are to be blackened and their eyebrows shaved for matrimony. When we breakfasted, all Fujisawa, having heard of the event, ran to our doors, or gathered around us, to see us eat on our improvised table, with Jap wooden sleeping-pillows adopted for chairs; and if one thing more than another seemed to astound them, it must have been the enormous quantity of tea we drank.

But to the great god, *Dai-bootz*, and his holy temple! We fitted out, to visit him, a retinue you would have laughed your eyes out to see—six cangos and eighteen coolies as our equipage! The cango is a sort of bamboo basket, and two coolies carry you on a pole. Our coolies were in the livery of nature, save their straw shoes, cotton cloth girdle, and handkerchiefs around their heads. We men are heavy fellows, some of us over two hundred pounds, a heavy load for two coolies to carry in a basket for miles, up hill and down hill, over creeks, streams, and through ocean surf and sands, and therefore we took a coolie extra for every cango. Three or four bettos (boys that run with the horses) were our outriders. The hours I spent in that bamboo basket cango will ever be deeply dented on my memory. But Yankee trained as I was, I was up to it. "Our heels ever higher than our heads," is about the first posture we, when boys, learn in New England, and heels higher than heads in a basket is cango riding here. We lean back on chairs at home, and put our heels on the mantel-piece, and this is Japan cango riding. Japs do it easily, for they are short fellows, and squat; but for our long legs it is hard work, unless brought up to it. In these cangos we made our pilgrimage to *Dai-bootz*. We spied out "the great Buddha" at last, prettily situated in a small gravelled court, surrounded by a growth of bamboos, camelias, diospyros, oaks, and conifers, and approached it up a flight of steps and stone portal. The Buddhist priests were glad to see us. They were sure of extra boos (twenty-five-cent paper pieces), and welcomed us with smiles, tea, and a lithograph of their idol. We went inside of him, after running all around him on the outside. His inside is full of gilt Buddhist saints, with croziers, glories around the head, etc., etc. We threw tempos (cents) up into his head, to hear them rattle. The priests liked it, for we did not pick them up, though they were frightened lest the heavy copper tempos, falling back, might hit on their shaven heads. We skirted on the outside again, the better to comprehend this huge mass of bronze, fifty feet high, and thirty feet wide at its base, which rests on a pile of masonry, six feet high. We ran again into the inside to see how the bronze joints were put together, and these joints were almost imperceptible. We got up into the old fellow's arms. Six of us sat on his thumbs! We looked into his face, and saw there "the mournful repose," the lips closed, the eyes downcast, and the head slightly bent upon the breast. Great is *Dai-bootz!* I don't think much of him as a god; but as mighty work of bronze art, as a Colossus, in that way I worship him, as I did the Sphynx, near the Egyptian pyramids, and wish I had a week to give him, instead of this passing hour.

At Fujisawa we left the great royal highway of Japan, and went into the rural roads, where not even a *gin-rick-a sha* can go, only a pony, or a coolie-carried cango, strapped on a pole. This is my first *entrée* into rural Japan life. Hitherto I have been in the cities—now I am in the country, and my admiration of Japan rises and rises. I thought once, when on the Nile, that the Egyptians, who could turn sands into gardens, were the great farmers of the world; but the Egyptians made no such farming gardens as these. Proud as I am of the arts, sciences, and marvellous doings of my own country, I blush when I compare American farming with this! Here, are rice-fields artificially created, luxuriant in beauty now, terraced from hill-side, up and down, and watered by the hill streams, or not watered, as husbandman wills. There, are barley-fields, and bean-fields, and fields of all sorts of Japan agricultural productions. Forests cap all the hill-tops. It is said, the law or customs of Japan forbid a man to cut down a tree, unless forthwith he plants another. Hence these beautiful tree-clad hills and hill-sides. (Our tariff laws in America counsel an American lumberman to cut down his trees by making dear all lumber from Canada.) Two crops are raised in Japan in one year, even on the rice-fields, where the first crop is grain. The grain harvest is over in April or May. The rains come on in June and July, and now the new crops are up, and the whole country is one beautiful landscape in green. It is ravishing in beauty, and I am happy in looking at it, even with my legs up on the roof of my cango. The turnip or root crops will come by-and-by. December and January are here only the real winter months, while in June and July, after the barley harvest is over, it is rain, rain, ever gentle rain.

One reason, perhaps, why Japan has superb farming, is that the farmers here rank next to the nobility, only Koongays of the royal blood, or Daimios (princes, say), or Haitamotos (lords), above them. All merchants, manufacturers, traders, artisans, carpenters, etc., give precedence in rank to these lords of the soil. The farmers' houses I see about here are like Swiss cottages, thatched, generally, with bamboo fences around them, but with no fences on their fields. The tools they have would not pass muster in our land. Their hoe is more like our shovel than a hoe, though hung as a hoe on a bamboo handle.

Ploughs I have not seen, nor harrows. Man or woman seems to be plough and harrow here. The flail, the regular old American farmers' flail, is their threshing machine. They pound off the husks of the rice in a mortar, and man or woman stand on a level, and pump up and down, the pounding pestle in the mortar.

But on, on, though I would like to scribble an essay on farming, and expand upon the superb Japanese agriculture. Let me say, before I quit the topic, however, that nothing is wasted in Japan. Not a straw, even, is allowed to run idle. Compost of all kinds is cherished as a gold mine. Our city sewers, which draw off so much wealth, would break the heart of a Jap farmer, seeing so much gold run into the sea. In pails and baskets, on men's shoulders, is carried for miles the refuse of the great city, off to the fields of the farmer. These pails, on coolies shoulders, do not always sweeten the air, but they make bountiful the fields and the crops.

Our coolie-cangos now transport us from the green fields to the ocean-side, and among the surf, rolling up on the sandy beach. I am in Newport, or Long Branch, or Cape May. The soothing sounds of the unceasing billows that lave the feet and naked legs of our coolies, gladden us, while the spray, now and then, dashes up a little into our bamboo baskets, sprinkling our heads, perhaps, but never reaching as high as our heels. We are going to Inosima, where is an island cave. We are "dumped" from our cangos into a tea-house, and while dinner is preparing we propose to explore the cave. We go over a hill of temples, or go around the hill by water. We enter the cave two hundred feet or more—an earthquake-made cave, doubtless, for this I infer from the way the rocks are pitched together; and near the end, unless we choose to crawl and go further, is a Sintoo temple, with Sintoo priests to watch over the holy shrines, near which waters from above are trickling. We pay the priest, of course, to help to keep up his paper candles and wicks of oil. We look at the devil he has got chained in there, and we drink from the holy spring, one draught of which is to save us from sickness, from plague, or cholera, or typhoid. I took three draughts, in order to be sure, for I need them all in the long journey I am contemplating.

The tea-house dinner of Inosima was nothing remarkable. We borrowed some boards to make a dinner-table of, and we squat again on seats, the Japanese use for sleeping-pillows. Fish, fish, fish, make all the meals here—shell-fish, crab-fish, sun-fish, devil-fish, the funniest sort of fish and crabs I ever saw, the like of which we have nowhere in America. But I did find an old acquaintance in a clam, an eel, and in a mackerel, and in a clawy-looking creature, something like a lobster. The whole air here is fishy. There is no sort of an ocean or river-creature that the Japs do not eat, even sharks; and the uglier the creature is, the more appetizing. Fish markets in Japan are curiosities, from the oddities, eccentricities, frights of things you see for sale there. And most of the fish sold are not dead fish, but living, jumping, wriggling fish. You buy an eel all squirming. The fish-market men bring their fish to market in water-tubs, and the fishermen keep a huge bamboo water fish-tank on each side of the junks, into which they throw the creatures that they haul up, or in. So much is thought of the fish here, that, on a certain festival day, every family that has had a boy born (not a girl) during the year, hangs out a great painted fish to boast of it. If I knew any thing of ichthyology, I would be more particular in my description of the fish; but I am ignorant all along, you see. I am not only deaf and dumb here, but a "Know-nothing" in most of the *ologies* and *ites* a traveller ought to know—from ichthyology to entomology, and on, and on.

The tea-house fish dinner over, we return to Fujisawa by another and shorter route. Our gallant coolies clambered up the hill-sides, and brought down the most beautiful Japanese lilies to decorate the cangos of our ladies, so that they, in these, their bamboo baskets, look like travelling flower-gardens. The *flora* on these hill-sides were exquisitely beautiful. Thus adorned, we jogged on in our cangos; and as we reapproached Fujisawa, the coolies broke into a trot; and didn't they toss us up and down on their shoulders, as they thus hastened into the village, amid the greetings of their friends and neighbors?

I ought, I suppose, to dwell upon the ruins of

Kamakura, an old and once grand Tycoon city, and now a desolation; but the living things are more than I can write of, and silence must reign, therefore, over the dead. All the valley was once full of shrines and temples. In one of the old temples is a celebrated stone, supposed to possess the property of curing barrenness among women, and which, therefore, the Japanese women frequent from all parts of the country. Kamakura is the Babylon and Nineveh of Japan. Every hill, every stream, every valley has a story, but what care you for them? (*Mem.*, it is a glorious place for a novel writer to make Japanese romances of for the American or British market.) The yet brilliant, the really living and beautiful temple of Fujisawa we could not resist the temptation to visit. The Mikado stops there when he travels. We saw the room (of screens and mats) where the Mrs. "Mikado" stopped one night, when journeying here, and we tumbled down on the mats where she slept, in order, if possible, to be inspired with some of the reflected glory. The Buddhist priests here changed their religion to Sintoo (just like the politicians), as the great Buddha went down a little with the Tycoon, but they now come up with the Mikado. The polite priests gave us tea (we gave them itzibus). They showed us a kitchen where two thousand of the Mikado's followers were once entertained. By the way, when this awful Majesty travels on the Tocaido road, there is the greatest commotion. Every tea-house, dwelling-house, house or shop of any kind, is boarded up, so that no carnal eye shall look upon and be blinded by the splendor of his dazzling glory. Every human and beastly thing is put out of the way. The Tocaido is devoted to him and his retinue only, and that retinue are all the while squatting on their haunches, or tumbling on their knees and faces, as they come within the charming power of the consecrated Majesty.

All this, of which I have been writing here, we "did" in a day and a half only from Yokohama; but we worked hard, and, on the Tocaido, drove hard our horses, returning not in very early evening to Yokohama. All along the road the women, more or less, the men a little, the children for the fun of it, universally cried out, as our carriages were passing, "Ohio!" "*Ohio!*" "Oɴɪo!"—that is, "good-morning," or, "how do you do?" or, "anaka!" "anaka!" meaning "Mr.," or "you;" and then, as we left them, "Sia-na-ra," "sia-na-ra," "good-bye," in the sweetest of tones. We had no police, no guards! The people seemed so amiable that we could hardly persuade ourselves that two British officers were killed near that route, not long ago. We never felt the least apprehension. The people seem too kind ever to trouble any one.

## LETTER XI.

### *RETURN TO YEDO.*

In Yedo a Second Time.—Now under a British Escort.—The English Dragoons and Japanese Yakonins.—The British Student Interpreters.—Only a Hundred Caucasians among a Million of Japs.—Paper Windows.—Uneasy Sleeping.—Two-Sworded Loafers.—A Thousand British Troops in Yokohama.—Cheap Shopping in Yedo.—Fashionable Riding.

YEDO, *July* 10, 1871.

IN Yedo again! Could not help it! Irresistibly fascinated here by sights, shops, scenes, etc.! Japan, after all, is the country to stay in, as well as to travel over; and so I am once *more* in the capital, as the best place to see men and things. I came up this time, not by the Tocaido road, but by the steamer, under the British flag, which is doing the Japanese coasting-trade, as we do it from Yokohama to Nagasaki, by the U. S. Pacific line of steamers, which weekly run that way to Shanghai.

The British chargé, Mr. Adams, acting as minister in the absence of Sir Henry Parkes (who has just gone home to England *via* San Francisco), and who, during our civil war, was in Washington, attached to the British legation, and hence knows every thing about us, and kindly remembers almost everybody, was polite enough to ask us to pass some time at the British legation in Yedo. To show the style in which Great Britain keeps up her establishments in the East, let me add here, a British mounted guardsman awaited us at the steamboat—a British mounted guard also escorting Mr. Adams, next received us—and then we left for the palace of the British legation, which was a former Daimio's residence, with a large escort of mounted Japanese Yakonins, who made their swords rattle furiously as we drove like Jehus three miles through the narrow streets of Yedo. . A horse-boy on foot (the betto) cleared the streets for us, and Yedo looked on, as it ever looks, with astonishment, at the mounted stalwart English sworded men, with good revolvers, and at the British official, thus escorted, with his two Americans, in a carriage.

Life in Yedo, for Americans or Europeans, must be hard. There are not a hundred of them, in all, in this great city—and only two or three European, or American women. The British government has attached to its embassy here five or six young educated Englishmen, who are studying Japanese with all their might and main, and making good progress, too. The advantage of this to the British government is immense —for it enables the embassy to understand the people. Mr. Satow, the interpreter, is a very clever Englishman, a scholar, more or less, in many languages and literature, and speaks Japanese with fluency and ease. Hence he is the prop of the whole embassy. I have learned more correctly from him of the interior administration of the Japanese government and society, than I have been able to learn elsewhere. I should have written you, if I had written on the topic at all, that the Japanese have no newspapers; but I learn from him now, that each department has its gazette or bulletin, publishing edicts, regulations, and parts of its correspondence with foreign ministers, who, mercilessly, are vexing the Japanese government on "claims"—for, there being no civil courts in Japan, all American and British mercantile claims, or suits, are foisted upon the Yedo government, through the foreign embassies here. Mr. De Long, the American Minister, has a dozen such cases on hand; the British embassy, of course, many more, as the British have so much more commerce here than the Americans.

Sleeping in a city of a million of Japs, thousands of them low fellows, entrusted with two swords, who know how to use them, like lightning, too, and who are so keen with them, that, only three years ago, two crazy fellows attacked a whole British retinue, cut at, or rather cut up, nine Englishmen and two horses, before they were brought down—sleeping, I say, with paper windows and doors only (on the ground floor), that any body can open at night, is not as safe as sleeping in the eighth or tenth story of a New York hotel. But, nevertheless, we slept "like perfect tops." What's the use of worrying when you go abroad on the earth? Better stay at home, if your mind is not easy on such things, or if your appetites care for what you eat or drink. These two-sworded loafers, though, ought to be put down, and must be put down. The government is all ready to put them down, but is afraid so to do, for the sword is a badge of honor here, a title of nobility—and a vagabond clings to it more than to life. If he loses his sword, or his sword is dishonored, or if, in an insult, his sword does not do its duty, the poor devil *hari-kari's*, that is, rips up his belly. It is glory to die in Japan thus self-ripped up; but to be hanged, or strangled, that is a disgrace everlasting, and entails a bad heritage on the family—whereas to *hari-kari* wipes out all spots of ignominy, and makes a martyr of a man. The French minister has suggested to the government that, in order not to wound the honor of these rascals, when the sword is taken from them, a decoration be given them, to show their hereditary claim to honor, and the suggestion seems likely to be realized in a year or two. If I ever come here again, I hope to see no more of these two-sworded vagabonds. I don't like the looks of their steel, especially when saki (rice whiskey) is in the owner of the swords.

The British government has in Yokohama, just now, nearly a thousand British soldiers, with a ship-of-war or two, and the French government has a large body of marines on shore—while other nations have only their flag to protect them. True, the British and French have no particular business in arms here; but, nevertheless, they are a sort of protective police for Americans and Europeans. It seems to me, here in Yedo, more than in Yokohama, that some such protection from arms is necessary, where so few Caucasians are mingled among so many millions of Mongolians—more especially when so many thousands of them carry swords. I had indulged in the apprehension, from reading Allcock on Japan, that there was to be no safety in going anywhere in Japan without a large armed escort; but, in and about Yokohama, one seems as safe as at home, though at Yedo there is not that ease.

I spent half a day shopping here, and the crowds all around stifled me for want of air. . Yokohama has the curiosities of Japan for sale, the costly things—but Yedo only the little funny things of Japan, the toys, the mock-dragons, the mermaids, etc. Tooth-powder costs three cents a box—the very best. Powder for ladies, two or three cents a paper. Rouge, freely used by ladies, for the lips, one cent a box. Handkerchiefs about twelve cents. Decorated hair-pins, with tassels, two, three, and four cents. The prices current of Yedo would amuse you. A *gin-rick-a sha* ride costs twenty-five cents for two and a-half or three miles. There are ten thousand of these things in Yedo, costing from ten to fifteen dollars each, and they have become all the fashion within a year or two. Other parts of Japan are rapidly following this good fashion of the capital. But these cheap things do not indicate the extravagance of the nobility or royalty of Japan. No people are more extravagant, when they have the dollars to spend or spare. The Japanese robes for the high-born cost as much here as in Paris or New York. For the high works of art very large sums are paid, and the decorations of their one-story palaces are without reference to cost.

But adieu to Yedo—and now a final adieu to this curious city. I can not persuade myself it is a healthy city, this time of the year; and on that account I shall be glad to be out of it. The air is stifling. There have been no breezes since I came here. The mosquitoes have the sharpest sort of nippers, and the punka is used here, to keep cool during meals, and to blow away these creatures.

## LETTER XII.

*THINGS IN JAPAN.*

Women among the Japanese.—Their Position and Condition.—Promiscuous Bathing-houses.—The Theatre.—Ticketing Straw Shoes therein.—Jap Stump Orators.—Bamboo in Japan.—Japanese Art.—Shopping in "Curio" Street.—Can spend any Amount of Money.—The Steel of Japan.—The Government of Japan a Feudality.—Railroads, Telegraph, and Mint in Japan.

YOKOHAMA, *July* 12, 1871.

THE status or position of women among the Japanese is more puzzling to a foreigner than any thing else, and no one looker-on agrees as to what that position is. The Mikado can have but one wife, but is allowed, by law or custom, twelve concubines; Daimios and Hattamatos, eight; men, with other titles, five; officers and the soldiers, two. But, say the laws ordered by Jycyas, "The man is not upright who is much given to women." It is an error, they tell me, that the Japanese are indifferent to the respectability of their wives, and that they often prefer taking one from among the public courtesans. But there are wonderful exhibitions of woman-life in Yedo and Yokohama, such as I cannot describe—exhibitions under the sanction of, and controlled by, the Government, and from which the Government derives a large revenue. The laws against dancing women, etc., etc., says Jycyas, are not to be administered severely, though "they are like caterpillars or locusts in the country." "Out of regard for the nature of mankind, their offences are to be lightly passed over." Hence, this species of vice is made just as public as it can be, outwardly, decency, however, ever hovering over it. Women are sold in childhood, temporarily, for a purpose, and many of them afterward marry well without dishonor. But this is a topic upon which I cannot enlarge.

The baths of the great cities are very peculiar institutions. Men and women, if they do not exactly bathe together, come so near it that the difference is not worth talking about. Everybody bathes here, and not to be clean is considered disreputable. The cost of bathing is cheap in Yedo, about forty cents every day for a month. If mere cleanliness is godliness, there are not a more godly people on earth. The baths are warm, ever open to the public eye from the street, with no disguises about them. They are so common that they do not even provoke curiosity. In Yedo there were many starers, staring at me, when viewing the bathers, but not one staring in. Nothing is thought of this peculiar mode of bathing. Nothing mischievous seems to come of it. We must not forget that what people are accustomed to from their youth up, does not amaze and astonish them as we strangers are thus astounded.

I went to the theatre the other night in Kanagawa—a big institution with no seats, but with rails to lean on. We all squat. The natives leave their penny and two-penny straw shoes at the door, near the ticket-box, and take tickets for them, as we take tickets for our hats or cloaks. It was a very funny sight to see four or five hundred shoes ticketed with wooden straps attached to them, the straps written over in Japanese characters. No American can stand a Japanese theatre over fifteen minutes. It is not like the Chinese, all " bang," " bang," " bang," " bang," smash, crash, thrash, but it is, if possible, stupider—to us, at least. I sallied out to hear a Jap stump orator lecturing, as I suppose Plato and Aristotle did, in front of the theatre. He blew, fanned, roared, and snorted, as do some of our stump orators. I was told he was reciting Japanese story-history to what seemed to be a very hungry crowd of admirers, two or three thousand in number. Scandal whispers that the Government employs these orators to uphold the Mikado Government against the Tycoon discontents. Perhaps so; we do the same. The rain began to pour down. It rains here in summer without the least trouble. We tried to hire a *gin-rick-a sha* to haul us home, but coolies, naked as they are, won't work in the rain (for fear of getting wet?), and so we had to foot it home. When a coolie's paunch is full of rice, there is nothing to stimulate him to earn more, especially late at night, and when it rains.

Every country has something peculiar in it that every inhabitant makes the most of. Pine wood is an American institution, as the bamboo is a Japanese institution; and what would the Japanese do without the bamboo? The handles of all agricultural instruments are made of it. The gutters of houses are of bamboo. Paper is made of bamboo. Split bamboo makes curtains for houses, and screens, all beautiful, too, when colored or painted. There is scarcely a human avocation that does not call into requisition the bamboo. Paint on houses is unknown here. The bamboo garnishes them up a little, but there is no paint nor whitewash where I have been travelling. Wood is left of the natural color, and waxed often to give it polish and beauty.

What has really astounded me more, perhaps, than any thing here, is art. The little hands and arms of the Japanese seem to fit them for nice execution; but they would not make the pretty screens, or pictures, or inlay copper, or lacquer as they do, if taste did not accompany them: I have just seen a big boy, only thirteen years old, who is painting for foreigners Japanese costumes, and his execution is wonderful. The paper-hangings of Japan are unrivalled. I have seen nothing in the world, that I remember, which equals the famous fan room of the Hamagoten in Yedo. We, doubtless, got all our ideas of beautifying paper from Japan. The bronze work of this people is wonderful, as well as their lacquer. They put years of work often into a Daimio's room. When we of English descent were barbarians in art, these people were all they are now.

We see bells and bronzes and inlaid work hundreds of years old. The iron and steel work of Japan, too, is far in advance of many "civilized" nations. The famous Damascus steel, the renowned Toledo blade, does not surpass, if equal, the steel sword of the Japanese officers. It may not bend as the Damascus blade, but it has a strength and tenacity beyond it. The old armor of the old Japanese knights is wonderful work for the age and time. Their work in silk and satin is wonderful, and also in crape. These people, farming people too, who use only the old spinning-wheel and the reel of our grandmothers, who have no Lyons or Aubusson looms, turn out real works of art in embossed silks and satins. I tell the administrators of Government here, if they will only send out their artists to study and copy Lyons fashions, or to imbue themselves with European tastes, their silks and satins and crapes will command the markets of the world. What they most want to please us now is the knowledge of our caprices and fashions and tastes. From their long non-intercourse with the world they have not advanced in all that, and it is hard to persuade them to do aught save what their great-great-grandfathers and mothers were brought up to do. The (foreign) Curio Street of Yokohama is a gallery of art. I could spend days there, if I had time, to study them up. A people who have their capacities can be taught to do any thing, and the marvel is, when they learned it or who taught them. Is not art inborn?

But shopping in Curio Street is an unutterable bore. The price asked for any thing is no sign of what you can get it for. Two or three shops only, it is said, have fixed prices, and hence foreigners largely patronize them. Elsewhere you sit and haggle and bid, and waste hours of precious time. About one-half of what is asked may be set down as the fair price; but this being understood the Jap shop-keeper triples often on that. Knowing nothing of the real value of things or real cost, and but little of their merit—as in lacquer ware—there can be the greatest deception practised, and hence we haggle at random—are laughed at by the Japs, and laugh at ourselves in concord with them. The custom-houses in America will think we are all cheats in our invoices, even when they are *bona fide*—all Japanese work being comparatively cheap, from the low price of labor. What is dear at home is very, very cheap here. The profits in San Francisco and New York, on Japanese curiosities, must be three and four hundred per cent., and hence their infrequent sale there.

The Government, or the form of Government which this country has, it is almost impossible for a foreigner to understand. The Mikado, or emperor, is the head to whom all the real estate of the country belongs, and from whom spring all landed titles, such as they are. And then there are Koongays, with the Mikado blood in their veins; the Daimios, or Yedo nobility; the Hattamato, or the lower class of Daimios. These people now make up the Government of Japan, which is the old feudal system of Great Britain and Europe eight hundred years ago. These feudal lords were in frequent collision up to 1600, since which time they have had tolerable peace, save in the recent rebellion when the Mikado overthrew the Tycoon. The Government was a dual Government up to the arrival of Commodore Perry, seventeen years ago, when differences began to arise between the Mikado and Tycoon respecting the admission of foreigners.

The Mikado did not assent at first to the treaties of Perry and Townsend Harris, and parties were created by these differences of opinion, which led to the overthrow of the Tycoon who made the treaties. We have, therefore, now a Mikado Government, risen into power on the overthrow of treaties, and yet obliged by foreign arms to uphold and maintain those treaties. These treaties expire the coming year, and there will be much difficulty in renewing them. The spectacle of a feudality of the middle ages now, in 1871, is a novel and interesting exhibition to the American eye. We are taken back, as it were, into Europe eight hundred years ago, and see the life our British ancestors led, with their serfs, villains, and retainers. But I must not weary you by writing a treatise on Government.

The Japanese are making great advancement in certain kinds of our civilization. They have warships like ours, which it is doubtful if they know how to handle. They have a mint organized like ours, but their currency, like ours, is only paper money—oblong pieces of pasteboard printed on, in Japanese. They have a telegraph from Yokohama to Yedo, which I have used two or three times and found as reliable as any in the United States. English messages are translated and transmitted in Japanese. They are also constructing a railroad from Yokohama to Yedo, some twenty-four miles, which the English engineers are making a very, very costly work—and this will cost so much that it will frighten the Japanese from extending their lines over the island as they were contemplating. Next year a telegraph from Nagasaki and Yedo to Shanghai will connect Japan and China, and enable even Americans, if they will pay for it heavily, to communicate with Yedo. The telegraph, by the way, has been extended over Russia in Asia to the border custom-house of Russia and China, some six or seven hundred miles only from Pekin, and in a year or two the communication will be completed from Pekin, so that St. Petersburg and Pekin can interchange ideas. This will be a rival to the English lines on the Indian seas.

## LETTER XIII.

### ON THE JAPAN SEAS.

Adieu to Yokohama.—The Foreigners and their Life there.—The All Sorts of Clothes of the East.—The Japanese Passengers on board the Costa Rica.—A Japanese Prince and his Retinue on board.—A Typhoon dodged.—Frightful Loss of Life and Property.— An Earthquake felt.— Curiosity satisfied.— Motley Cargo of the Costa Rica.—Butcher's Meat called Fowl.

JAPAN SEAS, *July* 13,
On Board Steamer Costa Rica. (Under United States Flag.)

ADIEU to Yokohama, and all its agreeable American population. We have been welcomed not only as countrymen, but as friends, almost as relatives. A New Yorker cannot but be at home here; for the town abounds with New Yorkers. I see the "Brooklyn Hotel," the "New York Hotel," too, and I eat meat from the "Fulton Market." The flag of the United States on the Pacific mail steamers dots the harbor. There are only about one thousand Caucasians in Yokohama (exclusive of the military), with a Mongolian population, including Kanagawans, of some sixty or seventy thousand, and all the while rapidly increasing. There are five or six little daily journals in Yokohama, rich in advertisements, but poor enough in news. One of these was sold the other day, I see, for twenty thousand dollars. As to news here, foreign news, there is not enough to keep a journalist alive. The wonder is that all do not die of *ennui*. The writers, of course, know nothing of Japanese, can therefore gather up no police reports, have no thrilling intelligence—no court records, nothing of etiquette in Yedo—nothing from the Provincial Princes. All we have is the editorial essay, and the everlasting, but all-important, prices current of rice, silks, sheetings, shirtings, freights, rates of exchange. But these are what men come to Japan for (to get rich, and then go home), and hence nothing is so important to them. The Caucasians live beautifully here, many of them near their places of business, right on the open Bay, and others, on the bluffs above; and five thousand dollars here in the way of living goes farther than twenty thousand dollars in New York City. They shut up shop at four; drive or ride till seven, and at seven and a half sit down to dinner, their evening amusement, after which, and a long sitting at dinner, they go to bed. Dinner is the great event of the day. Tiffin at one o'clock, as they call "lunch," the intermediate event—and therefore, the most is made of dinner. No theatres, no opera for Europeans, no libraries, nowhere to spend their evenings, they frantically dine, and unhealthily sleep after such dinners, with Chinese almost always for their cooks. The Chinese take to all trades, and Chinese make the best house-servants here—the Japanese not well taking to that sort of thing, save as nurses for children.

One of the curiosities of the East is the all sorts

of clothes everybody (of the male sex) wears. I am not writing now of the nature-clad Japanese; but they often get cast-off European clothes, which, when put on, amuse one to see. There's, a droll fellow, with nothing on but old trowsers and straw shoes! There, is another, with red European-made shoes, yellow frock-coat, Calcutta hat (a hat branching all over the head, forward and backward only though, and stuffed so thick with light stuff, that no sun's rays can pierce through it), spectacles on, too, and looking as wise as if some great philosopher. There, is another yet, with a frock-coat only, no shirt, no trowsers, no hat, no, nothing else! When European fashions are taken by the Japanese, they rush into them, as do the Central American negroes, or the North American Indians. But the hats of the Europeans in this country are of the oddest, drollest, most variegated kind you can well imagine. I bring here my American head cover, a poor concern, under a Japanese sun, or in a Japanese rain. I cover it all over with white linen, and a long veil down the neck, to shed off the hot sun rays. Another sports a big Calcutta, English-invented hat, made in imitation of the Turk's sash, wrapped round his head or cap (fez) on a hot day, also to ward off the sun's rays. Another yet, fresh come, to look jaunty, sports his American straw hat. In short, we have all sorts of hats human ingenuity has invented, and hence, we look like so many birds of passage, if not of prey.

But, once more, adieu to Yokohama. I am on

board the United States mail steamer Costa Rica, running between Yokohama and Shanghai (China), and touching at the Japanese ports of Hiogo and Nagasaki. The ocean is as quiet as an inner lake. This is the rainy season, and bless the rainy season, for the clouds, ever overhanging, keep off the hot rays of the sun. We Americans ought to be profoundly grateful to the Pacific Mail Steamship Company, for this weekly line of steamers to Shanghai, for it spreads the American name, and shows the American flag far and wide in these seas. It alone offsets, if not equals, British power and British fame here. We have a Prince on board, a real live Japanese Prince of countless generations, of the purest blood, with ten of his two-sworded retainers as body-guard—a Prince, too, of boundless green acres—but our Yankee-born captain, insensible fellow to blood, seems to think nothing of it. He carries Princes, he says, every trip. "Princes are nothing to him." Only a few years ago, these Princes all went to the Yedo Capitol with thousands of two-sworded retainers in their train, to whom everybody bowed prostrate in dust, as they passed by in norimons (sedan chairs), while now, they go on a Yankee steamer, under a Yankee flag, with Cape Cod, or Taunton (Good Lord!) captains. We have enough of these two-sworded fellows on board now to take the steamer if they wished to, but, says the captain, "What if they did? what could they do with the elephant if they had it?" Sure, they are well-behaved men. We have one hundred and fifty-five passengers, all Japanese but some six or seven. Some forty-five of them are cabin passengers, others in the steerage. I have just been visiting them. They sleep on mats, not in bunks, as the Chinese passengers sleep, but on their very peculiar wooden Japanese pillow—and with their women all stretched out promiscuously beside them. They must be the best behaved people in the world.

Magnificent green hills we are passing, clad with verdure to the ocean edge. The everlasting clouds and fogs of summer spread one universal green. I must repeat, it is the prettiest land I ever was in. England, in May, even, does not equal it. They do not know how to farm and to terrace in England, as do the Japs here. Many junks we are passing; more fishing-vessels. Their torches at night light up the sea. Torches, they tell me, lure fish. I am crediting about all they tell me, though, "they tell me," like Dame Rumor, is at times an awful liar. The light-houses, too, are on every prominent point of the coast. Thanks to the Japanese, for thus lighting up the shores. They light these houses well, keep them well supplied with oil, and their lights are as reliable as ours. Their innumerable junks profit by them, as well as our steamers.

We have just dodged a typhoon! The steamer preceding us, on which we were to go, took it, and weathered it at sea; but here in Hiogo, where I am writing now, the wreck and rack are frightful. Six steamers high and dry, three of them in utter ruins, are on the quay of Kobe. The ruins of junks line the shores. The sea wall (cut stone) is knocked all to pieces. A British bark, with almost all on board, is turned upside down on the shore. Verandas, bungalows, godowns (warehouses), are knocked up, or over. The lost of property has been very great, and the loss of life deplorable. The Hiogo *News*, our English newspaper, says :

"Between two hundred and fifty and three hundred houses have been destroyed along the shore, and six hundred junks reported lost. On one junk two hundred lost."

And all along the shore for one hundred miles, the rumor of the loss of Japanese property and life is frightful. One harbor, near here, is all filled. Every village between here and Osaca (a great city, fifteen miles off) is swept away. From one thousand to six thousand lives have been lost; but there are no Japanese newspapers, nor news-gatherers. One can only guess from what Dame Rumor reports. Thank the Lord, we are all safe.

Every traveller, of course, wants to know what a typhoon or cyclone is. My curiosity is amply satisfied, now, though where I was, was only a gale. My earthquake curiosity too is satisfied. I felt a little one —was shaken up in a little one at Fujisawa about two weeks gone by. There, in 1870, in May alone, were a hundred and seventy shakes. I am content with the little one I felt, only a little one, but it shook enough for me. This country is all volcanic. Its great mountain, the adoration and admiration of Japan, Fusiyama, is of volcanic birth. The soil is all volcanic. Hence its wealth. I shall feel a little easier as to shakes when I am on the other side of the Yellow Sea—for there are several sputtery hills and sulphur fountains hereabout. But there is no chance of dodging the chance of being hit by typhoons for three thousand miles yet. In the distance is the city of Osaca, where the Japanese Government have just established a *Mint*. Governor Ito, who was in Washington last winter, examining the *money-making* machinery at the Treasury, and afterward the Mint in Philadelphia, is in charge of it, and has organized it on the systems learned there. Governor Ito is well fitted for this position, as he possesses a clear business head, united with great financial ability.

The Costa Rica here (Hiogo) is loading for Shanghai, with all sorts of the odds and ends of things. We are taking baskets upon baskets of camphor on board—good to keep off the moths. (I hope it will keep off fleas.) The captain dare not stow it between decks, for it would endanger the flavor of teas, hereafter to come. We are taking in bales of isinglass; deers' horns in hundreds of bundles, sea-weed (our common sea-weed) for the Chinese to eat! (they love it) and *biche de mer*. There are a dozen steamboats in port now, several of them for sale to the Japs, who have been pretty well bitten by American and British boats. Two of them have been once old gunboats of ours. There are about three hundred foreigners here. The town is pretty, or was before the typhoon, that is, what is left of it is pretty, and the green hills over it are pretty, too. It is quite a place for a new cattle trade, that is opening. The Japs, I have written you, abhor butchers—won't let them enter the houses, and never eat cattle! Beef now is sold to them by these butchers under the name of fowl. The Prince of Satzuma, who keeps up an army of fifteen thousand men in European style, gives his soldiers three rations a week on this "fowl;" and he introducing the meat fashion, the desire for eating it is becoming general. But we are off, and adieu.

## LETTER XIV.

### ON THE INLAND SEA OF JAPAN.

The Beautiful Inland Sea of Japan.—Luxurious Travelling.—Prince Hizen.—Vampire Cat.—Bay of Nagasaki.—The Oldest European Settlement.—The Roman Catholic Priests.—Pappenburg Island.—Thousands of Christians thrown from the Precipice.—The Faith of Roman Catholic Missionaries.—Street Scenes in Nagasaki.—Needle Making.—Porcelain Painting.—Begging Buddhist Priest.—Street Actors.—Japanese Confectionery.—Japanese Woman's Toilet-Box.—Receipt for Blacking the Teeth.—Final Leave of Japan.

NAGASAKI, *July* 17, 1871.

THIS Japan, I re-declare, is the most beautiful country in the world—and I have now seen a good part-of the world. I have come down through the Inland Sea, by—what shall I say to give an American an idea of it?—through Lake Champlain, say, through Lake George, the Thousand Islands of the St. Lawrence, the Rocky Mountain ranges and the Columbia River in Oregon, Puget's Sound in Washington Territory, etc., etc. There is nothing that surpasses it, scarcely any thing that equals it, in our country. The Scotchman here has his Loch Lomond, or Loch Katrine; the Swiss, his Genevan Lake; the Englishman, Westmoreland; the Irishman, his Killarney. We have been sailing for twenty-four hours, ten miles an hour, through a succession of changeable scenery, an idea of which you can only have by bearing in mind the home beautiful spots I have named. The hills are covered to the very tops with the liveliest green, or these hills are terraced generally with garden spots, one overhanging the other. Along many of the hills, and on the very summits, are strings of lofty trees, so trained as to make a seeming continuous march of forest to forest over every hill-top.

There is no more luxurious travelling on earth than this down the Inland Sea of Japan. True, a hot sun is over our heads, often clouded, though, and affording a canopy. We are on the upper deck, on the bow of the steamer, under ample awnings, in bamboo chairs, made purposely to fit the human (extended) form. The moving air fans us. Ice, all the way from Boston, abounds for us. We can have iced tea in abundance, or, if we will, mint-juleps, even. The unknown Prince, whom I spoke of in a former letter as a fellow-passenger, turns out to be the Prince of Hizen, one of the eighteen chief Daimios of Japan, on his way to his estates near Nagasaki, where, as owner of coal mines, if judiciously managed, he is one of the richest princes in the world. I showed him, in "Tales of Japan," published in English, a wood-cut of "the Vampire Cat of Nabeshima," in which his family figured many years ago. The story is of a Prince of Hizen who had in his house a lady of rare beauty, whom a large cat throttled, then taking her form, and making the Prince believe she (the cat) was the real beauty.

The Prince kept on in love with the cat, but the cat sucked all his life away. The beautiful woman was at last found out to be a vampire cat, when a battle ensued, and the cat, worsted in the fight, re-turned cat, and escaping from the fighting room, was shot by the Prince's retainers. The Prince laughed heartily over the picture, and seemed to enjoy the fable.

The Bay of Nagasaki is, if possible, more beautiful than the scenery of the Inland Sea. The hills rise boldly from the water's edge, and land-lock the harbor. Everything here is fresh and silent now, as if there were not some seventy or eighty thousand human beings on the hill-sides. The sun had just gone, as we steamed inward, and people in these lands retire early to their mats, and rise early to greet the morning sun.

I sallied forth with that morning sun to see men and things, as then, they are best to be seen. The pomegranate and palm, the persimmon and bamboo, are here. There is a strange commingling of the temperate and torrid zones. Side by side, oaks and trees, and feathery bamboos and palms, flourish in equal beauty. The sober hues of the north are mingled with the more vivid verdure of the tropics. The brown fish-hawk, swooping down from the hills upon his finny prey, or poised in the air, makes the hills echo with his wild cry.

Nagasaki is the oldest European settlement in Japan, and yet there are said to be not over one hundred and fifty Europeans there now, which means

## ON THE INLAND SEA OF JAPAN. 123

Americans, too, for all here bear one name. The Dutch were pent up here for two centuries in the little Island of Decima, and allowed only once a year to visit a neighboring hill, and then under a strong guard. Xavier and his followers gained a footing here in the sixteenth century, to propagate the Holy Catholic faith. The galleons of Portugal and Spain, centuries ago, were here. Princes went from here to make their obeisance in Rome to the Pope. But a cruel Tycoon, alarmed by the triumphs of the Church over the people, fulminated an edict against all foreigners, shut up the Dutch in Decima, and then pitched thousands of Christians who would not repent (backwards), from the rocky cliffs of Pappenberg Island into the ocean below. Never since that period, when the Roman Catholics may have been said to rule the millions of Japan—ruling them more, perhaps, by their science, learning, and arts, than by the force of the Bible—have any Christians been permitted as missionaries to enter Japan, save in the four open consular ports. The rulers of Japan, even now, are energetically resisting all the representations and claims of Catholic and Protestant foreign ministers for "toleration;" and it is the very last thing, in the new treaty to be made in 1872, that the Japanese will yield. A French priest, passenger with me, mourns plaintively over the blows his church has received both in China and Japan, but is sure, nevertheless, the day is soon coming when God will open the highways and waters to the ministers of the *Propaganda fides* in Rome.  Nor is there any reason, if the masses of the people were permitted to be approached, why all should not become Christians —for the mere *outward* differences between the worship of the idol god, Buddha, and the Catholic altars, seem slight, while the Buddhist heaven, as defined in the classic books, is almost our God.  This very seeming similarity, though, makes the Buddhist priests bitter in their opposition, and they have of late had force enough with the Government to abstract some thousands of Catholics (the cherished relics of the old Catholic missionaries, that have in secret handed down their faith) to places unknown, but probably to the mines of Yeso, there to work out a wretched existence.

The streets of Nagasaki would afford to me endless interest, if I only had time to explore them, for every thing is done out of doors.  There are the manufacturers, by hand, of needles, and the needles are so much better than ours, that the Japanese won't buy ours.  There, too, are the workers on lacquer, painting with it on porcelain vases—work exquisitely done by men squatting on their haunches and nearly naked.  There is a little wheel, spinning cotton, that grandma is lazily turning—she, too, squatting, and naked to her waist.  Here is a splendid porcelain warehouse, that my eyes water to see, and that I would buy the whole of, if I had money enough.  For one pair of vases, some eight feet high, six hundred dollars is wanted.  The bamboo cups, the egg-shell saucers, I would buy scores of them, if they would bear packing in a trunk, and stand the rattle trunks have here—on poles and bullocks' backs; for there is only one road for wheels in Japan—the Tocaido—the rest for cangos, norimons, ponies, and bullocks, and coolies, with the poles, who bring on their backs, loads fifty miles to market. There are plays going on, even now, seven o'clock in the morning. The actors daub their faces all over with white powder, rouge their lips, tattoo their bodies with paint, and then "go at it" before any crowd they can collect in the streets. The streets are narrow, and so all walkers must go through the theatrical crowd. I followed a big bullock, heavily laden, and the crowd marvelled not over him, but over me set up a jolly howl—the bullock they knew; the wandering Yankee was unknown, and the jokes they cracked at my expense seemed to be many. There, come three Buddhist priests, collecting alms, rattling little bells on a pole, praying for tempos or cash, and then handing out a contribution-box. Everybody that had any thing seemed to give a little. I followed their example. Was this right, or wrong? Am I a heathen, or not? But, on the sands of the Dead Sea (in Palestine), I tumbled down, with my head toward Mecca, just as the Bedouins did—having long ago learned, even on the Adriatic, "when among the Romans to do as the Romans do." There, is a confectionery shop. The Japanese are as fond of candies as are our people. They make just what you want. I asked for a fish and got it—a respectable-sized fish—for two or three cents, with sugar enough in it to make a man sick a week. A merchant, who seems to be rich in the good things of the world, has just let one of our ladies peep into his wife's inner bed-chamber, and here is the brief result of her explorations:

Little or no furniture; no chairs; no bedstead—nothing but mats to sleep on. A toilet-box was on the floor, near the wall—about the only article of furniture in the room. In this box there were five drawers, and two lacquer basins on top. In the top drawer of this box there was a metallic mirror, like our hand-glasses. In the second drawer she kept her powder, paint, wax, brush, tooth-powder and brush. Two little drawers came next; in one she had her false hair, and in the other fancy pins, gilt paper, and other fixings for her hair. In the lower drawer was her pillow, which is placed under the neck when sleeping on the mats, so as to prevent the hair from being rumpled. It is made of wood, and covered with paper on the top. The powder looks like starch, and when they use it they mix a little water with it, and rub it in like paste; and they have two brushes that they use to rub it off with. The paint looks green, and turns red, when put on the lips and cheeks.

The following is her receipt for blacking the teeth:

Take three pints of water, and having warmed it, add half a tea-cupful of wine (saki?). Put into this mixture a quantity of red-hot iron; allow it to stand five or six days, when there will be a scum on the top of the mixture, which should then be poured into a small tea-cup and placed near the fire. When it is warm, powdered gall-nuts and iron filings should be added to it, and the whole should be warmed again. The liquid is then painted on the teeth by a soft feather brush, with more powdered gall-nuts and iron, and after several applications, the desired color will be obtained.

Whether the married women like thus to black their teeth or not, is disputed among foreign residents here. The men compel them, however, to do it, whether they like it or not, for it is the great sign by which a man consecrates and shows off his female chattel to the world. Whoever has blackened teeth is not to be touched by other men, on pain of death. The eyebrows of married women, I may as well add here, are shaved, and their lips rouged! (Needs there, then, this penalty of death?)

The Japanese women are not pretty; but they have charming natural manners; with beautifully shaped arms, and tiny hands. The young women are all as remarkable for their superb white teeth, as the married ones are for their hideous black ones. This custom originated some two or three hundred years ago, and is supposed to show the wife's devotion to her husband. One of the Mikado's wives (so goes the legend) was very lovely, and to show her indifference to her personal appearance, and to prove her love for her husband, blackened her beautiful teeth and shaved off her eyebrows. This was considered such a sacrifice, that all living wives (not to be outdone by Mrs. Mikado) followed her example. The custom has become compulsory.

In now bidding a final adieu to Japan, I feel a regret I never felt in leaving a foreign country before. It is so beautiful! The people seem so amiable! The happiness apparently so universal! But I feel that in my hasty skimming and sketching I know nothing of it, and, doubtless, I have blundered often in what I have so hastily pencilled, as you see by this manuscript, on mulberry (Japan) paper. Forgive, then, all blunders. A little is perhaps better than nothing, even if error is in it at times. Lovers of fruits and of vegetables will not find them in Japan. The peach is not fit to eat. There is nothing, in the fruit way, eatable but plums. The vegetation has no taste. Sheep cannot live in Japan. The grass kills them, after repeated experiments; and hence, we have no mutton, save what is imported from China. But the fish are excellent, and the beef tender and good. One, therefore, will not starve amid the beauties of Japan.

# LETTER XV.

## ON, AND OVER TO CHINA.

On the Yellow Sea, bound to Shanghai.—The Great Yang-tze and its Yellow Water.—Up the Whang-poo.—Reflections on entering the Great Gates of China.—Thermometer in Shanghai.—Hot, Hotter, Hottest.—Air wanted, a Puff or a Typhoon.—Things In and About Shanghai.—The Summer Costume.—Innumerable Mounds or Graves in the Cotton-Fields.—American Flag in the Yang-tze.—We are taking the Coasting Trade of China, etc.

SHANGHAI, *July*, 1871.

EXIT Japan! Lo, presto, China! Good-by, ye polysyllabic Japanese, Kotsuki no Kami Kuranosukie, Uzesugi, Kobayashi, Shimidgu Ikaku; and welcome, now, Ah Sin, A Pu, Sing Sing, Jung Ku, Ki Sam—nay, all of the monosyllabic Chinese vocabulary! I am on the Yellow Sea, or just south of the Yellow Sea, on my way to the islands of the Yang-tze, thence to the Hwang p'u, or Whang-poo, on, to Shanghai, the great Asiatic-European commercial city. The water is now so yellow, that I should have no hesitation in calling it the Yellow Sea, if they did not tell me that all this "yellow" comes from the mud of the great Yang-tze River, which begins somewhere up in the Thibet Mountains, and runs and crooks, three thousand miles to the ocean, with all the dirt and filth it can gather from innumerable cities, and all the mud it can sweep out from thousands of valleys and mountains. So many canals empty into this great river, that it may be said to be the inlet and outlet of the commerce of the three or four hundred millions of Chinamen—for, which is it, three or four hundred millions, the population here?—Nobody knows—at least, no one can answer! Three hundred millions, however, are enough for a nation, are they not? And hence, the river that draws off the dirt of these millions upon millions must be yellow enough to *yellow* even a sea. The Yankee steamer's wheels are splashing through these yellow-made waves, some forty, some sixty miles off from the coast—for thus, long before you get into China, you are upon its watery soil. Shoals, shallows of mud, islands under water and over water, at times, are all about us. Pilot boats, of course, are indispensable, and we greet, with no little pleasure, miles and miles off, a New-York-looking pilot-boat, with a John Bull pilot on board, who relieves the anxious mind of our Cape Cod Yankee captain, and conducts us toward the port.

Upon entering this vast portal, of this, the greatest empire upon earth, where so much of human life has been ebbing in and out, so many thousands of years, that history is blinded, and cannot number the many, one cannot help dreaming or thinking a little out loud. Here, is a country older than Jerusalem, older than Egypt, probably—a country which was comparatively civilized centuries before, when we

Caucasians were barbarians—once going ahead for centuries (nay, probably up to the time it touched our European civilization), but now going astern—a country that blessed us with the compass, the art of printing, and blessed us (or cursed us) with gunpowder—the land of Confucius and Mencius, whose heavenly teachings, though older than Christ's, seem, most of them, to have been almost as much inspired; and I, a Yankee, from a new world and long unknown, under a Yankee flag, with Yankee paddle-wheels, am coasting up into it, with the proud consciousness that this use of steam is my own countryman's discovery, with the telegraph, and hundreds of other good things more, but now far, far beyond the celestial Chinaman's dreams, nay, even despised by him, as he despises "the foreign devil," that outside barbarian, who is tormenting him with novelties. This is the land of the mulberry and of the busy silkworm, of silks, of satins, the luxurious prizes Roman matrons coveted, but yearned for often in vain, because of their enormous cost, and of the leaf that ships for three centuries now, have been risking every thing to win—the tea-leaf, I mean—a beverage, though coming from the Yang-tze, that every maid and maiden, as well as man, feels now to be a necessity of life, whether he or she lives on the Don, or the Volga, or the Thames, or the Liffey—by the Sacramento or the Passamaquoddy—in Oregon or in Nova Scotia. A boy emperor, now only fifteen, reigns over this vast empire, and these millions upon millions, in fear and trembling, all obey. *Exit*, this sort of ejaculation. *Enter*, China.

Shanghai is from Nagasaki (Japan) four hundred and fifty-nine miles, from Hiogo (or Kobe) three hundred and eighty-six miles, from Yokohama three hundred and forty-two miles; fare, one hundred dollars, first-class, other classes any price; for these one thousand one hundred and eighty-seven miles, time, including stoppages, one week. Shanghai is not on the great river, but on the Whang-poo, only a tidal river, some forty miles long, but on which great ships *do* enter, not without some fear, though, of being stuck in the mud. Indeed, the whole of this country about here is mud-made—like the Mississippi, or the Nile Deltas—and islands are ever popping up, and growing, where once great ships swam. The land-greedy Chinese bank up, and rob Neptune whenever they can, and the consequence is, that when a hot, baking July sun shoots down its rays upon vast areas of fresh mud, a malaria poisons the region all round about—so that, as I enter here, already I wish I was anywhere else; but I only mean to run the gauntlet, and be off in the first boat.

．　　．　　．　　．　　．　　．

The thermometer is the biggest liar that ever lived. It is only ninety-five or ninety-eight degrees here at night, and one hundred or one hundred and three degrees by day, and yet it is hotter, intensely hotter, than I have felt it in the Napa (California) Valley, coming from the Geysers, in July, at one hundred and eighteen degrees, or, on the sands of Egypt. Thermometers, therefore, I have no hesitation in saying, lie, not exactly in words, or figures, or letters, but in spirit, in substance, in caloric, at least. I am suffocating here! I cannot get breath enough! What would I give for a puff, and how much more for a typhoon, even if a destructive one? There is no air, night nor day, and, if possible, it is hotter by night than by day. There is no sleep in this oven-bed, and if there were, the mosquitoes would eat you up, if you did not throw over you the well-reticulated net. A mattress is unendurable; a mat has to be laid on that, or your perspiration would stick you to the mattress. Never, never, Yankee pilgrim, enter here in June, July, or August. They say you *can* breathe, and live, and sleep, in all the other months of the year; but if you will be such a fool as I am, and come, drink, and drink deep, not exactly of the Pierian Spring—not water, for that is poison here—but claret, hock, champagne, porter, beer, and eat ice, and little else, except bread and meat. Shanghai is nearly in the latitude of Northern Florida; but amid low lands as it is, on which are boundless fields of cotton, near the mouth of the great Yang-tze, doubtless, the climate is like that of New Orleans, on the Mississippi, with the thermometer ranging higher. What I know for a certainty is, you will never catch me here again in July, if there be any way of getting around it, or over it, or under it.

The foreign residents of Shanghai suffer not a little this season of the year; but here, then, they must stay, for now is the season of "tea," and "silk," the great exported staples of the country. In winter they can play, but never in the summer. They prepare themselves for being roasted as well as possible—not exactly in our Georgia, or the Japanese, natural costume, but as near to it, as civilization will permit. They go without shirts, to begin with. A white flannel frock-coat, closely fitting the body, somewhat fancifully made, with white linen trowsers, is the costume. No dickey is sported over that coat. No dickey could stand the drippings of perspiration here over five minutes, if on. They live thus, and do business with a punka, or wind-flap, flying over them, ever kept going by a half-sleeping coolie (Chinaman). We breakfast by punkas; we dine by punkas. Heaven giving us no breezes, men raise as many artificial winds as possible. No one ventures out, if it can be helped, till the sun is going down. A great two-story, long-tailed pith hat is then sported. They ride out toward sunset in "traps," low-hung carriages, drawn by one pony, or, in a California-made carriage, with California horses, where that costly luxury can be afforded; or, they go in sedan chairs, or, are wheeled by a Chinaman, two at a time, on a wheelbarrow, dog-cheap for such rides as that—the vilest invention, by the way, for going, I have ever seen yet—worse, if possible, than the Japanese cango.

The evening drive in Shanghai to the bubbling

spring seems to be the great event of the day. Then, the sweltering foreigners turn out into the country, to breathe the air—(but is there ever any?)—and in their various vehicles they make long processions, for the turn-outs are numerous here, and the foreign population is well-to-do in the world, if not wealthy, all. Woe! woe! however, to any poor wretch of a Chinaman in the way of one of these traps, or vehicles —for all drive with the fury of Jehus, among them, and through the thickest of their narrow streets, without any seeming regard to life or limb. The idea is, or seems to be, that "Shanghai belongs to us, not to you," and, "get out of the way, or we will ride, rough-shod over you." Wonderful to say, however, but few accidents occur, and when they do, the foreigners pay for them in a way abundant enough to satisfy the Chinese love of money.

On all these drives out of Shanghai, what most arrests an American's attention, especially one just now, with half a foot in the grave, from the diseases of the climate, are the graves or mounds of the Chinese, which seem to dot, if not to half cover, the great cotton-fields all about. These mounds or graves have been going up—how many years shall I say? four thousand? *Quien sabe?*—and in many places they seem to cover the ground, essentially interfering with and obstructing cultivation. The Chinese reverence, nay, worship their ancestors, and hence preserve these ancestral graves, mere mounds, with idolatrous veneration. Cultivation would be desecration, though they do use the grass grown over them to feed their cattle. At first, the dead are left on the top of the ground in two-storied coffins, and then, in time, over these coffins, the earth is piled. These mounds, now innumerable, these coffins, thus uplifted, are not exactly pleasant suggestions, under a July sun, and they mar the pleasures of the drive, till the eye is accustomed to them, as it can be to any.thing. They have become, too, great obstructions to the advancement and improvement of the country—for no railroad can be run through, or, over them; no telegraph, with the evil spirit on its wires, near them; nor common road, without a world of expense and negotiation. The race-course here is full of grave mounds, save on the track, and how the track was cleared of these graves, I have not learned, doubtless, by the omnipotence in China (as elsewhere) of the almighty dollar.

But, upon the whole, even in July, and to a half dead man, as I have been ever since I breathed what is miscalled " air " here, Shanghai is an achievement, a wonderful place, considering how it has arisen from the swamp in only four or five years. There are beautiful Italian villas all through it. There are churches that would do honor to New York. There are clubs with all the luxuries of the clubs of London or New York. British and American mercantile houses, mainly, with some German and French, have made good streets, good roads, and made good municipal governments—self-elected—all within five or six years. Some three thousand foreigners live here, enjoying all the blessings of life, except water and air —(don't laugh)—and make money, and grow rich, and then go home, if they don't die here, to enjoy it. They have daily and weekly newspapers—well-written ones, too—and doctors (of course), and lawyers, and courts. Every foreign nation, you know, has exclusive jurisdiction over its own subjects, and the British have their especial judges, while our judges are our consuls. Where commerce is by the millions, as it is here, the law cases are often of the gravest importance; and I see by the journals, the lawyers argue with as much force and ability as if in the United States or in England. We Americans have our gaol here; the British and other nations have theirs. The Chinese but look on—for Shanghai is foreign-governed in every sense, except the sovreignty territorial. It is wonderful that such mixed systems have worked so well; that the police is so effective, the pilots and harbor arrangements so good, and that so many nations live together in such harmony.

An American place is Shanghai now—far more than any other place in China; and though the British manufacturers have nearly driven us out of the market, in cotton and woollen goods, and driven our ships off the ocean, yet Americans "never say die," and work, and work well, despite the destructiveness of our tariff law. The Pacific Mail Company (ours) have nearly driven off, with their weekly lines to

Japan, English and French competition; and they have done it by the superiority of their steamers, and their superior management of them. They live, that is all; but they live in the hope of a better day, while the flag that they float here makes every American proud of his country. But a few years gone by, Americans sent out here some of our river steamers, to run from Shanghai to Hankow, six hundred miles off, up the great Yang-tze—the Amazon, the Mississippi, of China. Boats from Mystic (Conn.), and from other parts of New England and New York, were sent here. But that day is over. We can build no more ships in Mystic, or anywhere, under our laws; but the day for our flag to be emblazoned on the Yang-tze is not yet over. We are bringing out the workmen, and are going to build ships here. We buy the timber in Oregon, or Washington Territory, and put it together here. There are eighteen steamers under our flag now on the Yang-tze, running six hundred miles up and down, and coining money. There are others running once or twice a week to Tientsin (*en route* to Pekin), all under our flag, and floating it before millions and millions of Chinamen's eyes, who are thus taught to look upon "the flowery flag," so they call it, as omnipresent, everywhere, in the Yellow Sea and in the North of China. But some of these ships are already British purchased ships, with no right to our flag, save under consular authority. They have never seen an American port, and therefore, under our laws, can never enter there.

These American steamers, with their superior accommodations, have nearly monopolized the vast commerce of the great Yang-tze. Forty thousand junkmen, wails an official Mandarin, have been thrown out of employment in the coasting-trade alone! Perhaps so; but if so, they have increased the home value of Chinese teas and silks more than the worth of the useless labor of forty thousand junkmen. For a while they had all the freights to themselves. The British resisted at first, by sending their clippers up the Yang-tze to Hankow; but the navigation for sailing ships is so difficult and dangerous, that the insurance becomes more than the freight. Now they are sending quick tea steamers.

# LETTER XVI.

## *THE HEALTH OF CHINA.*

Where's Chefoo?—A Watering-Place in China.—Amusements There.—The American and Other Fleets.—The Noisy Salutations of the Fleets.—Church Service on the Colorado.—The Corean Expedition.—The Race of the Rival American Barges.—Rain here.—Breakfast by the Russian Admiral.—The English (Universal) Language.—Entertainments given us by the Russians.—Affinity of Russians and, Americans.—Admiral Rodgers's State Breakfast.—Divine Service on board the Russian Flag-Ship.—A Busy Week.—The Novel Assemblage at Chefoo about to disperse.

CHEEFO, *August* 1, 1871.

*Q.* WHERE'S Chefoo? *A.* Close by Corea. *Q.* Where's Corea? *A.* Look on the map and see. But the whereabouts of Corea all of you ought by this time to know—for our Admiral Jack Rodgers has just been thundering and lightning there with his little fleet, and is now back here, with lots of Corean trophies, battle-flags, jingalls, spears, etc. Corea is just across the Yellow Sea, about two hundred miles from this promontory of Shantung, and you can go there in a day. Chefoo is, in summer, to Shanghai and Pekin, the Newport, Long Branch, or Cape May of China. The Shanghaites send up here their wives and children, to live through the summer, and come occasionally themselves, while the Pekin-European residents come down here to escape, as they say, the terrible heats of Pekin. It is five hundred and twelve miles from Shanghai, about four hundred from Pekin, in about the latitude, and with the air, of Old Point Comfort (Va.), mosquitoes included—and a few extra fleas, and an occasional scorpion, added on! Nevertheless, Chefoo is the summer heaven of the Shanghai Hades. I feel as if I were in Paradise. I am revelling just on the borders of the ocean, surf, with nine American and European war-ships in the port, with their flags, all in the range and sight of our fair and comfortable summer hotel. This fleet must have on board, in all, some twenty-five hundred Americans, French, Germans, and Russians, and they make Chefoo, otherwise desolate—with not a road in it, or around it, for vehicles, and no communication but by sedan chairs—a very jolly place, at least for this summer. We go everywhere we can, by water. The coolies take us through the surf, in their chairs, to the boats, or, we get on the back of some lusty sailor, who takes pleasure in saving us from a ducking, as we go to visit the ships. We have nearly recovered our health, all of us—are ready for any thing—and these combined fleets, whose officers are all on good terms, the one with the other, are giving fun enough to everybody. The place, just now, is a second ex-Old Point Comfort, or, the regatta season at Newport—with breakfast parties, dinner parties, water parties, dances, serenades, etc. Three foreign ministers of the great powers are here—the Russian, General Vlangali, the British, Mr. Wade, the American, Mr. Low—with their attachés, retinues, etc.

Four bands of music are on board the ships—one, on the Colorado (American), one, on the Almas (Russian), one, on the Ocean (British), and one, on the Herther (German.) Here are materials enough for society, you see, in this great naval rendezvous—a place chosen for its health, and where ships congregate for the sake of their crews. There are two hotels here, a mile apart, the one inaccessible to the other, in consequence of creeks to be waded, save in sedan chairs; and in one or the other of these hotels, every evening, before dinner, which is at eight o'clock, P. M., one or the other of the four bands plays. I often ask myself, what do the Chinese say—patient, hard-working fellows—what do they think of these great, boisterous, ever ship thundering cannon salutations, and over this invasion of their otherwise quiet little Chefoo? Every minister has to be saluted—every admiral, every consul—and hence, from these nine ships-of-war, gunpowder, by day, seems ever exploding. The roar rattles in and around, and echoes from the Chefoo hills; and Confucius, born in this province, whose grave is not far off, must feel his bones shake, if there be any of his bones left.

SUNDAY.—We went to church on board the Colorado—the full Episcopal service, and nearly all the crew attending. It seemed strange, but reverential, here, in this far-off land, to be hearing that beautiful service, between decks, in our own native tongue, from our own chaplain. It transported us to our distant Sabbath home, and we felt as if we were there, when, on the planks of one of our ships, the chaplain prayed "for the President of the United States and all others in authority." The Colorado officers recited to us their unprinted and as yet unwritten adventures in Corea—as surveyors, as sailor-soldiers—and they showed the numerous little trophies they had taken. All say, "never were bolder, braver men than these Coreans," whose commanders' orders, "death or victory," they executed to the letter, by dying, save, when wounded, they could not continue the fight to die. Not a word, as yet, have our fleet heard from the Government in Washington, in reply to letters or telegrams; and now, they but await the coming mail due here, to abandon the expedition, and to start for Japan, to be in port as safe as possible during the approaching typhoon season.

MONDAY.—Rain, rain, nothing but rain! A long, dry season has been followed by a severe rain. Houses stand drouths here pretty well; but this rain is washing away our hotel. The builders here build of mud, and lime, and straw—much mud and little lime—and hence, when a flood comes, such as we are having now, the mud washes away, and down tumble ceilings, and walls, and plastering, and every thing else. Certain it is, our hotel is being washed down, and is running off into the Chefoo Bay; and, if it washes much more, we shall have to take to the Colorado, the Alaska, or the Benicia, the American ships now in port, for refuge from the flood. Pekin, I am told, whither I am now travelling, is pretty well under mud, if not all under water—for the floods above have been severe, while the Peiho River (the river near Pekin) is running over.

TUESDAY.—There was a great boat-race between the barges of the Colorado and the Alaska—and never did a regatta excite greater interest in New York, or in Southampton (England), than did this regatta. Two admirals—one American (Rodgers), one Russian (Federovski)—and two foreign ministers—Gen. Vlangali (Russian) and Mr. Low (American)—with aids, captains, lieutenants, too numerous to mention, were on hand. The crews of the three American ships were in the highest state of excitement, running to the rigging and manning the yards, as if so many birds—all, more or less, having staked something on the result, and all, therefore, winning or losing a little of that something. The barge of the Alaska won, and the Colorado, the flag-ship, was downhearted, of course.

THURSDAY.—Breakfasted with Admiral Federovski, on board his flag-ship, the Almas, in company with the American and Russian ambassadors, and admirals, and captains of all the war-ships in port—making a large party of us. The breakfast was in European style—French—prepared by a French restaurant-keeper here, and sent on board. A fine Russian band played during the breakfast, which lasted two hours or more. There were French, German, and Russian officials at table, but all spoke English—some well, all passably well. The English language, I see—and the more I see, the better I see it—is becoming the universal language of the educated world. Twenty or twenty-five years ago, or less, only French would carry you through the world; but now it is impossible to go anywhere, from the pyramids of Egypt to the mountains of Japan, that English will not pretty well carry you along. Chinese house servants, more or less, speak English—"pigeon English," as it is called—but, nevertheless, comprehensible English; and go where you will, in whatever society, English seems now to be *the* tongue. Such are the conquests of the almighty dollar, with the diffusion of English colonization in America, the Indies, Australia, and elsewhere. One of the Russians with us to-day, the secretary of the Pekin Embassy, was educated in Oxford (England), and speaks English better than the English themselves—that is, without their hemming, and hawing, and hesitating, and repeating, and re-repeating. The Russian ambassador and the Russian admiral both speak English; and what was remarkable, in a group afterward, when landed on shore, the German commander leading off in German, the whole group of Russians followed him, as if German were their native tongue.

The Russian admiral gave us, and the ladies with us, a novel treat after the breakfast was over; and that was the Russian (peasant) dance, executed with admirable effect by his sailors. One of the officers, too, threw off his uniform, and put on a sailor's garb, to enter into the dance, and in spirit, vivacity, and energy contributed to our common enjoyment of the strange spectacle of a Russian peasant dance on a Chinese sea. The band, too, played several Russian airs, and one, a national one, with great interest to us. The whole crew united with the band in singing the national anthem. To the Russian admiral, who made every effort to please us, we were much indebted; and we left, after enjoying one of the pleasantest days of life. The Russians seem naturally to "take" to us Americans, and we "take" to them.

FRIDAY.—Admiral Rodgers gave a "state" breakfast to the Russian admiral, the French captain-in-chief, the German captain-in-chief, the English captain-in-chief—to the Russian and American Ministers, and to your humble servant. These officers, all except the Frenchman and German, seem to be on confidential terms with each other, even in matters of their profession, and their conversation was prolonged for hours in mutual instruction and profit.

SATURDAY.—Visited the Alaska, entertained by Captain Blake, of New York, who distinguished himself on James River and in Texas, commanding the Hatteras, during our civil war, and who was commander of the late Corean expedition. By the way, I may say, this Corean expedition is given up, unless our Government orders to the contrary, which is not probable, before the intervention of Congress. The ships will next week disperse—the Colorado to Yokohama, the Alaska to Nagasaki, the Benicia up the

## THE HEALTH OF CHINA. 147

Yang-tze to Hankow, after a visit to Shanghai, and the Palos up the gulf here, to North China.

SUNDAY, 10½ A. M.—Revisited, by invitation of Admiral Federovski, the Almas, to attend divine service. A Greek priest, a very handsome fellow, in a black cassock, with a heavy-linked gold chain, upholding a golden cross, officiated. The service was in old Russian (Sclave). I could not profit much by it, in what was harder than "all Greek" to me; but in the extemporized chapel, flag-created, with its altars, images, candles, and incense, there was quite enough solemnity to be well understood. Another breakfast was given us here, after the service was over, with another Russian country dance.

Four and a-half P. M.—Visited, by invitation of Captain Hewett, the British ship, Ocean, larger than the Colorado, with two hundred more men on board —one of the large-class ships—with a very pleasant entertainment on board.

. . . . . .

I have gone into this recitative, personal journalism, only to give you an idea of the way we kill time in a little, dirty Chinese town, all mud and dirt, except on the sands where we are, and to show you representative squadron and diplomatic life in a summer European-coast city of China. There will be an infinite deal of gossip in the Chinese and Japanese English and American press, as to what all this assemblage means, of the American, British, Russian, French, and German squadrons, with their admirals and three ministers plenipotentiary. But all means only this—*Health*, in a not healthy country, in the unhealthy season—and nothing else. " Corea" is reported to be the great matter of consultation. I am said to have brought out secret orders from the United States Government. Corean junks have arrived here, as spies on our squadron; but there is nothing going on, save what I have journalized above. The British minister, in the morning, returns to Pekin. I go too—by water and by mud (this is yet the rainy season), if none of us break down under the weather in the interior. If nothing happens, you will hear from me again in about a month, and I will tell you something of the great capital of three hundred millions of Chinamen. I am thinking, too, of Siberia, and of going home *via* St. Petersburg; but I fear, in consequence of brigands lately reported on the route, I shall have to give it up.

## LETTER XVII.

### ON THE PEIHO RIVER.

Tremendous Flood on the River of Peiho.—Whole Villages washed away.—The People drowned out.—Widespread Desolation.—Living on the River on a Yankee Steamer.—The Grand Canal broken loose.—The Crooked Peiho River.—The Way we wound up the River.—The Year-ago Massacre of Europeans and Catholics in Tien-tsin.—The then Fright of all Missionaries.—Scare about going there.—Guns and Gunboats Commercial and Christian Guarantees.—An Exploration of the Old Under-water Tien-tsin, in a British Launch.—Innumerable Junks.—The Ruins of the Roman Catholic Cathedral.—The Tombs of the slain Sisters.—Terrors predicted for Tourists to Pekin.—Nevertheless, On, On to Pekin.

TIEN-TSIN, *August* 10, 1871.

LOOK on the map, and you will find where this place *ought* to be, when not under water, as now—on the Peiho River, the gateway to Pekin from the Gulf of Pe-chih-li, and where the British and French took their great points of departure, when, some years gone by, some thousands of them paid their respects to the celestial Emperor, in his celestial palace—respects not of the *kouto* style (nine bendings and three head-knockings), but respects with heavy cannon, big shot and little shot, sword, bayonet, and revolver. I am living on board a Yankee steamer, *built* in Glasgow (Capt. Hawes, all the way from Searsport, Me.), under the "flowery" Yankee flag, and all above me, and below me, and nearly all around me, is desolation, *desolation*, DESOLATION. The windows of heaven have been wide open for two weeks, pouring out nothing but water, water—and some say frogs—and all upper North-China appears to have broken loose, and to be flowing down here in mud, straw, bamboo, millet, sorghum, and other crops, etc. The Grand Canal has broken loose, and is pouring in the Yellow River, if not into the Yang-tze. Houses, mud and straw built, are tumbling down by the thousands. Whole villages are swept away, and all the inhabitants drowned. The desolation of the typhoon I witnessed in Japan is but a trifle in comparison with this universal misery. Thousands will starve to death, the coming winter, if not relieved by the Pekin government, and rebellion, as in such cases is usual, will probably follow.

But, I am not solemnly writing history, remember, only pencilling, as you see—scribbling; and, remember, too, that you print only a rapid traveller's journal. Come, go back, then, with me to Chefoo. The seventh of August, about midnight, in a big rain, we left the "Chefoo Family Hotel," in sedan chairs, two coolies only to each, to track three miles along the seacoast, by the surf, now rolling, and over the then mountain rivulets, to embark for Tien-tsin. And such "a ride!" such "a ride!" The Lord forgive me if I ever again take it at midnight, in a rain storm. The steamers that run from Shanghai to Tien-tsin (about eight hundred miles) always take passengers on board the night before, as they leave at daybreak in the morning, to see the islands, and to dodge the shallows.  We came up from Shanghai to Chefoo in the rolling "Manchu," Capt. Steele, from Townsend, Mass., a jolly, rollicking, capital fellow, with a fair library on board; and we came up from Chefoo to Tien-tsin in the not less rolling "Shantung," with the Maine Capt. Hawes I have before spoken of, one of the best sailors in the world, and delighted to see one of his own State men in this far-off land.  The boats of this American line are long, thin, shad-like screws, built to run over the Yang-tze shallows and the Gulf of Pe-chih-li flats and bars, and up the mud of the narrow Peiho —charming boats, when the heavens smile, but only rocking-chairs when a storm gets up, as it did for the long, lean, but otherwise beautiful "Shantung."  A fog hid every thing from our eyes, ten feet off.  We anchored off the bar of the Taku forts.  We shook, we trembled, we tumbled, we pitched, we danced— but the strong iron chains and the strong anchors clasped fast hold of the jocund "Shantung."  For twenty-four hours, thus, in blissful ignorance of our exact whereabouts, we capered, we frolicked, we starved—yet, in our starvation, fed the fishes of the sea.  Storms, however, never last always.  The fog cleared off, and we found ourselves in the company of junk upon junk, waiting for the fog rising, to find the mouth of the Peiho.  Now, however, alas! the river was all mouth.  The whole country was under water.  The lofty Taku fort embattlements, with their ugly-looking Chinese cannon, were not yet drowned out, and taking them for our landmarks, we crooked and wound about, and steamed backward, up, and forward, down, on our way up to Tien-tsin, sixty-four miles by water, and twenty-four by land. But what navigation! Our long, lean, lank Shantung, as long as the river is wide, would be swung by the current right across the river banks, and then we would plough *into* the banks with her nozzle, and root off perch after perch of the celestial soil. Ruins were all along the shore. Miserable inhabitants, abandoning all, were getting into junks with hogs, cocks, hens, and other household gods, while over the tombs of their idolized ancestors were pouring the wild, wild waters from the broken banks of the Peiho and the Grand Canal. Through twisting and turning, however, pulling and hauling, wading and poling, and by using steam and the windlass, our persevering captain managed, in the light of a long August day, to reach Tien-tsin, and to find all the inhabitants, Europeans and Americans as well as Chinese, wailing, if not weeping, over their common misfortunes. A Russian fellow-passenger with us, who had been to Hankow to buy teas for Russia, not only found his house washed down and his furniture destroyed, but teas of his, in warehouse, damaged to the amount of twenty thousand dollars, or more.

If I had put much faith in stories and warnings, as I came along, since I left home, I never should have put foot into Tien-tsin. Only a year ago in July the whole European population in the Chinese city was swept off by assassination and murder. Roman Catholic priests and nuns were slaughtered without mercy, with the French Consul and others, including two Russians. All in the new city, the European Tien-tsin, were spared. Mischief-making and revengeful Chinese leaders had put it into the heads of the ignorant Tien-tsiners (four hundred thousand, about, is the population of the city) that the Roman Catholics were kidnapping children in their orphan asylums, to use their eyes, ears, and the more vital or mysterious parts of the human body, as charms, philters, potions, spells, to bewitch the Chinese and their children. The zeal of these Catholics to fill their schools with children, whom thus they hoped to make instruments for propagating Christianity, and uprooting Paganism, lent credence to these wicked tales, and the end was the terrible mob that destroyed the beautiful little cathedral, the nunnery, the hospitals—nay, that rooted up, and rooted out, the whole French population in the old Tien-tsin. Others were murdered, not Roman Catholics; a Protestant church in the vicinity was destroyed, and all missionaries, of all denominations, everywhere in North China, were put into terrible fright. Chung How, then chief mandarin of the city, caused to be paid all the French losses, and is now in France, trying to propitiate the French people, to save Tien-tsin, hereafter, from bombardment, or the French bayonet.

But into Tien-tsin I came, nevertheless and notwithstanding. "Where others go you can go," is reason. If a traveller did not guide his steps by this species of logic, rumor would scare him off, often, from many an instructive route of travel. Guns, guns, guns, however, are here now great guarantees. Two French and one British gunboat are now here, with American, German, and other gunboats often looking in. Fulminating powder, I am sorry to say, seems indispensable to secure trade and commerce; and Christianity, guns, and missionaries have to go together in China. The steam launch of the great British iron-clad, the Ocean, which cannot get within fifteen miles of the mouth of the Peiho River, has just escorted up here, on his way back to Pekin, Mr. Wade, the British Minister, and the captain of the Ocean invited us to use his launch with him, to explore the ruins of the water-covered Tien-tsin. We steamed up the river, to the consternation of the Chinese junks, where steam never went before, and hundreds upon hundreds, if not thousands upon thousands, came out from their junk holes, as bees from hives, to see what this puffing, snorting, little steam devil was doing. A tall Tartar fellow, some great mandarin's great man, was lent us, to scream the Chinese junks out of our way; and as we spurted and spouted, junks scattered, as fast as pole, or line, or current could scatter them. Such an ocean of water-craft, such cities of masted craft afloat, such acres upon acres of shipping, my eyes never beheld before! One traveller playfully reports, "I counted a hundred millions of junks, and then stopped." I did not count. There was too much to count, and too much to see, to waste time to count. The launch steamed up to where the Roman Catholic Cathedral was. Nothing but the walls are left now and the cross, yet golden, on the tower's top. We dropped a tear of sympathy beside the graves of the good Sisters of Charity, buried near by, and heard a Chinese-born Catholic recite who was interred here, and who, there. These poor Sisters were flayed alive by the infuriated mob! One saved herself for a while in Chinese dress, but her European shoes betrayed her, and she was slain, too. The British officers with us sympathized earnestly with the captain of the French gunboat, who was also his guest. Strange it is, but so it is, we Americans, Frenchmen, Englishmen, Germans, here, in this heathen land, are all one. We have no nationalities not forgotten the moment we meet one of our own race, in these remote spots. A pic-nic in the launch—a tiffin is the Eastern name for a lunch—was given us near the ruins of the cathedral, and when that was over, we explored, as well as we could in a steamer, the drowned-out streets and tottering houses of this unhappy Tien-tsin. "Heaven has inflicted this upon us," say some of them, "because we killed the God of the Christians."

Of this country, under water now, of course I can see nothing. "Go back," says everybody. "Don't go up to Pekin." "You can't get there." "You will be fifteen or twenty days in going." "The land route is all under water, all impassable." Never were reports louder in traveller's ear, or so discouraging. Nobody could take us in at Tien-tsin. All houses were drowned down, or uninhabitable from rain, save that of the British Consul, whose house, the largest by all odds in the place, was filled with the Pekin British diplomats and retinue, just then. The "Astor House," the famous hotel of the place, established by some California Yankee by the name of Smith, was washed out—billiard, bar-room, all. "Come with us in the gunboat," said Frenchman and Englishman, both. "A gunboat is no place for a lady." "Go back with me to Chefoo," said the captain of the Ocean. "The fact is," I answered, "I have come over two thousand miles, from Yokohama, in Japan, only to see Pekin; and if I stay here, I shall have to live in a Chinese sampan (a covered house-boat, some twenty feet long), and as *motion* is more satisfactory than *station*, to Pekin I will go." "But the Russian courier has just been robbed *en route* from Pekin to our Minister, now at Chefoo," said a Russian Secretary. "The flood is making robbers of the hungry Chinese," it was added. Nevertheless, on, on to Pekin, was the impulse within me, and to Pekin I will go, for I do not believe the perils held up before me.

## LETTER XVIII.

### *ON, TO PEKIN.*

Arrival at Tung-Chow.—Lodged in a Temple.—Ice in Abundance now.—On to Pekin that Night.—The Gates of Pekin at Sunset.—The Infernal Road to the Celestial City, in a Mule Cart.—Bump, Thump.—No Getting Out, no Living In.—The Sights on the Tung-Chow and Pekin Road.—The Wheelbarrow Gentry.—Caravans.—First Sight of the Bactrian Camel.—The Great Walls of the City after Sunset.—What John Chinaman thinks of an American-dressed Woman entering his Capital in an Open Sedan-chair.—Difference of Opinion as to Pekin and New York Fashions.—Happy Welcome in the Russian Legation.—A Cossack Porter opens the Great Gates.

PEKIN, *August* 18, 1871.

TUNG-CHOW, one hundred and twenty miles from Tien-tsin by water, not eighty by land, was reached at noon. This is the port of Pekin, sixteen miles, though, and very, very long miles, you will see. Russian letters, written in Chinese to Russian agents here, secured us excellent lodgment in quite a grand temple, where we expected to pass the night. The Buddhist priests were as civil as lambs, and gave us sacred places to repose in, or to eat ice in, the greatest luxury we could have on a hot day. Ice, by the way, here is "cheap as dirt." The Peiho and the swamps around are all thick ice in winter, and there is no luxury like it to an American. Besides, all the little animalculæ in Chinese waters are thus frozen up and frozen out in winter, and you can safely eat ice, when you cannot drink the water. We tumbled down our weary limbs, and rested close by the Buddhist altars, with all sorts of images over us and about us—dragons and other scary devils—but nothing could scare us from sleep, rising, as we had, at four in the morning, and roasting, as we had been, in crowds of odoriferous Tung-Chow junks with hundreds of the population looking on, marvelling where such creatures as we are, came from. These Chinese temples, by the way, are curious, but quite comfortable structures to live in. The entrance is not exhilarating—through the kitchen, and near by all the washing utensils, through crowds eating, drinking, and smoking; but when in, there is magnificence in some temples, certainly in parts of this.

To Pekin, on to Pekin, however, was yet the burning impulse within me, and I was bent, if possible, in crossing the only sixteen miles, and on being that night in Pekin. At three o'clock they told me, "If you go, you can't get into the gates of Pekin tonight." "What, not get over sixteen miles," said I, "from three o'clock to sunset?" "You will be brought up all standing," it was added, "at the closed gates of Pekin, and be compelled to sleep on the road, in the dirt, and amid the vermin of the gateway." "On to Pekin!" said I; "on, on to Pekin!" Three carts, the springless ones I have spoken of, were hired for me and my traps, and a young lady with me, was put in a sedan-chair, carried by four coolies. The sedan-chair was loaned me in

Tien-tsin, and brought up on a sampan; and we started for Pekin, the great celestial capital, the earthly home of an emperor that Heaven has loaned to govern and to bless the millions upon millions of mortals in China.

Some two or three hundred years gone by, some emperor of China (plague on him!) took it into his head to make a road of granite blocks, some five or six feet long by two wide, upon a raised mound of earth, over the sixteen miles of distance from the port of Pekin to Pekin itself. It was the Appian Way to the Chinese Rome. It was a New York Boulevard—a Pennsylvania Avenue, as recently made in Washington. But, alas for me, in my mule cart, with no springs, the granite-road has not been repaired for two hundred years, or more, and "the Appian Way" has dropped out, and dropped in, to such an extent that only a mule could navigate a cart over it, or through it. The Turks have nearly such a road now, leading to Jerusalem, but no Turk was ever fool enough, as are the Chinese, to put carts on it! There was just such a road, some years ago, between Acquia Creek and Fredericksburg, Va., but the Virginians were never blockheads enough to pave it. I have ridden over corduroy roads in Maine, in rough wooden spring wagons; through black mud prairies, in olden times, in Illinois; over mountain passes in Nevada; but never, never, over such an infamous, infernal hewn granite quarry as this, all topsy-turvy. "*Bump,*" *that,* hit the shoulder, and made me shiver all over. "*Thump,*" *that,* was only the ribs. "Bump," "thump," "smash," "crash," *that,* hit me on the head, and made my eyes sparkle like rockets! Hat off, and then off guard, while fitting it on again, came another "thump," "bump." Hands give out holding on, wrists ache. Whew! there goes my head again, up against the sides. "Let me out," says I. Mule nor Chinaman understands English! I was afraid to break my legs, if the cart did not stop, when I was getting out. Thump, bump—in short, it was sixteen long, endless miles of "bump," "thump," "smash," "crash," such as the Spanish Inquisition only inflicted upon heretics, save only the breaking of their bones. I am only jelly, thank a good Providence. Every bone is where it was. But I would not take another such drive for one hundred dollars per mile.

Emerging from Tung-Chow, where the Russian and Mongolian caravans start with teas for Russia, on the Siberian route, we first were "stuck" on the Broadway of Tung-Chow—a way about ten feet *broad!* The wheelbarrow gentry—one man wheeling, on one wheel, two men holding on, steadying the burden on either side, and one mule pulling ahead—blocked up the great street of Tung-Chow. Our drivers and the wheelbarrow men, laden with goods for Pekin, bellowed and yelled, and thus cleared the way, in part, after near an hour's delay in reaching the outer gates of this walled city. The sidewalks, a foot or two wide, were high up, and we, in the street, were low down, in mud and mire, often, there wallowing like hogs. My cart was water-tight, and no matter, therefore, for the splash. It was well covered, mule and all, and no matter, therefore, for the blazing hot sun. Donkeys brayed hard in our ears, but no matter for that. The Bactrian camel, with his sprawl feet, all the way from the Mongolian deserts, obtruded his ugly neck into our presence, but no matter for that. Every thing was strange, new, and novel; and if it had not been for the tears in my eyes, started by the eternal banging of the springless cart, the journey would have been delightful. We crossed the great dragon bridge, where a French general won his hard-pronounced title of duke of something. The graves of "our ancestors" were innumerable, and pretty well kept. Temples there were, and not a few. Houses lined the road almost the whole way, and coolies, and mandarins, and servants, and farmers so filled up the road, that it would have been hopeless to try to count them.

At last, when the sun was set, and darkness covered the face of the earth, we approached the great walls of the great city of a million or two millions of people—nobody knows, or seems to know here, for the census has not been taken for over fifty years. Our servant-pigeon-English interpreter had shot ahead before dark, and on announcing, with gravity, "great people were coming on, under a Russian escort, with Russian protection, bound to the Russian Legation"—lo, presto! the heavy gates were open, and we were let in. All Chinamen, except ours, were shut out; and thus, for the first time in my life, I found use in trousers, hat, coat, and shoes, over the more natural habiliments of the wiser-clad Eastern man—for the first sight of us proved to the gate-keeper we were a race of European men, and doubtless, as he thought, Russians. Once in the gates, then scenes ensued. The four coolies who had brought the young lady's sedan-chair, mile upon mile, needed rest, and took it within the gates. When they set down the chair, hundreds upon hundreds gathered about it, as if to see a mermaid, with flowing ringlets, thus gliding through these gates. The crowd became first stifling, then earnestly curious, not only to see, but to feel of the novelty. They were greedy to know what such a funny thing was made of—whether of wax, or poplin, or muslin. Lanterns went up in all directions; the crowd increased, and grew more curiously noisy. I acted as policeman, looked amiably terrible, with only an umbrella for a baton; but the umbrella was wand enough to keep the peace. I did not much marvel over the curious Chinamen. What would New York think, if a Chinese woman, with her little bits of tiny bird-like feet, were dropped down on Broadway? And yet, our ringlets, our flowing frocks, our queer, strange top-knots that the world calls bonnets, the broad, emblazoned, unveiled face, are more astounding to Chinese eyes than the little bird feet of the Chinese women are to ours. American women have not often enough entered the streets of Pekin to accustom the strange spectacle to Chinese eyes. When the sedan and its burthen re-started on, the great crowd sent up one great jeer, and I did not much blame them, though I was glad to be rid of them, and to hide in the darkness, now increasing.

It was five *li*, nearly two miles, from the gate we entered to the Russian Legation, where was to be my hospitable home. The American Minister has gone to Japan, and General Vlangali, the Russian minister, now absent in Chefoo, ordered his house to be our home. Through these five *li*, in the now muddy streets of Pekin, we were a long time wandering— now, in the slough of despond, and now, on the dry land. Theatres were on the street side. Story-tellers filled the ways, with recitations to the crowds, holding lanterns. Shops were brilliantly illuminated. Songs from all sides seemed to be pouring out from the houses of a happy population. At last, near ten P. M., we reached the Russian Legation, in the Tartar part of the city, all walled in; and knocking at the gate loudly, we startled up the Cossack porter, and soon were welcomed by a hospitable meal, and, what was more important to us then, hospitable beds.

## LETTER XIX.

### THE JOURNEY TO PEKIN.

How he got to Pekin in a Springless Cart, over a Granite-Paved Imperial Road, Thirteen Miles long when first made, and passable, now thirty, or more, from the Holes in it, and the Crooks to dodge these Holes.—Bones all aching from Pounding, but Bone-Pounding Good Medicine at Times.—The Fit-Out for the River Peiho Journey in Sampans.—Hospitality of the Tien-tsiners.—Bad Water.—Must Liquor or Tea.—Dead Chinamen by millions, and Graves everywhere bad for Wells.—Catalogue of a Peiho Boat Outfit.—The Terrors of the Route all exaggerated.—The High Water a Help.—Cut across Lots.—The Supplies *en route*.—Beggars.—A not Disagreeable Journey.—All Sleeping Unprotected.—No Real Perils.—Coolie Comforts.—Sights on the River.—British Manufactures.—The Cock keeps Time for the Coolie in the Morning.—Life in a Junk.—Toilettes there.—The Countless Babies here.

PEKIN, *August* 18, 1871.

EVERY bone in me aches. I am black and blue, nearly all over! What importance, ask you, perhaps, is that to the public? Why, to keep the public at home, minding their own business, not making fools of themselves, as I am, in being pounded and pestled here, with muscles aching and brains half beaten out! "Fools go to Pekin, wise men stay at home," is my conclusion to-day, after my adventures of yesterday, over a Chinese granite-paved road, in a springless cart, drawn by a mule, in a straight line, two miles an hour—in the crooked line, three or four miles (by these holes), but up and down, five or six miles per hour. Nevertheless, I feel all the better for this pounding internally, though externally I groan every step I take. It is good for the torpid liver this climate creates. It stirs up the bile, is superb for digestion, and capital for the dyspepsia. The best medicine we house, home, newspaper-scribbling men can take at times, I am sure, is such a stirring up. If the Shanghai doctor had given me a Chinese cart to ride in, over a Chinese granite road, I should not have half died over his boluses, nostrums, and liquid concoctions. I feel to-day as if I could eat Pekin up in a week, and all this comes, I am sure, from the pounding of my flesh and bones.

Well, come back with me to Tien-tsin. When the good European people of this drowned-out city heard me crying, "On to Pekin," despite the flood, and when they saw the sampan boats, with the boatmen all engaged to go, their hospitality, in pity for our rashness, became unbounded. The captain of the British gunboat Lieven loaned us beds and bedding, and gave us a big cask of water, condensed and purified by his steam-engine. And, by the way, this is no country, this never can be a country for temperance men, unless you are born and brought up, from youth and childhood, to drinking mud, or water without mud, full of little live creatures, that dance about so briskly in the well water that you cannot get rid of them. All of us Maine-born men here, captains of steamboats, and all, abjure water and the Maine law. We drink it boiled and flavored with tea; but the pure article, as handed over to us by the Creator, never enters our mouths. The fact is, China is so dirty, so full of the essence of dead ancestors' bones, that even the wells are impure. Four hundred millions of Chinamen, dying generation after generation, seem to poison and corrupt all the streams. Hence, I was under great obligations to the captain of the Lieven for his big beaker of water. But what would not I give now, even, for a cupful of pure mountain iced water, like that, say, which runs gurgling through Salt Lake City, or, that comes trickling down from the snowy sides of the mountains of Oregon. A dollar a cupful would be cheap, very cheap to me; but, nevertheless, I drink, thankful, for the manufactured water, in tea, in claret, in porter, beer, Rhine wine, or any liquor that can be got, bourbon and brandy not excepted.

Should you like to see the outfit our new Tientsin friends provided for us, to ascend the Peiho, I give it for the benefit of future travellers here:

| | | | |
|---|---|---|---|
| Crackers, tins | 2 | Peaches, cans | 3 |
| Sardines, boxes | 3 | Candles | 6 |
| Strawberries, can | 1 | Salt, pepper, mustard, can | 1 |
| French preserves, cans | 2 | Cakes, assorted. | |
| Sugar, tin | 1 | Sponge cake. | |
| Tea, tin | 1 | Ice in abundance. | |
| Cheese | 1 | Ketchup. | |
| Pickles, bottle | 1 | Matches. | |
| Vinegar, bottle | $\frac{1}{2}$ | Corkscrews. | |
| Roast turkey, tin | 1 | Teapots. | |
| Cold meat, dish | 1 | Towels. | |
| Soup, cans | 6 | Napkins. | |
| Condensed milk, cans | 2 | Eggs— | |

with tumblers, cups, saucers, plates, saucepans, pitchers, soap, wash-basins, and other things too numerous to mention, but all useful to new housekeepers, in a sampan boat, going, one knew not, how or where.

The "sack" was more abundant, if possible, than the provender (particulars omitted), and if we run hungry, we could not well run dry, even if we were twenty days, as some predicted, in poling or tracking up this now turbulent Peiho. Other friends loaned us mosquito nets and pillows, and thus provided us to meet the outer enemy as well as to supply the inner man. No traveller, even up the Nile, could have been better supplied for a long journey.

And it has not been much of a journey after all—only four and a half days up to Tung Chow, the head of Peiho junk navigation, and a half day more overland, rather over stones, to Pekin! We paid our coolies extra to pole hard, track quick, or row with zeal; and the very high water, in lieu of being a disadvantage, turned out to be an advantage—for we cut across lots, here, there, and everywhere, through fields of sorghum, by acres of millet, through sesamum, and castor beans, and Indian corn, so that I do not believe we sailed over a hundred miles, though the distance by the banks of the river is reported one hundred and twenty, from Tien-tsin to Tung Chow. We reached half-way, Ho-si-Woo, in two days and a half—the hardest half, though. Our Chinese servant boy, who, with his "pidgen English," acted as interpreter, cooked for us, and bought what he could for us from the bluffs of the unwashed-out part of the country. We bought chickens, but we could not eat them, they were so fishy. (They feed them on fish.) We had made the nicest of omelets—not with butter, or milk, but with, I fear, the oil of the castor bean, or sesamum. "Like'e lice?" our cook interpreter boy often asked. I always said "yes;" but don't marvel, for the Chinaman ever turns "R" into "L," and rice was all he meant. "Bread" was "bled" —and I liked "bled" too. Pidgen English, even, is hard English to understand, till you have been long used to it; but we are becoming accustomed now. We paid only fifteen dollars for each sampan boat— double, nearly, the usual price—forty-five dollars for three boats, with four persons to work and to wait in each, and this included every thing, except little *cumshaws* (presents) in "cash," a cash being something like a farthing in value. Wherever we stopped, beggars innumerable turned up, or salesmen of eggs, grapes, peaches, apples, plums, and other fruits. We never stopped off towns or villages at night; but in fields of millet, or sorghum, or sesamum we anchored our boats, and slept as well—the hard beds excepted —as if we had been in our own homes. Life, however, is all trust here. The boats were all open to let in the night breezes. The coolies slept and snoozed right about us. There were no watchmen to protect us. I never carry revolvers in travelling, for I think they are more likely, in the rough handling they have on such voyages, to kill you, than to aid you in killing anybody. All the weapon I had was a dagger, a friend insisted upon my taking, for some short, quick fight, if one should become necessary. The Chinese, however, seem to be, in the main, too honest to steal, when acting as servants about you, and too peaceable to fight; so that everywhere I have felt myself as safe as if in New York, even under lock and key there. We started at daybreak, and rowed or tracked as long as we could see —the poor coolies in water almost all day, but happy at night, in their improvised suppers, when rolled up in their padded comforters, to sleep; and they probably get not even two dollars from the owner of the boat, who gave them this four and a half days of employ. From fifteen cents to twenty cents per day is coolie boatmen's pay on the Peiho, with the privilege of working eighteen hours in mud and water, and finding one's self. This, however, pretty well supplies his wants. Their clothing is cheap and sparse—only cotton cloth—and their food is millet and fish, when the latter can be got.

The boat sights we saw on the Peiho were many, the land sights few, and they were nearly all in, or under water. Many, many junks were floating down the rapid current of the river; some of them, stylish, three stories high, with flags, and handsome exteriors, but the great body of them, transports. The foreigners' coasting trade ends at Tien-tsin, and the native craft is exclusive from thence upward and inward, and all about. The transportation upward was mainly British Manchester goods, with which many a junk seemed to be laden. Once we had a lion's share of this great trade, and the cotton goods of Lowell, and Lawrence, and Lewiston, and Biddeford were floating freely upon these waters, for Chinese consumption, in company with these British drills, sheetings, and shirtings; but now, my Yankee manufacturing countrymen have so constructed their tariff laws as to destroy all this, and to give the whole to John Bull and the Germans. Do not tell me of cheaper labor in England; for, if "that's what did it," nobody could compete with the ten cents a day Chinese manufacture of their own cotton. Steam could be as cheap a workman with us as in England, if our Yankee countrymen did not love high duties on coal, and fish and potatoes (largely their food), and on machinery and the raw material for machinery of all kinds. But, whew! I'm shooting off on a tariff tangent!

Among the boat sights on a Chinese river is the everlasting cock, who is ever kept there to do *cock-a-doodle-doo* in the early morning, and thus to note the time, and to wake up the crew. At the cockcrow all start from their lairs, and go to work. The cocks are probably well-taught cocks—taught only to crow when the day is breaking. With the cock are hens, and with the hens, dogs, cats, etc., a whole menagerie. Life on a junk is just like life on land, with the doors more open, though. We see the Chinese women making their toilettes, and the men combing their own hair, and then binding on their long boughten cues. The longer a cue is in China, the greater "the swell;" hence, false hair is more for sale to men than to women. "I can't employ you with that cue," said a Russian friend of mine, the other day, to a Chinese boy, with a short tail. "I have no money to buy more," said the boy. "Take that, then, for a fit-out, and turn up grand." The boy took the money, and turned up with a tail that stretched to the ground. We see all these toilette operations going on—combing, washing, braiding; and we hear *up*-braiding, too—scolding, I mean. Never were greater scolds than these Chinese boatmen seem to be. Their monosyllabic words have a terrible ring, when they are mad—short, sharp, cutting. There was a row on my boat. A big fellow beat his brother, a lesser fellow. The little fellow smothered his rage till we reached a bluff, and then ran away; but the father, in another boat near by, ran after him, and though the father could never have overtaken the little fellow, by running, yet such is the force of parental authority here, over children, that only his command from a long distance brought back the runaway. The row that then ensued between the brothers, the father all the while interfering, became so boisterous that I thought it wise to show my dagger to keep the peace. I did not unsheath it, only stamped and yelled, and that restored order in the boat fleet.

One of the first things impressing a traveller in China is the babies, the countless babies. Malthus, evidently, is not read here, or the new New England native American non-propagation creed. "Multiply and replenish the earth," in our Bible, is, in the Confucian classics, in another paraphrase, "Beget children, to be sure of having your bones well taken care of." "The more sons you have, the better off you are in heaven." Girl babies, however, alas for the poor things, are deemed rather curses than blessings, more especially if you have too many of them —such curses, that often the little lasses are tumbled away to perish—boy babies, never. All the junks we passed, or saw, were more or less filled with babies—naked babies, mixed up with the cocks, and hens, and dogs, and kittens. Fathers were as often fondling them as the mothers. This love of babies, it is, that makes up the Chinese countless numbers, ever populating the land, and forcing the poor often to starve, or to live on kitten cutlets and puppy steaks. What we saw people eating most of, on our boat journey, were watermelons, pretty good ones; a species of cantelopes, that they nibble, as monkeys would; then peaches, that nobody else could eat, they are so bad—with onions, onions, onions innumerable. Indeed, the whole population hereabout seems saturated with onions and opium.

## LETTER XX.

### *FROM PEKIN.*

The Guide-Books of Pekin.—The "Ji-hia-kieu-wen-kau" and the "Chen-yuen-chi-lio."—Three Cities within Pekin, the Manchu or Tartar, Chinese, and Imperial.—Shopping in Pekin.—Great Fur Market.—Mongolia, Manchuria, Corea, and Siberia Sables, Ermine, etc., etc.—Precious Stones.—Jade.—Greek Chapel on the Grounds of the Russian Legation.—Life among Chinese Russians.—Catholic and Protestant Missionaries in Pekin.—Visit to the Roman Catholic Cathedral.—French Priests and Sisters of Charity.—School for Chinese Children.—Money and the Missionaries.— Conflicts between them. — Foreign and Anti-Foreign Party in China.—Chinese Efforts to create Prejudice against Christians.

PEKIN, *August* 20, 1871.

WHEN you first get into a new, great city, you ask for maps and a guide-book. Maps I have none, save in a Hong-Kong guide-book, but works on Pekin are numerous. The "Ji-hia-kieu-wen-kau" is before me—one hundred and sixty chapters only—four chapters on the beauties of Pekin (I can't see them yet;—it seems to me an infernal hole—no sidewalks, no gutters, the privies in the streets, in open sinks, and the accumulated filth of centuries rising up in terrific stenches; through mud over boots two and a half or three feet long);—twenty chapters on the public buildings (I am going to hunt them up); eleven, on the palace of the emperor (no outside barbarian like me is ever permitted to enter that *sanctum* there); one chapter on a large monastery, containing one thousand one hundred Lama priests; four chapters on the Imperial city; twelve on the Tartar city. The Confucian temple has two chapters. Then, there are three more on the ten stone drums, three thousand years old. As the "Ji-hia-kieu-wen-kau" is all in Chinese, reading backward and upside down, I fear I shall not profit much by it in my ardent pursuit for knowledge under difficulties in Pekin. "Chenyuen-chi-lio" is another guide-book here, only eight volumes! It tells, *not* me, but the Chinaman, who tells me, that "I can visit the principal objects of interest in a month," but even then shall obtain only very imperfect ideas! I have only a week, two weeks at the most, for staring, shopping, curio-hunting. What, then, can I see in or about these twenty-five square miles, within the walls?

My first outstart has been, under the auspices of a clever young Englishman, who speaks Chinese sufficiently—a student interpreter of the British legation, preparing himself for future Chinese consulships—into the Chinese city. The legations are all in the Manchu or Tartar city. There are three cities within a city—the heart, the Palace, the Castle city, the *sanctum sanctorum* of Chinese autocracy, where the Emperor of Heaven and Earth sits and breathes, nearly all alone by himself, save with his wives and concubines—the Imperial city, this is called. Then the Tartar city, where the Manchu or Tartar population reside. Then the Chinese city, the city of the Tartar or Manchu-governed Chinese—for the Manchus or Tartars, only a few hundred years gone by, you may remember, if anybody ever cares to know, overflowed the great wall, and then ran over all China. We went a-shopping! Where did a woman ever go that she did not go a-shopping—that she did not want something, and to buy something? I found that out, years and years ago, on the Upper Lakes, even among the then Pottawotamies, and in Vancouver, and in Jerusalem, and in Gibraltar; everywhere, the women *must* go a-shopping. Pekin, I had fancied, had not a temptation on earth for shopping; but what a blunder I made the moment I was introduced into the shops of the Chinese city. This is one of the greatest fur markets in the world. Mongolia, Manchuria, and Corea, as well as Siberia, send down here their sables, their ermines, their leopard and tiger skins, the white fox, and gray fox, and all other species of furs. The climate is fiercely cold here in winter, and, fuel being scarce and costly, the mandarins and wealthy classes wrap themselves up in sables and ermines, while the poorer classes put on sheepskins. The market *is* tempting. Sables, the best skins, can be had from five to seven Mexican dollars each; a mandarin's sable robe from two hundred to five hundred Mexican dollars, often even less; ermine mantelets for about twenty-five and thirty dollars, with leopards, tigers, and foxes in proportion. But "cheating" is a Chinese as well as European art. The furriers color and dye their sables, and who can tell? Not I. Look out that you don't buy cats in lieu of ermines. I hinted I might buy a mandarin sable robe. And now, though the thermometer is about ninety, I have been enveloped, surrounded, tormented by furriers ever since, and buried up in my rooms table high with all sorts of furs from the steppes of Siberia, the forests of Manchuria, and Corea, and the deserts of Mongolia. Curios—that is, Pekin curiosities—have been rushed in upon my rooms, by Chinese, in platoons. "Precious stones," such as rubies, sapphires, amethysts, etc., were spread before me in abundance. (Don't buy, you are sure to be cheated.) Jade, however, seems to be the precious stone of China, not much valued with us, unless it be in little cups, but here costly, next to sapphires. The fact is, China, or rather this, the court city of China, is getting poor, and is selling out its old curios, its sables, etc., etc. I have half a mind to turn merchant, and to rush home heavily laden with furs for Gunther & Co., and precious stones for Tiffany & Co., or Ball & Black. I have no doubt I could pay expenses ten times over—but I am going, just now, not home, but to the great wall; and I have not yet given up Mongolia and the camel, Siberia, the Baikal, and Ural Mountains, and the route Europeward, overland, through Asia. Where does not a man want go, when he begins to go? What end of the *passion* for going, when one once begins? . . .

It is the Sabbath, and, amid Russian surroundings, with a beautiful Greek chapel near my rooms,

I ought to worship in that Greek church, but the priests have departed with the ambassador, and the chapel is closed. Formerly, a Russian Archimandrite held possession of this now beautiful spot, who, in addition to his duties of ecclesiastic, took care of the political interests of Russia; but in 1859, when the new treaties were made, an ambassador, not an ecclesiastic, was appointed, with full powers. A magnificent establishment was created for him, and the priest departed to another part of the city. French is our language of intercourse with the student interpreters, dragomans, and secretaries, left here; and, as the Chinese servants speak only Russian, not "pidgen English," even, we manage to have from them, by pantomime, all we need—with a few Chinese words, every day increasing, representing the necessaries of life.

There is an English church, on the English legation grounds, near by, where we were invited to go; and there are several Protestant missionaries in Pekin—but the Roman Catholics had such large establishments here, and their history for three centuries in China had been so great and brilliant, that I resolved to see them worship on the Sabbath day. The distance was nearly three miles, and the service began at eight A. M.; and a fit-out to go anywhere in roadless Pekin is so serious a matter—to rally the coolies for the chairs, the ponies, etc.—that, no wonder, the service was nearly over when we got there. The French priests, however, most graciously received us, and welcomed with warm hearts European faces from so distant a region as America, and the Sisters of Charity came out in full numbers and showed us all parts of their great establishment. The Chinese children, some two hundred and fifty in number, "all Christians now," were drawn up for us to see. Their nice embroideries, as well as their spinning and weaving, were shown us. These good Sisters seemed to be happy in their isolation and their Christian mission—happy in the seed they were sowing, and the harvest they were reaping, and earnest for the propagation of the faith throughout all China. The priests wore their hair as the Chinese do, and, but for their priestly robes, would be taken for Chinese. The Sisters preserve their home Catholic costumes. The cathedral itself is a wonderful building for such a distance from civilization. The organ in it cost some forty thousand dollars here. Many Chinese worshippers were about, and the spacious grounds seemed to be teeming with Chinese people, some of whom were Sisters of Charity, too.

There is a great conflict now going on in this country, not only between the Roman Catholic missionaries and the mandarins, but between money and the missionaries, Protestant as well as Catholic. The almighty dollar feels itself damaged by the everlasting pressure which the missionaries are making upon the Chinese government, and constantly dooms them to some bad place. Commerce and religion *do* travel together, but they are often very troublesome companions. The missionary, especially the Catholic, asks for a status here, the exterritoriality, it may be, of the Consulates, or a sort of *imperium in imperio*, which the mandarins refuse to yield. The mandarins declare, now, there is scarcely a Chinese rascal that does not turn Christian in order to have missionary protection for his rascality. The money-men live in constant apprehension that these charges, and counter charges, and prejudices will lead to another war. A *quasi* foreign party, and a thoroughly anti-foreign party, exist in China. All think foreigners are over-exacting, overbearing, and insolent, in which respect the Chinese are not far from right; but the peace party in China want no more war with foreigners. The money-men are for bearing, and forbearing, with Chinese restrictions upon intercourse, and trade, and with Chinese prejudices, and ignorance, as long as they can make money, while the kingdom of Christianity is not of *this* world, but is aggressive, and full of fight with Buddhism, Lamaism, Tauism, and all the religious *isms* here.

After the massacre of French missionaries at Tientsin, Europeans were naturally led to inquire what has produced this feeling against Christianity? And this brought about the discovery of a book written by a Chinaman in high authority, and circulated by mandarins and others secretly.

Extract therefrom:

"This religion (meaning Protestant and Catholic both) has its headquarters in Italy. It has a succession of Kings of the

Church (popes), who assume, in behalf of Heaven, to communicate instruction. When a king of any of the Western nations succeeds to the throne, he receives his authority to rule from the pope. In all important matters the kings receive commands from the pope."

Then follow accounts of the conduct of priests, which are worse than any thing described by Maria Monk, or ever imagined in the English language.

"In case of funerals (of Chinamen), this religion's teachers eject all relatives and friends from the house, and the corpse is put into the coffin with closed doors, both eyes are secretly taken out, and the orifice sealed up with a plaster."

The reason for extracting the eyes is this:

"From one hundred pounds of Chinese lead can be extracted eight pounds of silver, and the remaining ninety-two pounds of lead can be sold at the original cost. But the only way to obtain this silver is by compounding the lead with the eyes of Chinamen. The eyes of foreigners are of no use for this purpose."

The following is probably the reason why the Chinamen beat their gongs so furiously in their fights with the English and Americans:

"Foreigners have the art of cutting out paper men and horses, and, by burning charms and repeating incantations, transforming them into real men and horses. These they use to terrify their enemies. They may, however, be dissolved by beating a gong, or by spouting water over them..... In creating a man, to be the progenitor of the human race, God ought to have created him completely virtuous and absolutely perfect, and even then there would have been danger that he would not be able to transmit his virtues to his descendants. Why should He create such a proud and wicked man as Adam, and allow him to bring suffering upon his descendants in all generations?"

These extracts give but the faintest idea of the abuses and misrepresentations of Christianity. Further extracts would be so indecent, or infidelistic, as not to bear publication. The object of the work was avowed to be "the expulsion of the race human," that is, the European species from all parts of China.

## LETTER XXI.

### *FROM PEKIN.*

Paradise in-doors, Tartarus out.—Pekin Holes, Mud, Dust, Dirt.—No Noses in Pekin.—Sights and Smells.—Wealthy Chinese.—Sumptuary Laws in China.—Sedan-chairs.—Marriages and Funerals.—Women of no Account.—Polygamy.—Women's Fashions in Pekin.—Dr. Williams, the Secretary, Bibliophilist, and Encyclopædist. — The Chinese retrograding. — Confucianism losing its Influence.—Christianity.—Roman Catholics, when starting here, teaching the Material as well as the Spiritual.—Conflict of Christ and Confucius.—The Chinese Classics.

PEKIN, *August* 23, 1871.

IN the Russian legation here, inside, there is every luxury or comfort the heart could desire. Some ten or twelve acres of inclosure, walls, gardens, fruits, flowers, birds, books, horses in abundance to ride on, chairs to ride in, etc.; but *outside*, in the streets and highways, what sloughs, pits, sinks, holes, stinks, mud, dirt, dust! To go out is like going out of paradise into Tartarus. The pope, by-the-way, nicknamed all these Easterners, when they first visited Rome, as from Tartarus; hence, the word Tartar, unknown here but in foreign mouths. Nevertheless, one must go out. There are no roads for carriages; hence, no carriages of any kind, except that villanous, springless, wooden-axled cart, mule-hauled. The Mongolian pony, a furious, fiery beast, that turns down his ears and turns up his heels, when you go to mount him, is your pleasant companion. You must go with the pony through the streets of Pekin, or not go at all, unless you "foot it," and the distances in the hot sun now are too great for that. When I came here, the other day, the city was all mud, mud—mud, two feet deep, or more— and hopeless sloughs in that mud, if you were not taught the Pekin arts of mud navigation. Now there are many dry places, for an August sun has been pouring down some days, and the dust is from one to six inches deep in some places, while in others the mud is about as bad as ever, and the rivers of undrained water render whole streets impossible to cross. For example, I rode a mile to-day under the great walls of the Imperial Palace on a raised mud sidewalk, dusty now, and so narrow, a Chinaman could hardly pass me on horseback, while six or eight feet below was a mud river, a monstrous ditch twenty feet wide, of mud and water, no mule or pony cared to sound or to explore. This mingled dust and mud is a strange sight in a city; but in our own capital of Washington, during the civil war, the streets often were not unlike those of Pekin; and even now, where the street-builders are working, in the upheaved Washington, or, on the New York new avenues, say, things are very Pekin-ese.

How human beings live by the hundred thousands in such a city as this, is only to be accounted for by an utter insensibility to sights and smells; but they don't see, and they don't smell. Eyes and noses in China are, indeed, often as great curses as everywhere else, big blessings. I should like to dispense with a nose till I get back to America, or into Europe, if I could then buy it back again! No sewers, no closets, no drains! No way of letting out of a big city the filth in it! Streets uncleaned for two centuries, save by the hogs and vultures! The poor are unclad and unwashed, with skins the water seems never to have penetrated, and eyes that are sore—but why pain you to describe? Imagine the worst of every thing, in that way, and that worst is all here. Nevertheless, people *do* live here, and some live magnificently. There are some wealthy Chinese. There are many wealthy mandarins. The interiors of some of their hopeless-exterior-looking dwellings abound in a certain species of luxuries, and in a very few comforts. What Pekin is, therefore, one cannot see in the streets; and, as a foreigner can only with great difficulty get into a Chinese house, no stranger is likely to see more than these streets. There are sumptuary laws in Pekin that forbid luxurious indulgence. No mandarin ever can ride in a sedan-chair, no matter how many buttons he has won—what their color is, or what fans he carries, but by special permission of the emperor. The sedan-chair is the emperor's prerogative. Foreigners attached to legations use it as representatives of home majesty, and the "insolence" is tolerated from necessity; but no Chinaman ventures upon any thing beyond a cart, save on two great days of life, or death—the first, a marriage procession, and the second, a funeral. Luxuries are allowed then. The woman, then, the only day of her life, rides in a sort of sedan. Hence, now I understand the commotion made on the night of my entering the city with an open sedan and a lady in it. These sumptuary laws I speak of, pervade, I am told, all Pekin life, and are here especially kept up to keep the people as far as possible removed from the luxuries of the emperor. They do not exist elsewhere in China, only in this court city, where the emperor is. The mandarin has his especial sable robe, or ermine adornments, in winter. As for the women, they seem to be of no account here, save as mothers of children. The Chinaman takes as many wives as he can support—the emperor has them by the hundred—but the first wife is the real wife, the only mistress of the establishment, and the others are only her handmaids about the establishment, and they all obey her. The Abraham, Isaac, and Jacob mode of life is the life in China yet. They have not advanced, in this respect, a step beyond the patriarchs. What a field this would be for Mrs. Cady Stanton and the other bright, strong-minded ladies who, in America, are reforming the world — for woman is not of the least account here, save to be pretty and well painted with white powder and vermilion, in hair long, skewered, and well glued, so that a gale of wind cannot disturb it—the whole standing upon two little props, looking like birds' claws done up in sandals, and here called "feet." Alas, women's fashions are equally foolish everywhere! I bet in Japan, once, the woman's hair was her own, and was beaten in the bet. I would not bet on any thing about woman in China now, from her head to her foot-claws—from her long nails to the color of her face. Copper, I should have called her color; but I see so many powdered and vermilion faces, that I am not certain, now, the woman race is not white, with red cheeks, or cheeks a little reddened. Above the brows is often painted red, with the eyelids, too.

The British and French legations have quarters almost as luxurious as the Russian—the British, more ground. The Russian ground was a concession in olden times, the fee being in the Russian government; the British hire a grand Chinese palace, with right of lease-renewal, at about fifteen hundred dollars annual rent; the French say, the repairs they have made and make upon their palace pay the rent. The American legation is in the house and on the grounds of Dr. Williams, the secretary of legation and interpreter here, who bought and built all for himself. But for him, the American minister would have no place fit for a dog to live in. The houses and grounds are handsome now, and quite spacious. This Dr. S. Wells Williams, by-the-way, who came in from his summer quarters, "the hills," some sixteen miles off, to see me, spent the day with me, and is one of the most remarkable men I ever met with. He is the American indispensability, and the American institution in China. He has lived here some thirty odd years, speaks Chinese fluently, and probably knows more of China than most of the Chinese. He is a regular Bibliophilist, a Thesaurus, an Encyclopædia, and seems to know every thing. Just now he is making a Chinese-English dictionary,.on which he has been at work some years, and which he hopes to finish in a year. No topic turned up in our long conversation, whether of theology, cosmography, philology, or cosmogony, that he did not seem to know all about, and without the least ostentation of knowledge. And then he was as great on furs, sables, and fur-bearing animals, and where they come from, and on precious stones, as on the *ologies.* He went with Commodore Perry, as translator, to open Japan, and he speaks Japanese. What a pity such "books" have to die, and one cannot always have such living books with them, instead of being compelled to turn over leaves, and weary one's eyes with letters! Dr. Williams was a printer by trade, came to Macao from Utica, New York, as a printer, and for some years published and edited the *Chinese Repository* in Canton. Dr. Hepburne, of Yokohama, Japan, is another like man—an American indispensability there—who links and connects us with all we know of Japan. He, too, is making a dictionary—a Japanese-English dictionary. Of course, men thus long living with the native races here, become sympathetic with them, excuse them, palliate their blunders, errors, faults, even their crimes. Dr. Williams relies upon the Bible, and only upon the Bible, to reform China. The race has made all the progress possible, he adds, without Christianity, and is now retrograding because some of the principles of the Bible, which Confucius preached as well as Christ, are fading away, or being disobeyed. He thinks Christianity is making as rapid a progress here as could be expected, when first brought into conflict with the Buddhism and Confucianism of a thousand ages, and that it is now laying the foundation, by-and-by rapidly to go ahead. I do not see it, though he does. It seems to me, and such is the opinion of most foreigners here, outside of the missionary establishments, that if the missionaries would teach more science, the arts, etc., the quicker they would reach the Chinese soul, and convert it to Christianity. The Bible, and only the Bible, however, is what the missionary clings to, though some of these missionaries are, in some respects, learned men. The Roman Catholics, when first here, started as teachers of things material as well as spiritual, and they accommodated the spiritual to the material. Matthew Ricci, an Italian Jesuit, who came to China about the year 1600, put off the priesthood garb, and put on that of the Confucian literati. He studied their sacred classic books, and became master of Confucius and Mencius. Schaal, a German Jesuit, made himself an astronomer in Pekin. Verbiest, another German Jesuit, made logarithms, and cast guns for the Chinese. But, in time, the Catholics fought with the Chinese worship of ancestors, the system of polygamy, etc., and then the conflict of Christ and Confucius became so sharp that both the Jesuits and Dominicans were expelled, even after converting no small portion of China to Christianity.

I have been reading, now, for some weeks, translations of Confucius and Mencius, and of all other translated classics I could get hold of—these classics, with the commentaries upon them, are legion, filling great libraries; and I am in a great state of mental confusion over them. Only such scholars as Dr. Williams and the British minister, Mr. Wade, with whom I have made many talks, seem to comprehend the mysteries in them—but I am convinced they would be very profitable studies to us Americans, so far as they teach home-government, family-government, self-government, obedience to parents, sacrifice of self to parents, etc. *Morals* are the foundation of *politics* with the great Chinese philosopher. "How can a *mean* man serve his prince? (asks Confucius). When out of office, his sole object is to *attain* it, and when he has attained it, his only anxiety is to *keep* it. In his unprincipled dread of losing his place, he will readily go all lengths." How much suggestion in that for the American mind, just now?

But how I am wandering, and scribbling, and philosophizing, and on what dry topics! Enough for to-day.

# LETTER XXII.

### *THE TEMPLES IN PEKIN.*

The Temples in China.—Confucius and the Lama.—The Lessons of Confucius.—His Influence in the Government of the Chinese.—The Sages of China.—Tablets to the Disciples of Confucius.—The Competitive Students.—The Despotism and Democracy of China.—The Diagrams.—The Yang and the Yin.—Intelligence of the Chinese.—The Lama Buddhist Temple.—Mongolian Priests.—Contrast of the Lama and Confucius Temples.—A Chinese Mandarin's House.—Yang was his Name.—Sensation in the Streets.—The Interior of the Mandarin's House.—The Wife and Handmaids.—Description of the Wife's Dress.—Refreshments.—Walks on the Roof of the House.

PEKIN, *August* 24, 1871.

TO-DAY I have made two grand visits—one, to the living temple of the great Confucius; another, to the grand temples of the Buddhist Lamas, who here represent the Grand Lama of Thibet and the Lamas of Mongolia. I approach the temple of Confucius as I once approached Jerusalem, or the Areopagus, or the Pantheon, or Westminster Abbey, or the Sorbonne. It is the temple of knowledge in China, the light, the only light, where no Bible is read. Confucius was born about 550 B. C., and from the day of his death, seventy-three years after, his books have ruled the kings, the mandarins, the people of China —now about one-third of the human race. Christianity and Confucianism are yet dividing the empire of the world. Over two thousand years, Confucianism has kept together, under stable government, now the oldest nation on earth, and one which has survived all the empires and wrecks of the European world. Hence, one must go up to the temple of Confucius, as one goes up to the Areopagus, if not to Mars Hill and Jerusalem. Confucius was wiser and greater than Aristotle, or Plato, or Cicero, or Seneca. His political and social lessons, and obedience to them, have saved China from the wreck and ruin of countless other nations in Asia, Europe, and Africa.

There is nothing very remarkable in this temple of Confucius to look at. The association is the only inspiration. The hall is lofty, the roof supported by large teak pillars from southwestern China. The front is a broad and handsome marble terrace, with balustrades, ascended on three sides by seventeen steps. The inscription on the tablet, in Chinese and Manchu, is:

"THE TABLET OF THE SOUL OF THE MOST HOLY ANCESTRAL TEACHER, CONFUCIUS."

Tablets of other four distinguished sages—Mencius, Tseng-tsi, Yen-hway and Tze-sze—are placed, two on each side; and six more, celebrated men of the school, occupy a lower position on the side. On the walls are handsome tablets in praise of Confucius. Each new emperor presents one in token of veneration for the sage. Some of these are:

"OF ALL MEN BORN, THE UNRIVALLED."

"EQUAL WITH HEAVEN AND EARTH."

"EXAMPLE AND TEACHER OF ALL AGES."

On each side of the court is a range of buildings where there are tablets to more than a hundred celebrated scholars. On the east side are seventy-eight virtuous men, and on the west fifty-four learned men. Then, there are rows of tablets, or monuments, with the names of the successful competitive scholars, who, at the triennial examinations in Pekin, win their honors on topics given to them, when shut up for three days, with only pencil and ink for companions, all books and all other companions excluded. These tablets look as if they ran back for three or four hundred years; but the names of those over a century old cannot be deciphered, as time has obliterated the engravings made of them in the marble. What better shows the vanity of human pursuit, of ambition, of the love of glory? It reminded me of the Consular tablets on the Capitoline Hill of Rome —but what vanity is it all!

Nevertheless, these competitive examinations and contests have the widest and greatest influence over the Chinese Empire. They open the doors of promotion to the very poor as well as to the rich, and they make every humble person feel—"I *can* be a mandarin;" "I *can* have the government of a province;" "I can see, kneel by, and advise the emperor!" They convert the absolute, hereditary, and otherwise uncontrollable, supposed-to-be heaven-given despotism into an educated democracy. Learning must govern—not blockheads and ignorance. A man must *know* something, in order to rule. The government, in short, is put into the hands of the intelligent classes—such intelligence as it is! But what an extraordinary species of intelligence! What strange studies! What curious themes! In our barbarous ages, our European metaphysical fathers disputed long and loudly, "whether angels could see in the dark," or, "whether you could pass from one point of space to another without going through the intermediate points;" but here, the studies are of the eight diagrams of Fo-hy, or of the *Yang* and *Yin*, the active and passive principle of the mundane egg, etc., etc. The knowledge is great; the scholarism is wonderful—but, *cui bono?* It runs no railroads, raises no telegraph poles, creates no great power, military or naval, cleans no streets, makes no sewers, diffuses no practical knowledge! Once more, the whole system proves that reading and writing are not knowledge, and books are not knowledge. Even the unreading and unwriting may, by mere observation and practice, know far more than those who thus read or write.

But the competition, the study, the ambition, *do* reflect a wonderful amount of intellect, and a certain species of intelligence, among all the common people of China. Almost all the people look bright, active, and earnest. Their self-discipline is astonishing. They work with patience and assiduity, and seemingly discharge all their duties with content. None learn faster, if any so fast, by mere imitation. Their capacity in that respect is amazing. Their existing manufactories show what they could do, if they had the machinery and the capital. As writers, our diplomats find their mandarins hard to cope with. As servants, they are unequalled the world over. The Chinese waiter is about the only one in the world who can guess, by instinct, as it were, what you want, so that, though you have not a word for intercourse, you can get along pretty well by the fingers and eyes alone.

But, near as I am to the temple of Confucius, where there is not a god, nor an idol, nor an altar, I must not forget the large Lama Buddhist temple—with its thirteen hundred or fifteen hundred Lama Mongolian priests. Some three hundred of them there receive instruction in metaphysics, or the doctrine of "the empty nature"—that is, the non-existence of matter, being, and things, such topics as the crazy French revolutionists discussed, earnestly, in the days of Voltaire. Others study other things—one hundred and fifty of them medicine—but Mongols, or Thibetans, unlike the Chinese, do not study overmuch. The Mongolian Lama priests we saw, in their yellow robes, as thick as bees in a hive, did not seem bright enough to study any thing. Indeed, they are not expected to do much, if any thing, but to keep their temples in order, and this they do badly. The idols are dirty; the walls are ragged; the floors are dusty. The Chinese Government supports all these priests, to keep the Mongolians, whose religion they represent, in order. They buy their priests to keep quiet, and so keep their people quiet. I should weary you by describing here all the halls, altars, cypress trees, hundreds of years old, and a seventy-five feet high wooden Buddha, with steps inside of him. Understand, then, it was a "mighty big" concern, take it altogether, greater in extent than the Capitol in Washington (but only one story or a story and a half high); bigger than the New York Central Park fountains, bridges, and lake. Beautiful carpets, made far away off in the interior, somewhere, were on the floor. There were pictures all the way from Thibet, with all sorts of odd representations everywhere, wearying one's eyes to look at them, and confusing the senses to comprehend.

The *contrast* of these neighboring temples—the one to the yet living principles of Confucius, and the other to the idol Buddha—was what most impressed me. In the Confucian temple were active, lively, hard-studying, ambitious Chinese; in this Mongol Lamasery of boyish priests, were half-dead men, walking on legs, but without any inspiration in them, living on bread, and fruits, and meats, as animals live, but living only to consume the fruits of the earth (*nati consumere fruges*).

But I am scribbling with dulness on priests and scholars. *Paulo majora canemus.* Let us sing on women, and houses, and homes, and visits, and style and fashions. Through the negotiations of some of the Chinese student interpreters in the British Legation, we were introduced to-day, with two ladies, into the very heart of a Chinese mandarin's house—Yang was his name—and we saw there what men seldom or never can see in Pekin. To give *éclat* to our outfit, we started from the Russian Legation with two sedan-chairs, a lady in each, and sixteen coolies in stylish livery to carry them, with three European cavaliers, two of them speaking Chinese and English, to escort them, and two outriders on horseback, in grandee livery, to lead off and follow after the escort. Pekin, of course, opened its eyes, as such a cavalcade went through its streets. Mule-men, market-men, cart-men, shopkeeper-men, all stopped to comment on the show. We were crowded through two city gates, from the Tartar into the Chinese city, where the dust was terrible, the pavement worse, and the crowd, if possible, worse still. We entered a very narrow and most unimposing street, that led to our mandarin's rather palatial establishment. The mandarin, to be sure, was not a student mandarin, who had studied his way up on "the essence" of things, and won his buttons by his books—for he was a rich banker, who had won his way up by dollars, or Chinese taels (sycee), and who bought his rank and title therewith. The mandarin met us at the entrance, escorted us through a narrow passage into a courtyard, where were dogs, and monkeys, and flowers in pots. Passing over the court-yard, we met, in a reception room, the wife, with her handmaids. There were Chinese chairs and tables in this room, and we were invited to sit down. The wife and her handmaids, of whom there were three or four, were elaborately painted, in powder and vermilion. The under lip, about an inch wide in the middle, was painted a bright crimson. The hair of the wife No. 1 was drawn up in a peculiar knot, projecting behind some six or eight inches, with gilt and jade hair-pins fastening a white lily on the right side. Her ear-rings were of jade, and pearl, and gold. Rings of the same kind were on her fingers. The feet did not seem to be over three inches long—so short, that she could scarcely stand or step, and in the end we found she could not go up-stairs. The under dress was of blue satin, close to her lower limbs, and elaborately embroidered. The upper dress was a lighter blue silk blouse. On her arms were heavy gold and precious stone bracelets. Wife No. 2 was a Manchu woman, with a different head-dress, and an inferior style generally. Wife No. 1 did all the honors. The others stood, while she sat. All were painted, even a daughter of fourteen or fifteen years of age. We were ushered, then, into the mandarin's study and bedroom, where tea was served us. Many European scientific things were around. The master of the house was fond of electricity, and kept a battery to light his pipe. He was a photographer, too, and took portraits of wife No. 1, in her grandest state dress. This so attracted our curiosity that we asked to see it, and out it came—costly, magnificent, emblazoned with gold, of crimson satin, elaborately embroidered, and with an over-mantle more showy still. The head-dress was a sort of crown, six or eight inches high, on a gold wire foundation, with turquoise, rubies, and the like ornaments interwoven. Numerous pearl pendants hung below the chin. The pearls were magnificent, and cost—how much, who can tell?

We were then escorted into another room, where refreshments were given us, served in European style, with Chinese cakes and liquors. The children were then exhibited to us—the children of different mothers, but they all seemed to live harmoniously together. The No. 2 and No. 3 wives did not sit down, as did wife No. 1, but seemed content and happy to look on. There were a melodeon, and many books. Other rooms were then shown us, and as we became weary of them, we were taken into other court-yards, grottoes, over little bridges, spanning little lakes, with flowers everywhere about us, and grapevines, and amid little trees. Then, we were taken on to the roof of the house, where were pretty walks and promenades, with cool, refreshing breezes, contrasting favorably with the heat of the rooms below. All these places were within one wall, and this wall overtopped every point of view from the street and the neighborhood. I was much gratified with this inner view of a Chinese establishment, the like of which is seldom or never given to man, when alone, to look upon. Wealth thus exists, we see, even amid the dirt and dust of the streets of Pekin, and Fashion is as omnipotent and droll here as in Paris or New York.

## LETTER XXIII.

### THE GOVERNMENT OF CHINA.

The Great Wall of China.—The Overland Route to St. Petersburg.—Turned back by a Mohammedan *Émeute.*—Now too late or too early in the Season.—Can telegraph from here to New York in twelve or sixteen Days.—The Government of China.—Confucius a sort of Ben Franklin or Thomas Jefferson.—No Hereditary Aristocracy.—Public Sentiment governs here as in Great Britain and the United States.—Railroads and Telegraphs resisted by Superstitions, to be overcome.—China making Great Preparations for War.—Casting Cannon, etc.—China retrograding.—Corruption the Cause.—Mandarin Titles bought and sold.—The Literati Mandarins now dishonest.—The Boy Emperor, fifteen Years of Age.—His Future not promising.—The Dowager hunting a Wife for him.—The Pekin *Gazette.*

PEKIN, *August* 25, 1871.

ONE of the dreams of my life has been to go to, and to stand upon, the great wall of China. There were certain seven wonders in the world to be seen in the geographies of my boyhood, and the great wall was one of them. I have "done" the Pyramids, the Colossus of Rhodes, and the other wonders, I believe; but the great wall is yet to be "done" before I am done travelling, or there would be no content. Hence, I am preparing a start for the wall. What grieves me most, though, is, that there, I shall be compelled to retrace my steps, at least for a thousand miles, back to Shanghai, before I can again get on a new track. I have long been resolving upon the Russian overland route, homeward, through the Desert of Gobi, on camels, to Kiakhta, the border town of trade between the caravans of China and Russia — thence to Irkutsk, the Baikal, the Ural Mountains, the Volga, and on, home, *via* Novgorod, Moscow, and St. Petersburg; but there is fighting going on somewhere, thereabout (in China), or a terrible fright, because of the Mohammedans and their hordes inroading just now, so that I am partially talked out of it, though more scared out of it by the approaching cold weather. The distance across the two continents, Asia and Europe, is some five thousand miles, or more—one thousand miles of it nearly in China, where every thing is in disorder; but in Russia there is a strong government, with horse-posts everywhere, so that I think I could manage to go in safety, if once there. There is a railroad, too, one thousand miles long, from St. Petersburg *via* Moscow, through Novgorod, on to Kasan, and probably further now, as the Russians are building a Pacific railroad like ours, which will probably be driven through Siberia and Manchuria in about ten years. The work is not so difficult as ours. Already they have a telegraph line across the continent, the whole length.

But, alas, I must give up the dream of going over all this, and of thus going through the heart of Siberia, and so, well comprehending Russia. It is both too late and too early in the season to start on such a journey. The cool winds already coming from the hills overlooking Pekin, and the cooler winds soon to come from the mountains of Mongolia, admonish me that if I were to start now, I should be fighting floating ice in Siberia on every river I should be crossing there, not strong enough to hold horses, and yet obstructive enough to forbid the passage of rivers in boats. A month later the journey could be made on solid ice, and in good sleighing, the most of the way, with the thermometer some thirty or forty degrees below zero, to be sure; but what is that to a man "raised" on the Androscoggin, or Kennebec, in Maine, or that fears the Shanghai thermometer at ninety far more than forty degrees below zero in Siberia? The start for this Siberian journey should be made from Pekin in May, I see—the summer route, with clear rivers; or in October—the winter route, with frozen rivers to cross. It is hard, rough, long, but nothing killing in it, on a fair start, under good Russian protection. Two or three Americans have been over it—some Englishmen—and the Russian couriers from St. Petersburg to Pekin go every month, or oftener, if necessary. St. Petersburg can be reached from here in twelve or sixteen days, by telegraph, from Kiakhta, the first Russian town. I could telegraph home, I think, from here in ten days now, and from Shanghai directly.

Before I leave Pekin I must try to convey to you my impressions, or rather *guesses*, of what this Government is; for, after all, such travellers as I am, run on haphazard—only *guessing*. No American out of China, however, has had higher or better sources of conversational information than I have had, and am having. The British and French, as well as the Russian legations, have been as kind as possible to me with their *attachés* and interpreters. Our American Dr. Williams, too, I think, is better informed than any other man in China, though he looks at all things with a Christian missionary eye, and through Puritan spectacles, a little spotted with Chinese pebbles. The Government, as I have hinted, seems to be a democratic despotism, and hence, perhaps, the secret of its old age and long preservation. Confucius was a sort of Thomas Jefferson or Ben Franklin. He laid down great practical democratic principles, and they have ruled emperors and mandarins hundreds and hundreds of years. Confucius created a public opinion and a system of precedents that no despotism could ever safely ignore. Then, the common people, through their instructed mandarins, guide, and overawe, if they do not always sway, the emperor. He is afraid of the people, and the mandarins are afraid of the people, too. There is as much a public opinion here to be respected, as in Great Britain or the United States. No hereditary aristocracy of any kind exists. No mandarin can transfer even his buttons, to say nothing of his post, to his children. When these mandarins are made governors of the provinces of China, their power is quite absolute; but the emperor is omnipotent, of course, over them. The provinces are like our States, with certain provincial rights that mandarins must respect when sent there. Hence, the Government is nowhere absolutely absolute—that is, with safety to itself. Intelligent mandarins would like to build railroads and telegraphs, it is thought, but they dare not, it is believed, as yet. No mandarin feels potent enough to advise the emperor to run a railroad over the graves and through the graveyards of Chinese revered and worshipped ancestors. The trouble in erecting telegraph poles is, that a superstitious Chinaman believes (and all are more or less superstitious) that these poles will interfere with the *Fung-Shuey*, "wind and water," a species of geomancy, or a belief in the good or ill luck attached to particular local situations, that the poles may have struck. Geomancy is an occult science here, and professors study it, and tell you the plan for a house, or a grave, where the *Fung-Shuey* will bless it. To such an extent is this superstition existing in Pekin, that when the Catholics built their cathedral higher than the imperial wall, the wall was raised higher than the cathedral, to ward off the Catholic *Fung-Shuey*. To ride over such superstitions, rough-shod, is what even an intelligent mandarin does not like to do. Hence, circumstances and events must control the erection of telegraphs, so indispensable for the unity of a great empire like this, and not force. An event has just now occurred which will hasten the erection of telegraphs. The grand Pekin Council of Scholars awarded two competitive prizes to two Cantonese scholars, the highest honors of the empire. The news was sent from Shanghai by sea telegraph to

Hong-Kong, and reached Canton, days before the news could go overland. The Cantonese were astounded, and discredited the intelligence until the long-looked-for Pekin official *Gazette* came overland and confirmed it. Then there was wonder and marvel over that intelligence, and all China, from north to south, is asking "if it will do to give foreigners the means of more rapid intercourse with the exterior of our empire than we ourselves have." Interest, and trade, and commerce, I think, will soon dispose of that *Fung-Shuey*, and give China the telegraph. "The graves of our ancestors," scattered over every little field in China, will be more difficult and dangerous to be dealt with than this *Fung-Shuey;* but "the graves of our ancestors" will have to go at last. All these opinions, nay, superstitions, in a *freeish* sort of country like this, have, however, to be respected, even by emperors and mandarins. We have opened their great river, one of the greatest rivers in the world; and, by steam, we Americans do nearly all the coasting trade there with Shanghai. Mandarins now prefer our boats to their junks to travel in. Europe and America have taught Chinamen how to cast cannon and to make rifles. Their factories, under our auspices, are almost equal to ours. Their rifle is as good as our Springfield rifle. Their ships of war are now putting on formidable fronts. If England again comes into conflict with China, it will not be so easy a conquest as in her two last Chinese wars.

Why, then, you ask, perhaps, is such a people retrograding?—for here, in Pekin, amid the ruin of roads, and bridges, and palaces, and the wreck of almost every thing, this retrogradation is too visible. China is not what it was three hundred years ago, with as much civilization, perhaps, but far less material progress. The answer to the question propounded here is a most important one to us Americans—for *corruption* is the sole cause of Chinese retrogradation, and is, if not corrected, certain to lead to the downfall of the empire, and its subjugation to Europeans or Americans. I have pointed out, in another letter, how rich men buy mandarin honors. *That* does not give a mere rich man office, but it does give him rank, station, and social position, and the common people are angry that even thus their scholar competitive system should be interfered with. As yet, it is believed, though often suspected to the contrary, that the examination of the scholars for the mandarin places is honest; and hence, corruption may not have penetrated these schools. But now, even these scholar mandarins have ceased to be honest. They go to their provinces, and they "squeeze" the rich and the poor, and extort all they dare. They buy silence in the councils of Pekin with the money they extort from the people, and thus corruption in the provinces works corruption in the capital, till all, more or less, have become corrupt, and there is no confidence or honesty anywhere. Confucius terribly rebukes all this in his legacies; but Confucius is losing his hold on the great mandarins of the empire. The empire, just now, is in the hands of a regency, with the empress-dowager and Prince Kung at the head—with a boy of only fifteen training to be emperor. Upon that boy, whether he watches or not the corruption of the empire—whether he puts it down, or permits it to run—hangs not only the empire itself, but probably his own destiny, as well as his dynasty. The boy is reported from the palace as not very promising for the future. And how can a boy be trained for empire in such an exclusion, seeing nobody but the few, hearing only what they choose to tell him, and with women and eunuchs, in the main, surrounding him? The wild, fierce Manchu blood that conquered the empire is running to water within the walls of the palace, and amid the luxuries of the palace; and, unless the boy turns out to be a wonder, the dynasty will be tumbled over for a stronger one, as has happened several times before in the history of China.

Great efforts are being made to find a wife No. 1 for the boy emperor—and he can have as many as he pleases, after No. 1. The pretty girls, from hundreds and hundreds of miles, have been sent up to the capital as patterns for an empress; but his mother, the empress-dowager, has not yet found out a wife for him. (She picked out one, who was taken to the capital to be educated a year for an empress, but during that year she died.) Boys and girls in China have nothing to do with the selection of their own wives. They seldom see, the husband his wife, or the wife her husband, till the day of marriage. The emperor, even, has got to take what they give him; but if No. 1 does not suit or satisfy, No. 2, 3, 4, 5, 6, and so on, can be handmaids. Some of the richest provinces have just been levied upon, however, to furnish silks, satins, and embroideries for some grand nuptial ceremony soon to take place in Pekin. The richest silk province respectfully protests, I see by the Pekin *Gazette*, against the silk levy made upon that province. The mandarin writes the requisition cannot be complied with, without trouble there; and, what is stranger, the Pekin official *Gazette* publishes in full the respectful remonstrance. This Pekin *Gazette*, by-the-way, is the only real Chinese newspaper in the empire. It is published daily here, and the manuscript is furnished twenty-four hours in advance to the foreign ministers, if they desire it. It is an official record only, with no dissertations in it, no "editorials," only the decrees of the Government, and the reports and petitions of mandarins from the provinces.

But what a long, dull yarn! I am weary, and off to the great wall in the morning.

# LETTER XXIV.

### FROM THE GREAT WALL OF CHINA.

On Top of the Great Wall of China.—Droves of Sheep, Hogs, Ponies, Donkeys.—Mongolians and Manchus.—Speech-making on Top of the Great Wall.—Speech of J. B. to the Great Wall.—Tartars, a Species of Yankees, leaping over all Walls.—Outfit for the Trip from Pekin to the Great Wall.—Brick Tea.—Sheep's-tail Soup.—Eggs in Abundance.—Mule Litters.—Description of the Craft.—The Muleteers.—Mingling Mire, Mud, and Dust.—Sounding for the Bottom of the Bogs.—Dodging into Farms and Gardens.—Roads in China are Ditches.—The Pass of Nan-Kow.—First Night's Experience in a Mongolian Inn.—A Brick Oven to sleep on.—Journey to the Wall over a Rough and Terrible Road.—A Series of Walls.—A Lunch amid Ruins of the Wall.—The Comfort of a Cup of Cold Water.

ON TOP OF THE GREAT WALL OF CHINA,
*August* 27, 1871.

*Veni, vidi, vici.* I have clambered up on to the tip-top of the Great Wall of China! I have suffered some, especially in bones and the flesh—but what of that, now I am here! *Vidi.* I have seen lots of sheep, with thick, fat tails, that make (report says), the best of soup (perhaps, I have eaten some of it—happy ignorance—don't know), and have seen lots of lean, lank, long-eared, black hogs, all the way from Mongolia—intelligent black hogs, for they understand two languages (more than I do), the Mongolian and Chinese, and they obey their drivers, unlike other hogs; and I have also seen lots of Mongolians —fellows with fur caps on, this hot summer weather, and sheep-skin coats, working their way, with their ponies, and the truck on them, to the great imperial city. Well, I have got now on to the jumping-off place, and intend to stop, and *not* jump off. The Mongolian Buddhists tell my man, Cheng, " These foreign devils can't go much further, just now, unless they turn Mohammedans, for the Mohammedans are killing all Buddhists" (out there in Tartary). As I am neither for Buddha, nor for Mohammed (only a hard-shell Baptist), both sides might try to kill me unless I enlisted under one banner or the other ; and hence I return homeward-bound, now, and as fast as I can go in the round-about European way, by the Indian Sea.

When, last November, ex-Secretary Seward and his party, with Admiral Rodgers and his party, were here, the ex-Secretary made a great speech to the Admiral, which has been duly recorded in the Shanghai (English) *Gazette*, if not in the Pekin (official Chinese) *Gazette*. It must have been a funny speech, *funnigraphically* reported, thus made up here to the crows, and the sparrows, and the black hogs, and donkeys, and mules, and some half-dozen Americans. Nevertheless, standing upon this great precedent, I propose to make a speech, not to Admiral Rodgers, for he is now off in Japan, but to the Great Wall itself. And here it is :

"Mr. Great Wall of China :

" I've come some fifteen thousand miles, from the Antipodes, mainly to see you, but I don't think you are worth all that trouble. You are a big thing, that is certain, a mighty big thing ; but I could have bought a photograph of you for a

Mexican dollar, and it has cost me many, to get up here. I won't come again, till, in the metempsychosis, I become younger and greener. I don't know how old you are, and can't find out—only that you are not half as old as Cheops' Pyramids, in Egypt. You were only begun, it seems, B. C. 213, and you were not done with till A. D. 1368, if then. You are very long, to be sure—some say two thousand miles. Fifty thousand workmen were at one time, so it is stated, at work, only repairing and extending you. But what's all that to the great Pacific Railroad, Mr. Wall, as long as you are, and going *through* mountains, not up and over them, as you do! Nevertheless, I don't mean to say you are not a very respectable, nay, a very wonderful Wall.

"But, Mr. Wall, you were built, you know, to keep off the Yankee Tartars from running over you into the flowery land of China. Have you kept them off? No, never! The Mongolian, Manchu and Siberian Tartars are very like all Tartars, everywhere, from New England to Old England. Put a lot of people down in a country only half made when the world was made, such as Old England or New England is, where nothing grows except with a great deal of trouble, and then very sparingly—where you need furs and fires to keep warm, and strong meats and strong drinks to keep alive—and do you think such an uneasy people there will not leap over walls, in order to get down into the golden grain, the silver rice, the flowery land of milk and honey? The Tartar peeped over these mountains, and, tired of sheep's tails, and sheep-skins, and bear meat, and tiger and leopard soup, and beef and butter, he determined to have something better; and hence he jumped, by thousands and thousands, over your wall, just as we home Yankees jumped over the Alleghanies, and the Potomac, and the Rocky Mountains, into sunnier countries and better lands. Man, by nature, is an indolent animal, and does not like to hoe rocks, or fight Jack Frost, ten months in the year. He is not content with crab-apples, but wants persimmons, grapes, figs, oranges, bananas, and *will* have them. Man was born with the devil in him, north, and the devil is only melted out of him under the hot suns of the south. Hence, Mr. Wall, the great Khans of Tartary, from Genghis Khan and Kulla Khan, on, and down, never much minded the great piles of granite and brick you have put up here. They scaled the mountain tops, and jumped over, or banged through the granite and brick in the valleys. There is no stopping Yankees anywhere—Yankee Tartars in America, or John Bull Tartars in England, when you show them a better country to live in, than they were born in. Thus, Genghis Khan (A. D. 1212), and Timour the Tartar —Yankees, undoubtedly—starting up here, somewhere, among these rocks and caverns, tired of black hogs, and sheep's tails, and a nomad life, with no cabbages to eat, nor onions, determined to overrun the world, and nearly did it. They ran over the Russias, ran down the Turks and Huns, and scared the Germans half out of their wits, while they scrambled over all China. The Chinese, however, did what most Southerners do with Northerners—captivated (not captured) them, sweetened them, took the barbaric out of them and put the gentle in; softened, humanized, civilized them, till the Tartars themselves became Chinese. Walls, then, Mr. Wall, have not half the influence over Yankees as a softer civilization. Granite and bricks and the bow and arrow are nothing in comparison with flowers, fruits, fields, figs, fans, etc., etc. The pretty fans of China fanned the devil nearly all out of all the fiery Tartars, and they quitted their horses, and took to the hoe and the shovel. If Mazeppa ever rode down this way, through the mountain passes, he is digging now, not horse-vaulting, and singing Chinese ditties and chants, not yelling and bellowing after hordes, and horses, and asses, and bullocks and calves. Mazeppa is no longer a nomad, but a farmer, now, in China.

"Mr. Wall and Mr. Mountain Pass—if we had you now in Yankee land, we should run a railroad right through you— (make bridges of *you*, Mr. Wall)—and drive off these camels, who are bringing on their backs coal from your miserably-worked mines, Mr. Mountain; and all these asses, donkeys, mules, and horses, that, by the thousands, are now bringing things, in panniers, from, and to Mongolia, and the region beyond. What a shame to keep these thousands of men thus employed, when one locomotive on an iron rail would do all their work? If you, Mr. Wall, had fought the present Manchu Tartars now ruling China with a locomotive and one big gun on it, you, Chinamen would not be obliged to be wearing pig-tails, and a shaven head, as you are—a fashion these Manchus imposed upon you when they broke through this wall. True, you have imposed upon them all your other fashions, except the little squeezed feet—(the Manchu women have ever refused to have their feet thus squeezed up)—but these bare heads, these pig-tails, the emblems of your subjection to the Northern Yankees, are very, very bad.

"Now, Mr. Wall, you have an expression of my mind. I shall take home a piece of "a brick" in memory of you—a whole brick I would take, if my carpet-bag were big enough for such big bricks as you are made of; and you must consider this a particular compliment, for if I should take home a brick of all the wonders I am seeing, I should have to take home a caravan of camels, too, to carry the load. Good-by!"

But how did you get from Pekin to the Great Wall of China? Listen, and I will tell you. Our "fit-out" was cold mutton, and beef, and chicken, and sugar, and tea, and liquors as needful; beds, sheets, blankets, mosquito nets, pillows, plates, cups, saucers, with knives, forks, spoons, etc., etc., for there is little to be had on the route that an American would like to live on. Brick tea you can have—the refuse tea-dust of China, baked into a brick—sheep's tails and mutton grease, made, some say, into candles, and then mixed in a soup of the tails, with the tea; but to such as are not thus brought up, the fare might be hard. Eggs, there are plenty of, *en route*, and hens and chickens; and where they are, even an American need not starve. Our carriages were what in Turkey they call Taktaravans—here, a mule litter, a large palanquin suspended on the backs of two mules, lengthwise. Strong leather bands connect the points of the shafts resting on the saddles of the mules. An iron pin, fixed in the top of the saddle, passes through a hole in the leather, and so keeps it in its place. The shafts are, of course, long, to reach from one mule to another, and to leave the animals plenty of room to walk. The motion is not at all disagreeable—nay, luxurious, when compared with all the other means of locomotion I have seen in China. The saddle looks as if it weighed a half cord of wood, and the litter a full cord. It was so heavy that it took four men to lift it. I stretched out and slept in it pretty well, when out late at night; and it was not difficult to read novels in it, when there was nothing to see, or nothing else to do.

The muleteers, two men to each litter—one for the front mule and one for the rear mule—started from Pekin early in the morning, and, at the rate of two miles per hour, contrived to get out of the city walls in two hours. In turning a sharp street corner, one litter turned over—for the shafts are so long that sharp corners cannot be turned with them; but no particular damage was done, even to the crockery ware, and none to us, save the fright. We blocked up a Pekin narrow street, and strung along a mile of carts, front and rear, before we were extricated—with an anxious crowd looking on and marvelling where such strange "critters" were going in such vehicles. The roads, just now, were in a mixed condition of mud, mire, and dust. Heavy rains had saturated the earth, and a hot August sun was drying them up, and turning them into dust. Whenever our muleteers saw a bog of mire ahead, in fear and trembling they sounded for bottom with the handles of their whips—(for, four hundred pounds on a mule's back, eight hundred pounds on two mules' backs, are likely to sink them, if once they get into a Serbonian bog). If the passage was found safe, *through* we floundered; if not, we ascended the banks, and made long circuits through farms, and gardens, and crops. Occasionally we were lost in the tall millet, or Indian corn, or sorghum, and the dogs barked at us, and the children rushed out to see what had come. Occasionally, too, a farmer would turn out, and "swear" we should not tread down his crops with mules, and threaten a fight; but when our man-of-all-work, Cheng, pointed to our European faces, and the liveried coolie who accompanied us, and who gave his rank and dignity by his livery, we were permitted to trample down millet, or beans, or peas, or corn, or any thing. Nevertheless, we had a hard time in these by-ways. The impassable bogs were numerous, and we threaded passages where mule litters never went before. The roads in China, I may as well tell you here, have become excavations, tunnels, ditches from long, long use, and the practice of gathering up the loose dirt in them to manure the fields; and into these ditches, whenever there is rain, the water pours and gathers, and soon makes stagnant pools and bogs. These bogs in the road were our terror, and hence these long farm detours.

Our "breakfast" was taken at four P. M., at Sha-ho, a village sixty li, or twenty miles, from Pekin—a distance, with the detours, we had been since seven A. M. travelling over. Nankow, the mouth of the mountain pass, some fifteen miles more distant, was to be our sleeping place, and we made for it, after breakfast, with all possible mule speed, then two or two and a half miles per hour. A blessed moon lighted up our stony, rough way, or we never should have got there that night. After passing by and around, I can scarcely say over, two splendid stone bridges, now pretty well in ruins, I did not see much after leaving Sha-ho. In spite of the horrible road, and the perils of mule litter travelling at night, I was rocked to sleep, and I slept soundly till we reached Nankow, eleven o'clock at night. *There*, there was a terrible row. The whole caravansera, pretty well filled with travellers, donkies, asses, was dead in sleep, and it was only after a loud, long knocking that we could wake up the master of the domicile, and make him understand we wanted water, hot and cold, and a place to lay our heads in, and to feed the mules in, that night.

Let me now introduce you to a Nankow hostelry, the kind existing all the way now into Russia, and far away, *in* there, certainly through Siberia. The donkeys and asses have troughs to eat in, under about as good a cover as you have, and close by your sleeping chamber; and you have an oven to sleep on, and over the oven, a mat, to keep the bricks from burning your skin, if the oven by chance gets too hot. Thank the good month of August, there needed no fires in our oven, and we were not roasted, nor baked, as travellers sometimes are in December or January. You, if you are old enough, remember the old Russian (brick) oven stoves in New England, before the days of iron. These brick stoves, especially in the New-England school-houses, were lit up, say at four A. M., for the school, beginning at nine A. M., by which time the school-house had become so hot, from the quantity of wood consumed within the stove, that only salamanders could healthily live in the schoolhouse building. The Yankees got that stove idea from these Mongols and Tartars up here. The difference is, that the Mongolians turn them to double use, for beds, and blankets, or comforters, while we only use them to warm rooms. On top of the mat, which was on top of the dirty bricks, that had not had a sweeping since they were laid, and full of all sorts of harmless creatures, that only nipped a little, but did not bite, we laid our beds. I never slept better. The donkeys brayed; the mules uttered their most plaintive lays for more fodder; the muleteers, roused up at midnight, and wondering what new fellows had come, sputtered monosyllabic yells that would have scared a traveller out of his wits if he had not been hearing like yelling from his own muleteers all day long. Nevertheless, after drinking my tea, after eating my omelette (I never ask now how omelettes are made, without butter or milk, and there are none here), and nibbling my bread, I never slept better. The New-York Fifth Avenue has better, that is, softer beds, to be sure, and a better table; but our railroad cars and steamboats do not prepare a traveller to enjoy them, as the litter did me, in this Yourt, with the horses, the mules, the donkeys, the Mongolian and Chinese muleteers. In a cold night, I can well fancy, there may be a comfort on the hot bricks of the oven you are sleeping over; but my "windows" were open, and the pure air of heaven was coming in from the mountains, and not even a blanket was necessary. We all waked at 5 A. M., men and donkeys, and we all breakfasted, I may say, together. Early hours, the Chinese keep. They are no laggards in the morning. Even the emperor gives audience to his mandarins at 5 A. M., who get their tea before they start for the palace, and have their breakfast on their return at 8 A. M. Our breakfast over, finished before 6 A. M., we started off, through the mountain-passes, for the wall, fifteen miles off—the ladies in sedan-chairs, with four coolies to each chair, and I, on the back of an interesting mule, that would do what he pleased, and, I soon found, knew so much more than I did, about mountain travelling, that I suffered the better informed beast to do as he pleased.

What I saw—what cuffs, kicks, shakes, thumps, over, amid, and on, the loose rocks, and huge bowlders, and mountain-torrents of this terrible road—no matter! Bells were tinkling on all our mules, and on all the leading animals we met, the one to warn the other, so as not to be caught in an impassable pass. The muleteers kept up a wild chatter with their beasts, and the beasts seemed to understand them well. We met great flocks of black-headed sheep, with heavy, short, fat tails, and otherwise very white fleeces. We met hogs by the thousands. Droves of horses and donkeys, too, were *en route* for the Pekin market. Thousands and tens of thousands of people are daily passing over this great highway from China to Mongolia and Russia, and over such a road, not as good as that old horse-path up and down the White (New Hampshire) Mountains, on either side. Not five miles out of Nankow I began to see one of the series of walls that have been erected in this great pathway to keep off Tartar invasions. The terror inspired by the outer tribes of the North has been such that the Chinese have fortified almost the whole gap in the mountains. A handful of men, with modern artillery, with European handling, could now keep off Genghis Khan or Tamerlane; but not with only spears, and bows, and arrows, once the weapons of war, as here, even now, to a great extent. There are four or five series of walls, running up even to the tops of the hills, before one comes to *the* Great Wall. All over the hills, by the valleys, are the ruins of old forts in the direction of the road. Bloody battles have been fought here—many of them—but the story of them is lost to us, for there is no historian before Agamemnon. When, in olden times, the Mongols were coming, the intelligence was transmitted into China by beacon-fires, lighted on the towers, and the signal flashed through the Chinese dominions, and the mandarins assembled their hosts from the south to repel the invader.

At last, as I have already written, we were up an ascent of rocks, over which the Great Wall towers, some thirty or thirty-five feet high, with a granite foundation and a brick crenellated topping thereon. We let loose our mules here, freed, *pro tem.*, our chair-men, and then, spreading our blankets on the grass created by the vegetation grown around the ruins, reclined to eat and to drink—a lunch, or tiffin, as it is called in the East. The cup of cool mountain water that for weeks and weeks I have been longing for—water freed from impurities, and fresh as the torrent just springing from its native wells—was here. No one knows how good water tastes unless one has been living, as I have been, for weeks, on claret, beer, porter, and tea, feeling it not safe to drink the water of the country below; and hence, I now drank mountain water by "the wholesale," and became as good a temperance man as Neal Dow in Maine.

# LETTER XXV.

### RETURN TO PEKIN.

The Ming Tombs.—The Grand Approach to them.—All going to ruin.—The Summer Palace of the Emperors.—" Yueng-Ming-Yuen-Ching," the man-of-all-work.—Letters of Credit no Service in Pekin.—No Coin or Currency in China.—Sycee.—The North of China.—The Emperor gives Audience at 5 A. M.—The Marble Bridge and the Lotus.—The Temple of Heaven.—The Temple of Earth.—The Sacrifices in these Temples by the Emperor.

*September* 1, 1871.

FROM the Great Wall of China I went to the Ming Tombs (the Chinese imperial burying-place, what the Pyramids were to the Egyptians). The Ming dynasty was a pure Chinese dynasty—no Tartar blood in it—and one of the Mings created, in a beautiful valley here, just under the mountain road about, a series of burial-places, now one of the wonders of China, though half in ruins, as every thing is here. The approach from Pekin (thirty miles distant) into the valley is, or rather was, once, magnificent. There are six great stages, or notable places, in the valley, to the tomb of Yung-lo—a marble gateway, constructed of fine white marble, ninety feet long, fifty feet high, carved with squares of flowers; then, a stone bridge; then, the Dragon and Phœnix gate, and seven marble bridges with elegant balustrades; then, the avenue of animals, cut in bluish marble in colossal size—two pairs of lions, two of unicorns, two of camels, two of elephants, and two of horses. The elephants are thirteen feet high and seven wide. Beyond the animals come the military and civil mandarins, six on each side. These are all in grand costumes. Our mules found these lion and elephant figures so life-like that they shied at them, trembled all over, and refused to pass by. We had to blind their eyes, and then make them follow a donkey who did not appreciate sculpture as well as the mules. Gradually, then, over a paved road, we came through persimmon, or wild mulberry orchards, to the great resting-place and tomb of Yung-lo. I could fill a page with an interesting topographical description of the vast hall, two hundred and ten feet wide, and thirty feet deep—of its pillars of teak wood, twelve feet round and thirty-two feet high to the ceiling—but who, in America cares for the Mings, or the dead Mr. Yung-lo, whose remains repose in the august mausoleum in the rear of that hall? I only hint of what I saw, in order to impress you with the idea that the Chinese were as proud of mausoleums as the Egyptians were, or, as New-Yorkers are of Greenwood Cemetery. But Mr. Yung-lo's and all the other Ming tombs are rapidly going to grass. Another (Manchu) dynasty is on the throne. Grass is growing all over the roofs, and wild weeds are in all the courts, and often in the halls. By-and-by, it will be as hard to find where Mr. Yung-lo was buried as where Augustus, or Julius Cæsar, or Titius Livy, or Demosthenes, or Thucydides rested.

Dollars are wasted on great mausoleums. A thousand years after a man is dead, who cares for his dust and ashes, if any of them are left? I ate eggs and cold mutton, and drank Bass's London beer, on the floors of the Mings, within the sacred enclosure, and paid the keeper a few cash (cents) for the privilege. A dozen Chinese muleteers would look on to see how a Yankee ate eggs and mutton with a knife and fork, all hankering after the *to be* empty bottle, invaluable to them as a bottle; and such is life, and such is death, among the Ming Tombs!

If one will go to see where Chinese emperors are buried, one ought to go, next, to see where Chinese emperors lived. Hence, we went over a few miles, some twenty, perhaps, or more, to Yueng-Ming-Yuen, the once wonderful summer palace that the British and French burnt down, or blew up with powder in 1860. You will remember that in 1859 the Chinese declined to execute the treaties which let foreign ministers into Pekin, and that Sir Frederick Bruce (who died in Boston, after being the British Minister in Washington), and our Mr. Ward, were not permitted to reside there. The British and French concluded to fight their way into the capital, and were successful in the fight. The Chinese violated a truce, and murdered some Englishmen and French, whereupon, in revenge, the summer palace of the emperor was sacked and destroyed in part. It is said ten million dollars' worth of valuables were found in it by the soldiers, who were permitted to sack it, which many of these soldiers, little understanding values, sold for trifles. Gardens, palaces, temples, and pagodas on artificial hills, were all sacked. Judging by what is now left in ruins, it seems to me that the famous gardens and parks of Versailles, and Wilhelmshöhe, in Hesse Cassel, are not more beautiful than this summer palace, Yueng-Ming-Yuen, was. Here the emperor resided five or six months in the year, with his wives, and his eunuchs, and servants—Pekin, some eight miles off in sight—and every thing about him that could give a human being luxury, ease, effeminacy. There was a lake for gondolas to glide in. There was an artificial island, with summer-house on it, and a bridge, magnificently arched, leading by a circuit to it. There are groves and tangled thickets, left purposely wild to contrast with the artificial structures all about. Statues of many kinds, in marble and bronze, are numerous, some mutilated, but enough left to show the once great grandeur of the twelve square miles within the inclosure of the palace. We lunched within, near dragons in marble, on a terrace, under cedars and pines; and here, in the life palace of the Emperors, we had our little feast, as the day before in the Ming Tombs. Travellers must eat and drink, no matter in what high places their meal-times pick them up.

Weary and worn, after four days of hard excursions, we returned to the great city, and the mud we had found in it two weeks ago was now dust and flying dirt, and flying dirt and dust. I am beginning to think my first *entrée* into Pekin in the mud has made me do injustice to its streets. One does not need seven-leagued boots now to get over its ditches and pools. The springless carts are endurable where there are no pavements, and it is the fashionable vehicle I see now, with curtains, and covers, and paint, and vermilion; and therefore not so very bad to look at. But custom fits the eye for almost any thing. Pekin looks vastly better to me than it did at first. I think I could exist here, if there was no other place to live in. The air is exhilarating, and the climate has been beautiful since I came here. So much in apology for first impressions in Pekin.

I have written of "Cheng," my dragoman, interpreter, cook, valet, waiter, man-of-all-work, and a genius besides, who only asks ten dollars (Mexican) per month, and *pickings*. The ten Mexicans turn out to be the very smallest part of the pay—for I am wholly in his power. I cannot enter a temple without him, or get out of one, or do without him at any time, anywhere. Cheng's genius is best displayed hereabout on currency, and I can recommend him to the President for his Secretary of the Treasury, as long as the paper-money system exists in America. Cheng will turn a Mexican dollar into nothing, by the exchanges, through the bankers, a little quicker than it can be done in Wall Street, New York, or, in Montgomery Street, San Francisco. I give him Mexicans, and he exchanges them for sycee, silver (chopped-up silver, generally), and he exchanges that into the paper money of Pekin, which is not current ten miles out of the city. They have paper money here in Pekin only, just as we have "stamps" in the United States—the lowest value, ten of our cents; but underneath and beyond this is "cash," in strings of copper, one thousand to twelve hundred of which make a dollar, and on a journey, you have to take, or ought to take, strings of cash weighing enough to load a mule. With a respectably big good bill of credit from New York or London, I cannot get a cent from it here, in Pekin (there are no bills of exchange drawn here on anywhere), and were it not for the kindness and trust of the Comprador (financial officer) of the Russian Legation, I could not have gone to " the wall," or get out of Pekin. I brought up from Tien-tsin, here, as many Mexican dollars as I dared to carry, but they were soon exhausted in the temptation of the shops of Pekin. The currency of China is in a most abominable state. The Government money is trusted in nothing but in its copper coinage. Even Mexican dollars will not pass among the country people. Silver only is used, and that, everywhere goes by weight. There are no Chinese coins; there is no mint. The Government would not be trusted to have one, so corrupt is it believed to be, or has been, in times gone by, in the coinage of money, or in the issuance of paper, which, in large quantities, it once put forth, as described in the travels of the Venetian Marco Polo.

11

Before I leave these regions of North China, from whence there is no emigration, save into Mongolia and Manchuria—none, certainly, to America—I must pay a passing tribute to the general apparent kindness of the people, and the safety for the European traveller. No one has designed or intimated harm to us, either in the lone villages or on the River Peiho, when exposed all night on the sampan boats, or *en route* from Tung Chow and Pekin to the Great Wall—far, far into China's interior. We have scarcely ever felt the least sense of insecurity. Our lives for days and days have been at the mercy of Chinamen, and no one has harmed us, on the contrary, all, though curious to see, have been hospitable to us. Ever since the wars between Great Britain and France, a foreigner seems to bear with him a charmed power for protection. Though provoked, as the Chinese must have been, by the burning of the Emperor's summer palace, even amid its ruins, the people all about were civil—so civil, that when requested to let us eat in peace, without the curious crowds usually gathering around, they all cheerfully departed, and peeped from corners only, at a distance, fancying they were out of our sight. I have no gun with me, no revolver, and I deem the carrying of them more unsafe to my own surroundings than any protection they would give from any imaginary perils from the population about me.

I have good opportunities now to see farm life, garden life, rural life, in general. The agriculture, especially the terrace agriculture, is not what I expected to see. Farming is not carried to such perfection as in Japan. Mountain land is not rescued from its barrenness where it might be; but every spot of good land is put under cultivation for millet, or sorghum, or corn, or peas, or beans, etc. The sorghum runs up to twelve or fifteen feet high, and its stalks and roots are used for fuel in winter. There is no grass land in this part of China, and hence few or no cattle are raised here. There are no green fields, therefore, though often green hills, and these are, now, as green as in Switzerland; and very Swiss-like among the mountains, with the Swiss disease of the goitre among the women there. And on these hills there are sometimes cattle and goats. A country thus all ploughed, and hoed, and cultivated, its plains, now full of crops and teeming with agricultural wealth, is a novelty to an American eye. I could see nothing but crops, for miles and miles, as I wandered through the fields, and the field paths, called roads. There are some few fruits here—the apple, now ripening, not bad—the peach, not good nor bad, and the grape, excellent as a garden grape. Figs and pomegranates are growing in the gardens of the Legation about me, but they are housed in winter. The winter here, indeed, must be terrible, judging from the good, thick ice I see on the table, and from the abundance of furs and skins of all sorts in the markets, offered for sale as clothing. The sun in summer is too fiery hot, and in midday, the safest way is to keep out of its rays. But the climate of Pekin I have found agreeable and healthy, and in the mountains not far off, the air is as pure as in Switzerland, or in Oregon, or in New Hampshire. Every one below in the unhealthy regions told me, "it was as much as a man's life was worth" to come to Pekin as a tourist in August; but, I have found myself improved in health and vigor. April, May, September and October, however, are the safest months to be here. Pekin is cut off from the rest of the world in winter, for ice blocks up every stream, everywhere, about here, and only long and tedious overland travel then is practicable.

. . . . . .

Pekin, at seven o'clock in the morning, is the busiest hour of the day. Later in the day, when the sun is hot, no one ventures out unless compelled so to do. After some difficulty, a horse was procured that would allow a lady to mount him (the horses here are so unaccustomed to women that they are frightened by them—their dresses, etc.). I started, with one of the gentlemen attached to the English Legation, for the celebrated marble bridge, about three miles from the Russian Legation. We met, just at the outside of the gate, a long train of camels; some heavily laden with bags of merchandise, others kneeling, waiting patiently for their load—all awkward, ugly things, and at this season of the year, they are looking their ugliest, as they are shedding their coats. The streets are filled with them, and in close proximity to them are the tiny donkeys, looking even smaller from contrast. There are no carriages. As we wound our way slowly in and out of this motley crowd, and through the dirt of Pekin, we attracted quite as much curiosity as the novel sights excited in me. In many places the women were chatting to each other on their door-steps. As we approached, some would rush in (or rather *hobble*, owing to their cramped, deformed feet) and shut the doors, but peep through the cracks until the foreign devils had passed. They were all, notwithstanding the early hour, painted with red and white; their hair arranged and glued with a vegetable wax, and elaborately decorated with artificial flowers. They make these flowers very prettily, and sell them very cheap. The old grayhaired grandmothers will have a bunch of these bright flowers on their heads. Carts were passing us, with outriders. These carts were painted red, the wheels placed farther back than the common carts, the attendants dressed with the official cap, surmounted by a long, red tassel. I found these were the mandarins —high officials—going to an audience at the palace. The emperor receives his ministers at five o'clock every morning, and has an audience until 10 or 11 A. M. We now reached the Roman Catholic Cathedral. But as we had visited the Cathedral and Convent a few days before, and the Sisters had shown us their schools and Chinese children, their embroidery, etc., we did not stop, but rode on to the bridge. We almost had to ride over the beggars that thronged around us—so dirty, so covered with sores, that it made one sick to look at them. Like all of that class, they make the most of their disgusting-looking ailments.

The marble bridge itself is beautiful, built ever so many years ago—I am afraid to say how many; and, wonderful for China, it is in fair repair. But the most beautiful thing, to my eyes, was the lake around this bridge, the whole surface of which was covered with the lotus flower in full bloom—of a beautiful pink shade, with large leaves, some lying flat on the surface, others coiled up, as we had seen them represented in so many of the temples, both in Japan and China. The lotus is a sacred flower. Near the wall of the palace was an odd-looking temple, very dilapidated and neglected. This proved to be a Mohammedan mosque, built by one of the Emperors for a favorite wife, who, after living here a few years, became so homesick that he built this Moorish temple, for her to look upon a home-scene; but even then she was only permitted to look from a tower built inside of the palace walls. Poor Chinese Empress. What a sad lot to be selected to wear the ermine in China! We then rode past and around the temple that the Emperor uses to pray for rain. As this temple is constantly used it is kept in good repair, and brilliantly decorated with many colors. Again we met many carts, horses, donkeys, and a crowd standing and waiting. This is the great palace. While I stood gazing—for we foreigners are not permitted on those holy grounds—a grand high mandarin drove up, alighted from his cart, and entered the sacred precincts. He was in his best robes, of dark-blue satin, embroidered with many colors; his cap surmounted with a long tassel and blue button. We next made our way through the market. The attendants of these grand mandarins were busy getting their breakfasts—men, horses, dogs, donkeys, pigs, and some few women, in a heterogeneous mass—and not one single foreigner had we met in all this long ride.

. . . . . . .

FRIDAY, *August* 25.

This morning, in our early ride, we decided to turn our horses' heads toward the Temple of Heaven, and determined to enter, if possible, by strategy or bribery. The Chinese strongly object to foreigners (especially foreign women) entering such holy grounds. They are reserved for the Emperor and high officers. The Emperor comes here to offer sacrifices and pray for his ancestors once, at least, every year. On one or two other great occasions during the year, he may come here to offer prayers. During the rest of the time this great park of many acres, full of beautiful trees, walks, lakes, and flowers, is shut up, and left to the care of a few Chinese, who neglect it, and allow weeds to overgrow all of the paths, so that the undergrowth spoils the beautiful avenues of trees. On our way to this Temple of Heaven we rode through the Pekin fish, vegetable, and fruit markets. The trades-people are totally regardless of the comforts of either pedestrians or equestrians, as they erect their temporary tents in the middle of the streets; and in our winding way we were often compelled to bend our heads to our horses' necks, to pass under these tents; but they were all good-natured, and I felt amply repaid by the many new sights it gave me of Chinese life. The fruit market was particularly attractive, and the fruit was arranged with quite an idea for effect as to color and variety. As we passed on to the south of the city, we met a funeral procession, the mourners (the men of the family) dressed in long, white robes; then a crowd of hired servants surrounded the cart holding the coffin; and the musicians follow. This was only the funeral of a very ordinary individual. The higher the man's position, the greater the funeral procession. On our right, we now see the Temple of Earth (or Agriculture), where the Emperor goes every spring to plough; on the left, the Temple of Heaven. We rode rapidly across the open field, hoping to conceal our advance to the temple gate by the walls, and so to approach near enough to the gates to ride in before they could be closed upon us. But the "Heathen Chinee" were too quick for us, and triumphantly slammed the gates together, one minute and a half too soon for us. We talked, bribed, threatened; they held out to make us bribe more, and at last slowly swung back the heavy gate. We found this first wall enclosed many acres; the trees, evidently, many hundred years old, and a beautiful avenue, formed of large trees meeting overhead, extended from this first gate to the second, a distance of a quarter of a mile. Here, again, we were refused admittance, until further bribery was resorted to. Even then they insisted upon our dismounting, as the grounds were too sacred for horses. The distance from the second to the third gate was twice as great as the first one; and then, mounting some dozen steps, we were on a raised terrace, running from the north to the south of the temple grounds. At the south was a large circular marble altar, built in three terraces, each terrace raised nine feet, and on the top, it is thirty or forty feet in diameter. Partially surrounding this altar, on the southeast, are the urns for burning the sacrifices, and offerings of silk, etc. The animals for sacrifice must be selected with great care. They are bullocks, two years old, without blemish—the best of their kind. They are fed in the park which surrounds the altar. The Emperor, every December 21, proceeds to the Temple of Heaven in an elephant carriage. Since the death of the last Emperor all the elephants have died; and as the boy Emperor will be inaugurated next year, the King of Siam, it is said, is to send him two white elephants to draw his carriage when he goes to offer his prayers and sacrifices in the Temple of Heaven. On entering these sacred grounds, the Emperor first goes to the Tablet Chapel, on the north side of the grounds. Here he offers incense to Shang-ti, and to his ancestors, with three kneelings and nine prostrations. This chapel is one of the best preserved I have seen in Pekin. The roof is richly ornamented with carving and brilliant coloring; the columns (that support the roof, which is made pagoda-like, three stories high) are more than two feet in diameter, made of wood, plastered with crimson, and painted all over with gold beasts, birds, and fishes, as well as I could decipher. The marble terraces and steps, both at the north and south altars, are handsomely carved; but weeds are growing up, mouldering, and covering even these beautiful things. Next year, I suppose, all will be made as bright and beautiful as thousands of workmen can make them. The sacrifice at the north altar takes place at the beginning of spring. The Emperor goes from his home in the city to the altar, to meet there the new-come spring, and offer prayer to Shang-ti for a blessing on the labors of the husbandman. Here, also, as at the south altar, are seen the green furnace for the bullock sacrifice, and the eight open-work iron urns in which the offerings of silk are burnt. An urn is added when an Emperor dies. A plain, uncolored, and coarsely-woven silk cloth is preferred for these offerings. Prayer for rain is offered at the south altar in the summer. On occasions of drought the Emperor sometimes goes on foot to the "Hall of Penitent Fasting." This is to indicate that his anxiety of mind forbids him to seek bodily ease while his subjects are suffering. The anger of Heaven is a sign that there is a fault in the prince. He, therefore, lays aside his state for the time.

The distance to be walked is three English miles, and it may be at a time of year when the heat is great (and it is certain to be, when the dust is many inches deep). He may, however, return on horseback. This is a special ceremony. There is also a regular prayer and sacrifice for rain offered about the time of the summer solstice. At this time the Emperor kneels on the top step or platform of the altar, and his officers arrange themselves on the twenty-nine steps and terraces behind him. The prayer is then presented and read. It is then placed before Shang-ti on the offering of silk. The prayer, which is written on silk, is then taken to the iron urns, and there burnt. The temples and grounds are full of interest. Still, you are never impressed with a belief in the religion of China. The mould, dust, and decay cover and penetrate every thing.

# LETTER XXVI.

### *RETURNING SOUTHWARD.*

A Traveller retracing his Steps.—Tung Chow, on the Peiho River.—The Wheelbarrow Traffic.—Death to the Coolies.—Processions *en route.*—Of Funerals and Weddings.—A Good Story told of Gov. Seward.—Mistaking a Funeral Procession for an Ovation to Himself.—Expense of Travelling as a Grandee.—A Temple for a Hotel.—Running the Gauntlet of the Junks to Tien-tsin.—The Noisy Monosyllables of the Chinese.—Huge Pyramids of Salt.—Home, Sweet Home.—The Szechuen.—Under a Yankee Captain from Maine.—The Grapes of the Peiho.--The Rolling Screw Steamers of the Yellow Sea.—Rivalry of British and American Steamers.—Chinese Customs collected by Foreigners.—The American Flag driven off.—Manufactures driven off.

SHANGHAI, *September* 10, 1871.

RETRACING one's steps is not a traveller's pleasure. *En avant* is the watchword in *going*, as well as in fighting. But in China an American sees so much of the new, that reseeing opens to him novelty after novelty. We left Pekin at noon, a hot sun on our backs, good for the rheumatism, which at this season of the year, up there, hits one, when sitting out and enjoying the night breezes. I was on horseback— no more springless carts for me, though Mongolian horses are rather tricky; and we had a handsome escort of young Englishmen, attached to the English Legation, as student interpreters, some of whom went sixteen miles, all the way to Tung Chow, where we take boats to go down the Peiho River. We *tea-ed* on the road. Inns, here, ever sell tea—none, whiskey, rum, or brandy—and tea, I am finding more and more, is a great refresher to the traveller, without cream or sugar, even. What most rearrested my attention now, was the immense number of wheelbarrows, *wheeling* merchandise from the Peiho River to Pekin. These wheelbarrows, with one wheel only in the centre, are so overladen that it would seem impossible for men to manage them, if you did not see them doing it. Tons seemed to be on them; and how the man in the middle, with a strap over his shoulders, over the wheelbarrow, handles or manages to live under the burden is astonishing. Forty years of age is said to be the oldest of this class of coolies. This middle man, though, often has a mule pulling ahead of him, and on the sides of the wheelbarrow, are two men if not more, to steady. Over the paved road, full of all sorts of deep holes, worn by years and years of wheeling, go these wheelbarrows, with their loads, for all the interior of this northern part of China, and for Mongolia and Manchuria. A steel rail, or iron, might be laid at little expense over this level-paved road, but it is not permitted. A locomotive rail would do the transportation for one-twentieth of the present cost. "But," say the authorities, " this would throw thousands of the coolies out of employ!" The reply to this has been, "So do junks; so does the Grand Canal." "Why not destroy junks and canals, and let coolies and wheelbarrows do all the work everywhere? Why endure horses, and camels, and mules?"

We met several processions *en route*, some funeral, some wedding. These are very imposing, both of them, very showy and very flashy. They tell a good story in Pekin of Gov. Seward, when here—doubtless a lie, but too good a story to be lost for *that*. The expectations of the ex-Governor were said to be great, when he entered the great capital of this great empire, with which he had made a great treaty; and he therefore indulged in great expectations of a great welcome. As he entered the gates of Pekin, a great funeral procession was coming out with music, catafalque, etc., etc., all as imposing as a grand procession of some great dead man could well be made. The Governor was entering with the marine band of the Colorado, mounted on donkeys, as this grand procession was going out. The great living and the great dead thus met. The Governor, naturally enough, concluded this was in honor of his grand *entrée*, and he rose, and rose, in his open sedan-chair, and bowed, and bowed, and then ordered a halt, and got out, and bowed, and bowed again, to the catafalque of the dead. The Chinese think all foreigners are rather mad, and hence did not marvel over it as much as they might; but when Gov. Seward found out what he had done, the story is, he was more mad than pleased.

My *exit* and my *entrance* were not thus grand; in, on a cart, and out, on a horse—but so much the better, for, to be a grandee, or to travel as a grandee, is a grand expense. The kindly Russian protection under which I had fallen, relieved me from the many annoyances of travel, all the way from Tien-tsin up to Tung Chow, and on to Pekin; but when the Russians delivered me up, on the return, at Tung Chow, to the tender mercies of the Chinese, the troubles began. Everybody wanted something—*what?* and what, *for?*—who can tell, that speaks no Chinese, or understands it less when spoken? One stately fellow, however, in a semi-official hat, extorted a few dollars by an appeal to our "grandeur." "Every thing has been paid," said I. "True," the translation was to me; "but great people always pay more than little people!" Who could help paying after that? The extra Mexicans were forked over, and without grumbling. (*Mem.*—If one would travel economically, never travel as "great people.")

At Tung Chow—a big, walled city, by the way—we were, by grace and favor, re-tumbled into the Temple of Fang-Wang-Meaow. The priests were as good (to us) as if they had been Christian priests, and we, first-class Buddhists. Wearied and worn, they made every thing as comfortable as possible for us, bargained for us, and provided us with sampans (house boats), to take us down river; and at midnight bade us good-by, as we embarked in them to return to Tien-tsin. We here regathered our "traps"—beds, bedding, blankets, dishes, and other household resources—and as the moon was rising, and we were bidding good-by in the distance to the Pagoda of Tung Chow, we went to sleep. What good philosophy this is, thought I, when going to sleep—in an open boat, amid countless Chinese boats on the river, full of all sorts of people! But what is the use of worrying? Between springless carts, mule-litters, and a hot horseback ride, on a hard-going horse, with every bone and muscle aching, I could have slept, I am sure, even in the City Hall park (New York), with a blanket about me; but I doubt if my pockets would have been as safe, or boots returned, if left outside the railing.

We were only thirty-six hours returning to Tientsin (one hundred and twenty miles), the current carrying us—(fare for three house boats, seven dollars each, twenty-one dollars in all). Nothing remarkable turned up until we began to run the junk gauntlet near Tien-tsin, and the junks now are not so crowded together, and crowding, as earlier in the year. But, me being judge, it is as much as a man's life is worth to run this junk gauntlet in this narrow river, at this season of the year; and yet this judgment of mine is not worth much, for very few accidents, I am told, occur. We went on—our crew shouting, screaming, squealing, and squeezing, a thousand other crews, with like shouts and screams, that shake tender nerves, but seldom scare. A Chinaman will make more noise for nothing than any other class of men on earth; and their monosyllables, on the key, *alto* and *altissimo*, here become terrific. I had so many new things to see going up, that I did not well see the huge pyramids of salt, piled up on the river for miles. Salt is a government monopoly here, as in more civilized nations—as in ours, too, with this difference, the monopoly, home, being *tariffed*, while the Pekin government here has all the profits. This salt is sent all over the empire, up through the Grand Canal; and hence, these huge pyramids of salt on the shores of the Peiho, ready to be transported, everywhere, on the internal waters—as far as Canton, if necessary. Here, then, perhaps better than elsewhere in China, in these innumerable junks, one can see the vast coasting, and internal traffic of the Chinese, in comparison with which their foreign commerce is but a drop in the bucket.

"Home! Sweet Home!" Tien-tsin was that home to us for a day, on this, our return from the great interior. The American flag was floating here, on a coast steamer built on the Clyde—the "Szechuen"—with a Captain (Patterson) all the way from the State of Maine; and, on this Szechuen we forthwith made our lodgment (the only "hotel" left by the rains), and from there we distributed the beds, the pillows, the mosquito nets, the books, etc., that the good people of Tien-tsin had loaned us for our river voyage. The American Consul here is a very intelligent Scotchman, with a Chinese wife and Chinese children, and speaks Chinese as well as he speaks English; and the American flag was pleasantly floating over his house. Mr. Moore, too, the agent for the American boats here, was kind to us, and his hospitality was welcomed in his own house, where a freshly-come American wife from Pennsylvania added graces to that home. The missionaries called upon us, and several Englishmen, and the officers of the British gunboats in port here—so that, on the decks and in the cabins of the Szechuen, we had every reason to feel "at home." By the way, these little British gunboats seem everywhere on the coast. They are so small that they creep into very small ports, and up very crooked and shallow rivers, as is this Peiho, while our bigger craft, more stately, it is true, are but ornaments for Cheefoo, Yokohama, Nagasaki, or Hong Kong.

But Tien-tsin was to be only a temporary "home," for the day after our arrival we were off at the earliest dawn, rethreading the mazes of the crookedest river I ever saw, not even excepting the Raritan (N. J.). We had laid in a great store of grapes—for this is the grape season, and Tien-tsin supplies Shanghai, Amoy, Hong Kong, and all the coast, with grapes—while we had plenty of ice;—and who cannot live on ice and grapes in a hot land, with a little good bread thrown in? But there is no stinting on board of these foreign ships on the China coast. All live like princes on the very fat of the land. The "fare" is enormous in price, but enormous in the supply of eatables therefor. As to the steamers, though, I cannot say much for them—for, how they do screw, and roll, and pitch, and twist, and turn over, and turn *under*, almost! I have stood the Atlantic and the Pacific without much fuss; but these shallow waters of the Gulf of Pechili, and of the Yellow Sea, how they do swell and tumble under you—for, if there is a typhoon, or a storm, hundreds of miles off, these sympathetic shallows twist and twirl under it, as does a fish when there is not water enough to cover him. The "*rolling*" Manchu (Captain Steele) has had famous poetry made upon the capacity of the ship to roll, and thereby has an envious preëminence in that bad way; but the Manchu rolls no more than the Shantung or the Szechuen. They all roll, and roll, when there is a breath or a zephyr to roll them, and will forever roll.

We had a sort of a race from Tien-tsin to Chefoo, and from Chefoo to Shanghai, some eight hundred miles, or more, in all. The British flag is in opposition to the American flag on this coast, and the opposition steamers start together, on the same day and the same hour, with the understanding, however, that they are not to consume too much coal, drive too hard, or lower freights or fares. The British steamer "Appin" (screw), however, could not screw as fast as the American, naturally, which left her ever behind; and hence, in order to avoid this disgrace, the British owners ordered more coal, more fire, the more to hurry up on the course. The American steamer could not permit the honors of the past to be withdrawn, and so we piled on more coal, and had more fire, for at least three hundred of the latter part of the eight hundred miles, and beat, of course, in the arrival at Shanghai, only a half hour, not an hour at the most. The race then became very exciting, for, except at night, we were always in sight.

We stopped at Chefoo only two or three hours on our return, long enough, though, to see the American Consul, Mr. Wilson, and to have long talks with other Americans, among them a very intelligent young man (Mr. Holwell), who is employed in the Chinese custom-house, which, by the way, is run altogether by foreigners—an Englishman (Mr. Hart), in Pekin, at the head, and Englishmen and Americans, and Frenchmen, and Germans are scattered everywhere through the treaty ports, to collect Chinese customs. The Chinese, I infer, have reached the conclusion that they themselves were not sharp enough to match smuggling Yankees and John Bulls; and hence they employ foreigners to collect their duties on imports and exports, who, save in, and about Hong Kong, have now stopped all smuggling, except in opium, the duty on which is so high as to be irresistibly tempting. Mr. Holwell is one of the employés at Chefoo.

This place, Chefoo, in the province of Shantang, where Confucius came from, is one of the rich provinces of China. Its exports for foreign use are mainly Pongee silks, which cost here, from three dollars and fifty cents to six dollars for nineteen yards—silks, by the way, admirable for our Southern and Western climes, and for umbrellas and sun-shades, and for travelling dresses in the North;—and straw braid, of which our straw hats and straw bonnets are made in Connecticut and other parts of New England. It is cheap enough here, but with the thirty per cent. duty on it in America, and with freight and other charges, it becomes dear there, and thus doubles or triples the prices of our hats and bonnets.

I am grieved to say that I have not seen, since I left Shanghai, the American flag on but one vessel, save those on the American line of steamers, no more of which can now be built in America—all, alas, hereafter to be built on the Clyde, or elsewhere in Europe! Our sailing vessels have been recently driven off the Chinese seas, which, originally, under Boston and Salem enterprise, were once almost *our* seas. But few or none of our drills now clothe the millions of the Chinese Empire. Our cotton manufactures of all kinds are being superseded by England and Germany. True, *man* is a little cheaper in Europe than in the Northern and Western parts of America (not South)—but *machines*, not *men* make drills, and sheetings, and shirtings; and they make them so cheap that even the Chinese and Japanese, where *man* is not worth half as much as *horse*, or *mule*, or *donkey*, cannot compete with *machine*. What make our drills dearer are taxes on coal, iron, steel, wood, food (fish and potatoes, the great food of the Eastern manufacturers), for *machine* work is so much cheaper everywhere than *man*, that man nowhere can come into competition with machine. We make the machine dearer and dearer, and hence we are driven off the seas, and, alas, off the land, too! But for the American lines of steamers here, now run, under American captains, by Chinese and Malays, mainly, the flowery flag (the name the Chinese give our stars and stripes) would hardly be seen on the Chinese and Japanese seas. These live independent of *home*, free from the tax oppressions of *home*, and spread far and wide the American name and fame, despite the ingratitude of that *home*. Their ship stores cost not half ours cost at home. Their copper, and rigging, and machinery, not half of ours. The Germans, I may as well add here, are engrossing, in their sailing vessels, much of the coasting (treaty port) trade of China. Their merchants live less expensively. Their vessels are sailed cheaper, and they have smaller craft for navigation in the smaller ports of China.

But, this is out of place. I am a traveller, not a political economist, now—a sketcher, scribbler, only, if you please, not an essay writer.

## LETTER XXVII.

### *THINGS IN SHANGHAI.*

Shanghai.—Its Enterprizes and Surroundings.—The Hot Sun of Shanghai.—Turning White Men Yellow.—The City Government of Shanghai.—Eastern Hours for Breakfast and Dinner.—The Great Commerce of Shanghai.—Much of it passing into Chinese Hands.—Tea Trade.—Tea-Tasters.—Telegraphs to, and from Shanghai.—Tea Steamers up the Yang-tze.—Foreign Schemes to dodge the Fung Shuey.—Hostility to Electricity.—The Telegraphs from Shanghai *via* Nagasaki and Vladivastock, in Russia.

SHANGHAI, *September* 12, 1871.

SHANGHAI I gave a bad name to—sick, as I was, under the red-hot flaming suns of July. Fresh from the North now, full of the breezes of Mongolia, with some oxygen in my veins, not all hydrogen, as in July, I begin to think the place habitable, not infernal (from its sun); and the thickly-scattered dead Chinese, in coffins, above ground, all about the drives of Shanghai, do not look so like having me soon among them as they did six weeks ago. Nobody that I knew in July is dead since I went North; and hence, I reason, death is not the inevitable fate of all who enter Shanghai in July. Upon the whole, the place is a model place, save and except that sun —that red-hot, fiery, furious sun—that only a two-story pith hat, a double umbrella, and goggles, enable you to live under, with white shoes on, in white linen only, and no shirt, nearly as Japanese and as Chinese as possible, free from that European discipline, which has established the unnatural law that clothes in hot climates are indispensable. By the way, what is the matter with these Eastern suns? There is not a hot place in the United States, from New Orleans to the Geysers in California—though the thermometer makes nothing of running up to 118—where a straw hat, under that sun, is not endurable; while here, you would soon run mad, in a straw hat, under the same sun. The sun is the Caucasian's mortal enemy here, while the Mongolian (has he a thicker pate?) needs no hat, seldom has a hat; nay, on the contrary, with shaven head, accepts harmlessly the full blaze of the noon-day sun. The atmosphere here must make these Eastern suns so much hotter than our Western suns, under the same indications of the thermometer. The very reflection of them, sometimes, gives the Caucasian the heat-apoplexy, and almost instant death. I was constantly threatened with it in July, though never venturing out of doors till the sun was setting, or, before it was much risen in the morning. This very reflection of the sun, however, which I have seldom faced, has almost made a yellow man of me, and I expect, hereafter, to stand high with my colored brethren.

But to redeem Shanghai from my July injustice, I must say, it is a charming little Pedlington. Everybody knows everybody, and everybody talks about everybody. The people are all " tip-top," and all are aristocracy, and there is no commonalty. It is a community of clever merchants, with the prettiest wives they can tempt out from America, and England, and Germany, all struggling to get rich, and all fighting for Sycee and Mexican dollars, and all happy in the surety, they will be rich some day—then go home, and be buried under ground, not as here, on the surface, in a two-storied coffin, with a cord of wood or more in it. Shanghai, I think, is the best governed little city I ever saw. The whole Caucasian race, with an exceptional French "flare-up" now and then, live in perfect concord, and govern the city family, not as politicians, or statesmen, but as Abraham, Isaac, and Jacob governed their flocks of sheep, and of men and women. The streets are as nice and neat as a parlor. The police drive away, or ward off nearly all crime. The charitable institutions are many. The English Episcopal Church here is a sort of cathedral, in a large, open ground, which must have cost thousands and thousands of Mexicans to build. There are few handsomer churches in New York than this Episcopal church here. The merchants, though thinking only, and struggling only, for Sycee and the Mexican, nevertheless live like princes. But what abominable hours they keep—breakfast, or tea, or coffee, and toast and eggs, at nine A. M.; breakfast again at twelve, or one, on every thing, with wines from everywhere, and dinner at 8 P. M. Then all go to bed after that, with overflowing stomachs, well prepared for nightmare that night, and dyspepsia or fever next day. They have no evenings. There is no social visiting at night. Their exercise and air are taken as the sun is setting, and after that they eat, and eat, and drink, and drink—and why don't they die? But, the fact is, this hot climate is an exception to ours. The more you eat here, the better you seem to be off. As hog and hominy are indispensable for our Southern negro, even in July, so beef and mutton, if not pork, seem indispensable here. The drinking that would kill us Americans is here done with apparent impunity. The water itself not being fit to drink, everybody drinks soda water, or Bass's beer, or London porter, or claret, or sherry, or port, or brandy, and none seem to kill. London porter, half death in our bilious climate, in July, is here, in July, the staff of life. I think I owe to a bottle of it per day (which I could not drink at home) the capacity to exist here, in July.

The commerce of Shanghai reminds one of New York in its better (shipping) days. The river is full of ships from all parts of the world but ours. Now and then, there is the American flag, or an American sailor (A. A. Low & Co. keep the flag alive), but few and far between are our ships. England is here in all her ocean glory. Shanghai is to this land, with its great river (the Yang-tze), what our New Orleans was to the Mississippi, in its palmier days, and before its trade was diverted by railroad. The commerce of the world rushes here to gather the teas and silks of China, and the exports and imports are enormous in value, more especially to and from England. Hence, the operations of exchange in banks are very large, and the mere commissions upon transactions make the fortunes of many. Trade, however, here, as everywhere in China, is rushing from the foreigners more and more into the hands of the Chinese. They buy all the tea from the farmer; they pick it, and sort it, and sift it, prepare it for, and bring it to, market; and some of them now are thinking of establishing their own agencies in London, Liverpool, and New York. They sell now to foreigners by "musters"—that is, by sample—and every tea mercantile establishment here has its tea-taster who tries the tea, and buys it from these "musters." No merchants are keener, or sharper, not even the Yankees, than these Chinese merchants. The "tea-tasters" here are great institutions. They arrange twenty or thirty tea-cups in rows, with covers over them; then pour on water of a given heat; then take a minute-glass, and, measuring the time, keep it just so long under cover, when they taste and smell, and then make record of the quality and value of the tea. And now, don't let every old lady in America turn up her nose at tea, when I tell her that, in the packing of the teas in the tea-chests, the naked-footed coolie (Chinese workie) jumps on the tea, and tramples it into the chest with his feet and toes, just as sugar is trampled in elsewhere, or as bread is made, in hot weather, in a baker-shop, in Chicago, or New York, or Boston. Tea and sugar are good, nevertheless, despite the dirty coolie in China, and the dirtier African in Cuba—are they not? Teas, too, I have forgotten to state, are heated, toasted, and baked in firing-pans, the better to stand the long voyages; and hence, the tea we drink at home is not the uncured, the undoctored tea the Chinese drink here. The green teas are especially doctored, as well as the scented teas; but, as I never drink them, I won't hurt the feelings of those who do.

Shanghai is now, by telegraph, within the reach of "all creation;" and hence, this telegraph is making some mischief in the tea-trade, as it does, on the start, with all the trades elsewhere. The costly telegraph dispatches must fly often here, to and from London and New York. Reuter tells us the great news items, by telegraph, in joint-stock telegrams; but the prices of teas and silks in the great markets of the world are secrets to the trade, which each house itself pays for. The British, this year, have run through here some five or six steamers, from Hankow, the headquarters of the tea-trade on the River Yangtze, to Liverpool and London, and they have made the voyage in fifty or sixty days, through the Suez canal. These movements threaten a revolution in the movement of teas. You have doubtless noticed how the Pacific Mail steamers to San Francisco have been crowded with teas this summer, while extra ships have been put on, and they have not been able to carry half away in the season when wanted.

The telegraph has recently been branching off

here in all directions, save that of China, where overland electricity is at a discount, in consequence, as I have shown you before, of its hostility to the "Fung Shuey," the wind and water superstition of "the heathen Chinee." There is a scheme on hand among some of the pro-Chinamen, which I think will, sooner or later, dispose of this superstition; and that is, to employ Chinese leading men on the routes to build the telegraphs, and *then to keep them in order*, paying them, for the guarantee and protection, more than it is worth. "The devil" (Fung Shuey), it is thus thought, will be "whipped around the stump." The god of silver (there are no gold gods here—we never see gold as money) will thus get around the god of wind and water. Shanghai, New York, San Francisco, Oregon, and Vancouver's Island are now telegraphically linked, under the Pacific and Atlantic Oceans. The Danish Company (it may be Russian, under cover), that stretched the wires by sea from Hong Kong to Shanghai, has now not only connected Nagasaki (Japan), but run a line from Nagasaki, by sea, up north to Vladivastock, a seaport on the Pacific (Russian) coast, whence already, six thousands miles nearly, is a wire to St. Petersburg, and thence all over Europe. Thus, Shanghai, Hong Kong, and Nagasaki have now two ways of reaching Europe—one by the Indian and Red Seas, the other overland through Russia—two strings to the bow. The indispensable link now is, though yet wanting, the link from San Francisco, by sea, over to Asia, then through Russia, so that in case of European wars there will be two strings to the American bow. Russia and the United States together must make that link; for no private company, for years, would it pay, in consequence of the sparseness of population. Two great friendly people like the Americans and Russians, with their two great institutions (the two D.'s), cannot afford thus to live apart, or to think and to breathe only through Europe.

## LETTER XXVIII.

*FROM THE ENGLISH COLONY OF HONG KONG.*

How Screw-Steamers roll.—Cabins, Hot, Hotter, Hottest.—Chow Chow excellent.—Sleep in a Stew Prison.—The Great English (P. & O.) and French Lines of Steamers in the East.—Hong Kong.—Typhoons here.—The City the Refuge of the Refuse Chinese.—Curious Intermixture of Population.—The Coolie Emigration here.—The Dialects of China.—Pidgen English.—Chinese Kitchens and Cooks. etc., etc.

HONG KONG, *September* 20, 1871.

THIS place is some fifteen thousand miles, or more, from New York—the way I am going home, *via* Europe; but, nevertheless, it is very European. I was "steamed" into the city at night-fall, just as the innumerable gas-jets were illuminating the houses on the side-hill streets, and the effect was very beautiful. The eyes long used, or only used, to oil or tallow-dips become electrified by gas-jets; and hence Hong Kong, as I entered into it by gas-light, seemed like fairy-land. The French steamer Phase, of the quondam Messagerie *Impériale,* now only "maritime" (a name that is likely to stand, as it may be both Cæsarian and Republican), was the steamer in which (some eight hundred and seventy miles) I came down south, to this, the latitude of Havana—(fare, $60)—in which the *chow chow* (that is the only word Europeans use here for feeding) was excellent, the seamanship good enough, but the sleeping, in the hot, sub-aqueous cabin, almost infernal. The steamer—long, lean, lank—was lawless when the wind blew, and rolled so that the port-holes of our stewing prisons were always shut, unless one wanted to be in a salt-water bath all the night. Think, in the latitude of Florida and Havana, of being thus shut up, and in a boat whose iron sides had been so heated by the Shanghai suns, that only an arctic winter can well cool them off! The fact is, while England and France may be, nay, doubtless are, great on "the hulls" of steamers, they know nothing, this way, at least, of interior accommodation. The "Phase" was superb above water to live in; but uninhabitable down under water, in the sleeping cages in which we were cribbed. The success of our American steamers on the Yang-tze, on the Peiho River, the Yellow Sea, and the Canton River, has arisen mainly from the fact that our carpenters know how to build cabins—a lesson yet to be learned in England and France, so it seems to me. There are two powerful lines of steamers running from China and Japan, through the Red Sea, to Europe—the English line known as the P. & O. (the Peninsular and Oriental), and the French line, the Messagerie. They run once a fortnight each, and so give the whole East a weekly mail between them both. Both are largely paid by their respective Governments—the French, however, pay the most, who, though they have the best steamers here, because the newest and latest styles, have the least commerce. Nevertheless, in silks they are well freighted, for their silks go up the Adriatic into Germany, as well as to France and Italy. The French gave us French *chow chow*, with light wines and beer; and John Bull, roast-beef, beef-steak, plum-pudding, etc., etc., but no wine nor beer. The P. & O. line is subsidized by the English Government, $2,500,000 per annum.

As for this British Colony of Hong Kong, all under the British Government—with Sepoys and Sikhs here for soldiers as well as Britons—it is difficult, in a small space, to sketch for you a comprehensible idea. It is a little island, built on the side of a great hill, which runs up to a peak, and at the bottom of that big hill, and on the sides and fissures of it, are some of the prettiest architectural displays you see anywhere, except in the palatial streets of Italy. You look out of one window, and you look on the harbor and the sea; and hence, at times, when the wind is from that way, you feel the fresh breezes of the sea. You look out of another window, and you look up the sides of the mountain, with houses overtopping yours, the peak overtopping all. The streets are as good as money can make them. Sewers are in all quarters, and water flows down in pipes from the hill sides, into your closets and bath-rooms; and that great scarcity of the East, and therefore that greatest of blessings, runs into your rooms abundantly, fresh, pure, healthy—so that, if you have been famishing for water as I have been, now over two months in

China, you drink and you drink here, and you bathe and you bathe, for the mere fun of it. Hong Kong, you thus see, is a beautiful little place, with some five thousand Europeans in it, including the garrison, with twenty Chinamen, or more, to one European. The Government buildings here are handsome, and the public grounds are handsomer. But my description may be rosy—for I have been so long wandering in nasty Chinese places, that this place not only seems to be a home, but a sort of heaven. The hot season is nearly over. The monsoon is changing, and brings down an occasional cool breeze from the north. The society is attractive and hospitable; but, perhaps, what is worth more than all to make a man's eyes see every thing in rose-color, is—I am well. Some of the dwellings of merchants here are truly palatial. I am a guest in a house originally built by Dent & Co., which cost here over a quarter million of dollars, where labor is so cheap—now, however, cut up, after the failure of that great house, into three establishments; but those left are all palatial. When money was made here, without rivalries—without Chinese or other serious competition—men could afford to build such palaces to live in; but that day is over now, never to return again.

Fortunately for me as a voyager, thus far I have dodged typhoons, as well as escaped earthquakes in Japan; but I see here now, as I saw in Hiogo, Japan, the terrible power and devastation of these typhoons, of which all in the East, but more especially the natives, live in affright, if not horror. About two weeks gone by, a typhoon knocked up here, the Praya, or Bund, or Quay, as we would call it, and spread devastation and death far and wide in the harbor. The crippled ships now in, and others coming in, show the typhoon's power at sea, while many have gone down—junks certainly—never to be heard of again. Steamers, however, escape them better than any other craft. The barometer forewarns the navigator, hours ahead, of their approach, and while a ship can only go as the caprice of the wind directs, the steamer chooses her own place to dodge the typhoon at sea, or the harbor to anchor in. Huge granite stones, well laid on the Praya or Quay here, were torn up from their places. Ships at anchor were drifted about as if playthings. The loss of life was small among the Europeans and Americans, but great among the Chinese, who have no newspapers to record in detail their calamities; hence, we never know any thing of the extent of their sufferings under these typhoons, or under the floods.

There is a great outcry here, just now, against crime and criminals, and the Chinese, and the police. All the rogues and rascals of China that can elope from home run·here to hide, or for protection against their own mandarins. Hence this city is full of Chinese burglars, and thieves, and murderers, even. I see to-day two or three hundred of these criminals chained together to wheelbarrows, at work, wheeling dirt to fill up the excavations created on the Quay by the typhoon. They were all under the command of negroes, mainly from Jamaica, who, with whip and musket in hand, keep order, and make the criminals work. The fact is, Hong Kong is a great "sore" in the Chinese system. European law does not fit Asiatic courts; the trial by jury is an unnatural graft here, and imprisonment for crime is often a blessing to a half-starved Chinaman rather than a curse. These burglars, some of them, are so expert that they grease themselves all over, in oil, and then enter naked the warehouses, so that, if caught, they can slide away—there being nothing to hold on to except the pig-tail, which is carefully rolled up. In walking the streets here, one sees the motleyest of all populations. There, is the American, the Englishman, the Scotchman, the Irishman, the Frenchman, the German; and *there*, are Ah Sin, Hang Wang, Hi Gang, Pe Tow, Tai Ling, Sing Shun,—with Parsees, Sikhs, and Sepoys from India, negroes from the West Indies, Malays, Manillamen, bastard Portuguese and Spanish, etc. There, is the Chinaman, with his pigtail and his fan, and the Parsee, with his long, black paper hat, or the Sikh, with his turban, or the Sepoy, in his cap; and there, comes the American, or English stove-pipe hat—a curiosity here, attracting attention, where all wear pith, or straw, or felt. The "stove-pipe" now looks as ugly, to my eye, as the "rough-and-ready" in America, or any other like ugly contrivance for the head. There is no universal law here—no fashion for hats, it seems. Every one wears what that one fancies. Linen is the great article of men's dress in these latitudes, and most of them appear all the time in white. The apparel is not costly here—pantaloons, $2 and $2 50; coats, $3; vests, $1 50, etc. But Hong Kong, you will remember, is a free port—no tariffs, no customs, nor custom-house officers—and it is the great smuggling *entrepot*, too, for the whole of this part of the East, more especially in opium, on which, out of Hong Kong, there is a very high duty, but not often paid by the Chinese about here.

This city, with Macao, some thirty miles off, is the headquarters of the coolie emigration to America. The Northern and Central Chinese do not emigrate by sea; but the Southern Chinamen long ago began to go off to Singapore, Cochin China, or elsewhere in the West; and hence emigration for him to America was not so serious a matter. From Shanghai and the Northern Yang-tze River, there is no emigration. No Chinaman there can be induced to emigrate to the United States. No Pekinese ever turn up in the United States, save those that once came over with Mr. Burlingame. The fact is, the dialects of the Chinese Empire are so conflicting, that one province can scarcely understand another; and hence there is little or no social communication between the North and the South, or the East and the West. The Cantonese cannot understand a word, or scarcely a word, of Pekinese, and *vice versa*. There is a mandarin language, which all officials understand, and, more or less, all the intelligent men of China; but, nevertheless, China is thus more cut up than Great Britain was thirty years ago, with its Welsh, its Gaelic, its Celtic, its Yorkshire and Lancashire dialects, which, though spoken then in the heart of the island of Great Britain, outsiders could scarcely understand. The common mode of communication here between the foreigner and the Chinaman is, in "Pidgen" (not Pigeon) English—the word "Pidgen" being the Chinese comprehension of the English word "Business." This Pidgen English is now the universal dialect between foreigners and the Chinese. All get along with it very well, though it is nearly as incomprehensible to my unaccustomed ear as the Chinese itself. The "Compradore," that is, the Chinese head business man of all foreign houses, who stands between the foreign merchant and the Chinese merchant in all matters of trade, always speaks Pidgen English. These Compradores, by the way, are great characters in China, and make much money outside of their regular business, and not exactly in its line. One of them, whom I saw in Shanghai, was a mandarin, and on extraordinary occasions he would turn up in his robes. The Chinese (Cantonese) servants, all over China, make the best servants in the world. They do the work of women as well as of men. They are most excellent cooks—the best of waiters—but it requires several of them to do what one American or English servant does in a house. Coolie (drudge man about house) will not wait. "It is not his 'pidgen.'" Waiter will not do coolie work, none of it, not in the least. Cook only cooks, but cooks as well as a Frenchman, and that is saying much in his favor. The butler, or head "boy" of a house, who is the universal genius of the house, and who has the capacity to do almost any thing, if he will—who acts as translator and supervisor of all the establishment, and whose "pidgen" it is to see and to keep every thing in order, is paid only from $7 to $12 per month, providing his own *chow chow* (food), and in all other respects taking care of himself. These servants often have little "larn pidgens" under them—that is, boys learning to speak "pidgen English," and to do what we call "chores." A Chinese kitchen, from which such good things are turned out for the table, is a wonder in its way. There is nothing in it but a cooking-stove or two, not longer than our American water-pail, with a few stew-pans, and many chop-sticks, from which few things come the many courses for the table, all well-cooked and garnished—nay, even the best of beefsteaks, so difficult to have cooked well at home. The more I go over the world the more I am convinced that Americans and Englishmen are far behind the rest of creation in preparing their food to be eaten. Our "civilization" in this is over a hundred years behind the age; and in this respect the Chinese are far our superiors. That devil's invention of ours, the kitchen range, ought to be kicked down where it came from, the lower regions—an invention which, in summer, roasts us out of our houses, and in winter consumes as much coal in a day as a Chinaman would need in a month, or a Frenchman in a week. Some rich man in America, some coming Peter Cooper, in lieu of teaching us how to draw, would do better to found a college to teach us how to boil potatoes, cook beafsteaks, roast mutton, and bake bread, for such a Peter Cooper would be the very greatest of American human benefactors. In lieu of giving $100,000 to Yale, or Harvard, or Princeton, to found a professorship of mineralogy, or geology, or other *ologies*, how much wiser would it be to give the $100,000 to establish a professorship for beafsteaks, or corn bread, roast beef, hog and hominy, etc. But—I am thinking of "home"—not in Hong Kong, now, I see. I am off to Canton.

# LETTER XXIX.

### *THINGS IN CANTON.*

What Canton is.—Its People, Streets, Sewers, etc., etc.—The Temples of Canton.—Sacred Hogs, Confucius and the Stalls.—Caging Students ambitious to be Mandarins.—Do Chinamen eat Cats, Dogs, and Rats?—The Manufactories of Canton.—The Silk Gauzes.—An Improvised Breakfast on a Pagoda.—No Beasts of Burthen in the City.—All Coolie Work.—A Sabbath in Canton.—Boat Life there.—Ducks and their Owners.—Gates and Police.—No Going Out Nights.—No Courting.—No Clubs.

CANTON, *September* 24, 1871.

WELL, I have never, never before seen exactly such a funny place as this is. If I had dropped into China this way first, I should have pronounced Canton to be a nasty, dirty hole, with streets so narrow that one could not move or breathe in them; but now, in contrast, I pronounce it to be New York (Fifth Avenue) and the surroundings, Boston, Philadelphia, Baltimore, Edinburgh—any thing, or any where, but Washington, which, if I am killed for it, I must say, in spring, and winter, and summer, looks very like Pekin, in its dirt, and dust, and mud. Canton is the Paris, as well as the Paradise of China. The streets are all paved (think of that for China!), instead of being full of mud holes, that you have to sound with a pole to see if it is safe to try to go over them. There are sewers under a good part of the great city;

and hence the smells are not frightful here as elsewhere. True, the streets are so narrow that no carriage can enter them, and two sedan chairs pass each other with difficulty, and the houses often overtop each other, across the streets, in order to keep out the sun; but this makes cooler streets in hot climates, though with less air. I often think, however, Chinamen have not our breathing apparatus, and do not need our air. Their lungs live on less; and where we should die, in the close streets of Canton, they seem to flourish, like the fungi, in the shade. There are eight hundred thousand people living in these streets, or in the boats on the river; and hence you can imagine the crowds that often must be in these narrow places. Whole strings of people, *en queue*, often form in the streets, to wait their chance to get along—the coolie with his two water tanks on a pole; the marketman with his greens and his onions; the merchant with his silks and satins, etc., etc. All classes wait with commendable patience, *en queue*, sometimes five hundred feet long, for the crowds to go by; and there is no pushing, no shoving, though an amount of bellowing that re-echoes from the hills about Canton as if a storm was roaring below.

Our party, in five sedan chairs, fifteen coolies to carry them, and the guide in advance, began the exploration of Canton. Didn't we make a "muss" in the streets! Didn't our train block up the narrow ways, stop trade and commerce, bother the marketmen, and the merchantmen, and all sorts of men!

And yet the Cantonese were patient to be kept ten or fifteen minutes, till our train could get by them. We filled up the Canton streets as a soldiers' procession or a funeral procession fills up Broadway; but there was no police to keep order, and we passed on only by the courtesy of the people.

We first "did" the temples; but I am weary to death of "doing" temples, and you would be wearier if I "*re*-did" them upon paper. Three, however, are worth a brief notice—HONAM, No. 1—and that, only because there is an artificial fish-pond on the grounds, and an eternal clatter of Buddhist priests praying all the time, and knocking their heads and noses on the floor, with an occasional priest burned up now and then, when dead, and a holy hog kept sacred to die of fat; the TEMPLE OF 500 GODS, No. 2, worth seeing only for the great number of gilt gods, and the odd-looking faces they have; and the TEMPLE OF CONFUCIUS, or Hall of Confucius, No. 3, well worth seeing, because every thing created and inspired by, or for, Confucius is all there is left of soul in China now. The Examination Hall—that is, the stalls and halls fitted up for the examination of the thousands of young men studying Confucius and Mencius, and the other sages of China, and thus aspiring to be mandarins—is also well worth a study. There are here about nine thousand stalls, in immense corridors—stalls about as big as horse mangers—where students are put, with only a pen, a paint brush rather, and paper, to write out themes given them, and kept there a day or two, with little or nothing to eat. Their essays, written on certain themes, are examined and commented upon by high mandarins, and the best scholars pass as fit for the Imperial offices, with tempting fields of promotion before them, if they win the prizes by well-written essays on the themes thus given. These nine thousand stalls are often all filled by the aspirants, who, when there thus shut up, go hard at work, without the least means of being aided by books or persons, and do the best they can. These examinations have been the life of the empire for hundreds and hundreds of years, and if corruption or favoritism do not control them, they may save China from foreign domination some years longer.

But more interesting, if not important, to me, was the great question, "*Do Chinamen really eat rats, cats, and dogs?*" Our guide took us to the markets to see. Sure enough, among beef and mutton, were dogs slung up by the hind legs on pegs; and cats, and rats, too! "Dogs," says the guide, in "pidgen English" "are very good!" The rich eat dogs as well as the poor. Dog meat thus is No. 1—first chop—while cat meat is No. 2, and rats, only for the poor. Mixed up with rice, and eaten with chop-sticks, the mess is said to be very good. I did not taste, nor try it,—though, who knows, when we were eating some of the nice, rich soup served us, that a rat may not have flavored it a little? Thus the fact was established in my mind that Chinamen *do* eat dogs, cats, and rats. We knew they ate almost every thing else.

Ducks' legs were for sale in the market—not ducks as a whole, but the legs, apart. Immense quantities of meat are sold, to flavor the rice dish; and the chop-sticks go from the rice to the grease, and from the grease to the rice, with a rapidity that astounds us, who try to make rice stick on these chop-sticks.

From temples to rats—what varied themes a traveller has to scribble of! From rats to workshops, now we went. The beautiful Canton gauzes we see, so aerial in a hot clime—the silks, the crapes, the shawls, the fringes—all are woven by the poorest people, in the dirtiest holes, and by the ugliest looms. It was almost impossible to wriggle in, among these looms, so as to understand well their work; but the principle of these looms is very like that in the looms of our New England great-grandmothers. The shuttle is the same, and the wool and the warp are the same in principle—the power applied a little differently. There, for almost nothing, work and toil these weavers, weaving their lives out to give the world luxuries they never themselves enjoy. The lacquer shops, where the pretty Canton tables and screens are made, were also visited—the carpenter shops, the china shops, etc., etc. And Canton is a large manufacturing city, living on manufactured work, more especially, though, on its chinaware and silks. There are great shops here, with rich merchants over them, who do a big business with the whole world. The Sèvres ware, the ware of Dresden and of Bohemia, and much of the ware of England, are now far superior to Chinese work; but all was learned from the Chinese, and the world even yet comes here to buy the original things. Here is the land of the fire-crackers, and here one eternal "4th of July" is kept up, in one everlasting "snap," "snap." I should never weary of shopping in Canton—(Paris in its palmy days was not fuller of pretty shops)—if I only had Sycee enough to buy a little of every thing. One could exhaust a little fortune in fans and ivory work. The jewelry, some of it, especially the fretted work, is not to be laughed at. One's eyes, especially if the eyes be woman eyes, water over the pretty bracelet and ear-ring work, carved from crane's beaks, and set well in fretted gold. But Europe has caught up with China, and Geneva now does this work better, and Vienna too, where fans are painted to be prettier than in China. The Chinese manufacturer stands still where he was hundreds of years gone by, while the European and American go ahead and ahead, and never stop "progressing."

But one must eat, alas, as well as see; and to show you how things are done in Canton, let me add here, we "breakfasted"—that is, had "tiffin," second breakfast—three or four miles from "home," on the heights of a five-storied pagoda, where the city was at our feet, and the country, if graveyards can be a country, behind us. Kwan-Yin-Shan is the Chinese name of our breakfast pagoda. What I call attention to, is the skill with which Chinamen will improvise you a meal anywhere. In the baskets of coolies, strung on poles over their backs, and through the narrowest streets, were conveyed to the tip-top story of this pagoda, the finest of crockery, the choicest of meats and wines — nothing broken, and all served up with skill and care. Thus you breakfast or dine almost anywhere, for your meals will follow you. You can sup on the river, and live luxuriantly in the house-boat, or breakfast, as we did, overlooking Canton, and enjoy the breezes of the country, unobstructed by houses or buildings.

Nothing more impresses a man in all China than the power of men to do business without beasts of burthen or vehicles of any kind. A coolie does not cost half so much to keep as a horse, or an ass, and will live and thrive on what a horse would not touch. There is not a cart in all this great city! There is not a road or a street for horses! Every thing goes on men's shoulders, or backs, or heads. The huge block of granite is taken up, and taken off, by six, or eight, or ten, or more, coolies, with poles. The hogshead from abroad goes on the shoulders of four coolies—that is, upon their bamboo poles. All the loading and unloading of junks is done by coolies with their poles. All the commerce and all the trade of these tens of thousands of people are done on poles, on men's backs. Hence, these coolies become wonderfully muscular. Their shoulders must be as tough as cast-iron, and the muscles of their legs as firm as a boxer's arms. There are no springless carts down here, as in Pekin—no wheelbarrows, as in Shanghai—only the sedan, for the transportation of passengers, and a most luxurious vehicle it is to be carried about in.

It is the Sabbath, and I go to hear Archdeacon Grey preach and pray for the royal family of England, in the very pretty little Episcopal Church, built in the foreign settlement of Shamien. As all foreigners here shut up shop on Sunday, the Chinaman, especially the servant, begins to comprehend our one Sunday, in lieu of the three hundred and sixty-five the Chinese have, or have not, every day in the year. Archdeacon Grey preached only to some forty of us (there are now not over one hundred foreigners in all Canton, so much has Hong Kong killed off the foreign trade of the city), but Archdeacon Grey has been in China now some twenty-five years, and has caught up, or been infected by, the rhetoric of China. I could not understand half what he said—nothing, when he was eloquent, and "eloquence," you know, is often the death of all sense. The Shamien settlement of Canton is the beautiful spot of the city. The houses are almost all palaces, the walks and gardens as useful and as pretty as taste and climate can make them. Shamien was built up by the English and French Governments from a mud-flat island, and the filling of it up cost some $325,000. All the merchants left in Canton are now there, except the two American houses of Smith, Archer & Co. and of Russell & Co., who have built upon the old original

Factory site, associated now with so much of Chinese Canton history.

The boat-life of Canton is "very peculiar." Thousands and thousands live on the river. What they do for a living I could not well find out, for there is not enough boating or ferrying "to pay," nor enough fish in the water to feed them. True, the ground-rent and the house-hire are nothing—and the wharf-rats, and cats, and dogs may supply the meat—but who will supply the rice? Nevertheless, these thousands live, and seem to thrive, and certainly look happy. Canton, however, is the happiest-looking city I have seen in China, and everywhere, the people seem ready for fun. Children are born in the boats, and live all their lives in the boats—and the mother of them often rows, or sculls, with a child strapped on her back. Upon some of these children are tied bamboo floats, so that, if the darling tumbles overboard, it is easily fished up and in. On these boats, too, they raise ducks and chickens; the ducks are sent out in the morning to feed in the marshes round Canton, and, just before sunset, the man who has charge of them blows a shrill whistle, and the ducks come hurrying from all directions by the hundreds. It is wonderful to see them separate, each duck going for its own boat, and the owner counts them as they enter (calls the roll); the last one is always taken up and beaten for being the *last*, and the next night they tell me, that that last duck is invariably the first. Then there are grand boat restaurants, where parties go, as to Delmonico's, to feast free from the dead air of the narrow streets, and enjoying the free air of the river. These restaurant boats are gorgeously fitted up with lanterns and with gilded adornments of many kinds, and they give the visitor the best the market affords, not excepting even the dogs. I think if I had to live in Canton, I should prefer the free air of the river to the close air of the streets. At night the river is gayer than the city, for the gates of the city—gates by the score within the great wall-gates of the city—obstruct all night locomotion, while the river is open and free. I loved to revel in a house-boat at night, breathe the free air, hear the squeaking guitar of the Chinaman, see his fire-crackers, peep into his restaurants, hear his babies squall, and the mothers and fathers snore. If you do not admire my taste for music, reader, you will enjoy the variety I had, will you not? In the streets of Canton you will see, every afternoon just before sunset, groups of Chinamen, seated on the highest points they can find, in order to catch the evening breeze, all of them with twigs in their hands, and pet birds perched thereon. You wonder why the birds do not fly away, but, on examining, you find they have a piece of cord tied round the leg and then fastened to the twig, allowing the birds to fly only three or four feet. Canton city is divided, by its streets, into hundreds of compartments at night, and in, or over each compartment is a gate, closed at night. For order and peace every little community within these gates is responsible to the authorities, for there is no local police. The system is somewhat like the old English system of the Chiltern Hundreds, and which it was proposed to introduce into the Ku-Klux Bill for the benefit of the South. It works in Canton well, or ill (?)—shuts up the shops at dark, sends people to bed early, preparing them thus to rise early in the morning, stops all night gadding, all theatre going, all soirees and evening parties, all courting and billing and cooing, brings home husband early at night, and keeps him from then straying off.* There is a river police, which cruises about the river at night, and bangs into you, if you do not sail straight.

I might scribble pages and pages upon these droll, these extraordinary Cantonese; but I must stop to tell you how I got up here, and how go I back—in American river-steamers, with American captains—boats reminding one of the North River navigation—fare $5 for ninety miles—but fifty cents for a lower deck Chinaman, and one hundred cents for an upper decker. The Bocca Tigris—that is, the mouth of the river, where the Chinese once had forts which they thought would bite like the mouth of a tiger—has not a soldier there now, and the British, French, and Americans, in years gone by, knocked the fortifications all to pieces. Whampoa, its pagodas, the shipping there (not much now) the cane-fields, the lychee-nut tree, the orange groves, the very many other (to me) unknown strange fruits, would be themes to fill letters, if I were writing a book—but I am on the wing now, and so must say "adieu" for the nonce.

## LETTER XXX.

#### THOUGHTS ON THE CHINA SEAS.

The Imitative Powers of the Chinese.—Their Love of Money.—Population of China over-estimated.—Pisciculture in Canton.—Chinese Dialects.—War Talk.—Superstitions of the Ignorant.—Singapore.—The Malay Divers.—Foreign Commerce.—The Census.—The Jungle.—Agriculture, etc., etc.

Off Cochin China and Siam, and on the
China Sea, *October* 4, 1871.

AFLOAT as I now am, I have leisure to recall some of my Chinese and Japanese reflections, and I am availing myself of it, in the British steamer Orissa, one of the P. & O.'s, as they call the line of the Peninsular and Oriental Steamship Company, which has now some sixty steamers afloat here, and on the Mediterranean—(fare, by the way, from Hong Kong to Brindisi, in Italy, the mail line, now about $450).

The Chinese impress the traveller deeply by their great imitative powers, powers of endurance, and wonderful industry. No people work harder, not even the universal Yankee nation. Their love of money is beyond what any other people seem to have, and they are willing to work for it. Very few nations could stand up in competition with them, if they had an American education and American training. As mechanics they are capable of any thing. Then, they can live on little or nothing—on vegetables almost altogether;—and their clothes cost little or nothing. Nevertheless, England, Germany, and America largely find them in these clothes—for, as I have written before, the spinning-jenny does not eat at all, or need clothes, and the Chinaman must have something of both. Luxury seems to be forbidden in China. Even the rich do not indulge in it, and it is hard to tell, by any outward sign, the rich, from the poor man, either in his exterior or in his dwelling.

But the Japanese are by far the most interesting people. They have not the solidity or stability of the Chinese, but they are a far more interesting people, and learn faster and more cheerfully than the Chinese, of all that is new, and of all that progress, the great outside world is making. Both their agriculture and manufactures seem to me quite superior to the Chinese. China is not near as well cultivated as I expected to see it, while in Japan, in most parts, agriculture is carried to a very high degree of perfection. There must be more people to the square mile in Japan than in China, and the farms must supply more food for the population. The population of China must be over-estimated by 100,000,000. There cannot be 400,000,000 of people there; and I doubt if there are 300,000,000. Pekin has no two millions of people in it, as some say—nay, not one million—while Canton must be much the most populous place. But, in many parts of China, the struggle for life, or to live, seems greater than in Japan. I omitted to state to you from Canton, as a specimen of life or living, how fresh fish were artificially raised in the artificial ponds, in, and about Canton, and how the surplus are sent to Hong Kong, by steamer, in huge fish-tubs, filled with fish and fresh water, and aerated by coolies as the steamer goes; and how, when these fish reach Hong Kong, they are "dumped out" into fresh-water boats, waiting for them, and thus kept for market—mainly for the Chinese, though, for Europeans do not relish them.

The Chinese labor under immense difficulties in their progress and civilization, from their language alone, to say nothing of their pride, vanity, and self-confidence, which teach them, yet, that no other people know half as much as they do. Their dialects prevent any real unity of the great empire, for the Northern people cannot understand the Southern people, and *vice versa*. What a Pekinese says is unintelligible to the Cantonese; and one province near by often, only with great difficulty, can understand the people of another. Where such diversities of tongues exist, it is the mandarin of the province that governs, rather than Pekin, the head of the empire; and these diversities are not likely to be done away for years and years, save through the agencies of railroads and the telegraph, which the mandarins are now disinclined to have.

All over China, among the Europeans and Americans, "war," imminent war, with China seems to be pending, judging only by what I hear them say.

I could not see any real causes, however, for this apprehension, and the diplomats in Pekin do not believe in it; but war may come, and come very unexpectedly, perhaps, if the superstitions of the Chinese are played upon by the more intelligent Chinamen—the third- and fourth-rate mandarins—as they have been played upon this summer in many parts of China. Thousands of the ignorant Chinese have been taught to believe that foreigners carry "pills" about them to poison the wells, and that the missionaries, especially the Roman Catholic missionaries, are engaged in kidnapping Chinese children. The Pekin government knows better than all this, and discourages all such talk; but the lower mandarins of the provinces often keep up these fancies and falsehoods, in order the better to have control of the ignorant people. Nevertheless, in China there is almost universal reading and writing, and that degree of intelligence which comes from these two "R's," and which, I think I have written you before, I do not deem to be education.

But I am now steaming far away from China and Japan, and going among another people—to India, to see the original Indians, and how their British masters govern them. Here afloat, then, I will but sketch of what I am now passing and seeing. To my right is Cochin China and Siam, the land of elephants, and tigers, and leopards, etc.; and on my left, are the Philippine Islands of Spain, and Borneo, British and Dutch, native, in part, and the rich Dutch island of Java—a gold mine to the King of the Netherlands, as Cuba was to Spain before the rebellion. The poor Portuguese who, after the Arabs, first discovered the East, seem now to have little or nothing left here, except Macao and Goa, while John Bull has gobbled up all, except Java and Sumatra (Dutch), and the Philippine Islands (Spanish).

. . . . . .

SINGAPORE, *October* 7.

We are just entering the British city of Singapore, 1,437 miles from Hong Kong, having made the voyage from a Friday to a Saturday the week after. As we enter, our first novelty is the Malay divers, who, in little boats, are swarming about our steamer, and diving after every sixpence or penny we throw overboard—sure to get them, too, before they reach bottom. They are the most wonderful swimmers and divers I ever saw, and one cannot help emptying one's pockets to see them dive after the coin. These swarms of swimmers seem to fill the water all around us, and their cries and clamors and intent earnestness in watching the passengers as they throw over their coins, can hardly be described, so furious and wild are they in their screams and cries.

Singapore is only a degree and a half from the equator, and hence we have here all the tropical productions—with fruits whose very names are unknown to us in America. The vegetation is all new to me, for I have never before been so near the equator; and hence I feel all the enthusiasm, and am inspired with all that wonder new-comers in the tropics feel. The place itself is beautiful; and the hotel where I am now, "the Europe," immense in its extension (but only two stories high), with all "the entertainments" a traveller could desire. Singapore is the seat of government for "the Straits Settlement," which includes Singapore, Penang, and Malacca, with its Governor and Chief-Justice, a British garrison, and all the other appurtenances of a British colony. There is here a beautiful Episcopal church, a Catholic church also, and the Presbyterians have a place of worship near by. As a free port, it is the *entrepôt* of merchandise from all quarters hereabout —of spices, of pepper, of nutmegs, of sago, of rattan, tapioca, etc., etc. There are two American agents here, who do an immense business for the United States, almost as much as all the English merchants do, taken altogether. Nearly all our rattans come from Singapore.

The "Straits Settlement" is a British colony here, of which Singapore is the capital. The census reports 306,776 inhabitants, but from all parts of Europe only 1,592, about one in 200 of the whole. These are:

| | |
|---|---|
| Malays | 147,684 |
| Chinese | 114,130 |
| Klings | 20,125 |
| All other Easterners | 23,245 |
| | 305,184 |

The three settlements are Singapore, Penang, and Malacca. The country all about is jungle—wilderness—full of tigers, and leopards, and other wild beasts; and we were told we should see them from the shores, swimming to our ship, but none have been so bold. This jungle is cleared by the Chinese, only by the Chinese—the Malays and Klings refusing to be much else than boatmen, fishermen, sailors, huntsmen, etc. The Chinese are, in the main, the only farmers; and the emigration here from China, encouraged by the British Government, is very great. Anon they "will make the wilderness blossom like the rose," while the Malays would never clear the land.

The cultivation in, and around Singapore is beautiful. All the equatorial productions abound in one eternal summer, with ever-constant rains. The sea breezes, however, temper all here, and make it a very habitable place. I visited the rich gardens of a Chinaman—Whampoa's, I think—in which, even more than in China, with greater opportunities in these tropical latitudes, were the peculiar tastes of the Chinese gardeners displayed; but their gardens, of which this is one of the best, if not the very best, are not to be compared with the landscape gardening of England and of the United States. Here we saw the pineapple, the cocoanut, bread-fruit, the orange, mango, jackfruit, mangosteen, custard-apple, coffee, chocolate, nutmeg, clove, cassia, etc. One boast of Whampoa, in his garden, is his hogs in their sties; and I must admit, none bigger or better are ever raised in any part of the United States.

# LETTER XXXI.

### *FROM CEYLON AND THE BAY OF BENGAL.*

England, Continuous England.—The Steamer Congregation in Ceylon.—A Grand Oriental Hotel.—Buddhism born here.—Sapphires, Rubies, and Pearls.—The Cingalese great Cheats.—A Monkey Story.—Curious Boats and Boatmen in Galle.—Men here mistaken for Women, and *vice versa*.—Madras, and Things there.—The Latin Races here crowded off by the Anglo-Saxon.—Englishmen here patronize the Shastra and the Veda, as well as the Bible.—Their Race kept distinct.—A Handful of Englishmen governing a World.—Juggling in Madras.—Golconda and Juggernaut.—Cyclones and the Church at Sea.—Hymns, etc.

ISLE OF CEYLON, POINT DE GALLE<br>
(THE COCK'S SPUR), *October* 15, 1871.

MORE British dominion! The everlasting English flag! From Hong Kong to this Ceylon is three thousand and thirty-one miles, and yet, almost all the way, it is "England," "England," "England!" The Dutch were cleared out of Malacca, and of this rich island of Ceylon, and here we are, now, in an extended England! Far beyond us here, and yet *en route* to England, are Australia and New Zealand—Melbourne four thousand six hundred and seventy miles off, and Tasmania and New Zealand further still! Here, once a month, five great British mail steamers meet—one from China, another from Australia, another yet from Suez and England, another from Bombay, and one more from Calcutta. The Point de Galle, every two weeks, is a busy place, when four steamers meet; but once a month, when Australia and New Zealand come in, it becomes a veritable watering-place, where crowds meet from all parts of the earth.

I am at the Oriental Hotel, landed this morning, and just fresh from the English church, where, including the British military, were some five hundred people, or more—the men all, or almost all, in linen, and the ladies in the showiest robes of summer. There is a Catholic church here, a Presbyterian also; but the island is the great fount of Buddhism, from whence it was mainly propagated into Japan and China. The Oriental Hotel now—which would do credit to Newport or Long Branch—is, on its porticos, a grand bazaar, Sunday though it is. Rubies, and sapphires, and pearls, glitter before our eyes, and chains and bracelets of tortoise work, too—with Ceylon laces of the Maltese style, quite tempting to ladies' eyes. The island of Ceylon is the headquarters of the pearl fishery, and rubies and sapphires abound in its mountains. When we remember, now, what the poets say of its spices (the odor of which they would cheat us into the belief we could snuff a hundred miles off), and of its oranges, and cinnamons, and lemons, and cocoas, and palms, and coffee, we see what a rich island it is—what a jewel in the crown of England! But these rubies, these sapphires, these pearls, it is almost impossible to buy here—for the Ceylon shopmen and hawkers are such abominable liars and cheats, that it is next to the impossible to trade with them. They start with demanding twenty pounds sterling for a ruby or pearl ring, and they may not refuse a rupee for it (fifty cents), if you venture to offer it to them. Ruby rings of glass and brass are made in Birmingham to sell here; and they are so mixed up with the real sapphires and rubies, that only a jeweller by trade can tell one from the other. And how these hawkers and shopmen on the porticos of the great hotel persecute you! No matter with whom you are talking, or what you are doing, they thrust their shell-work, and rubies, and sapphires, and laces, into your very eyes, and pertinaciously insist upon your making some bid to buy. One fellow so tormented me with a monkey, for which he wanted "only ten rupees," that, to get rid of him, and to keep his monkey out of my eyes, I offered him a single rupee, whereupon he jumped at the offer, and I had a monkey on my hands, ten thousand miles from home! The steamers do not take monkeys, even as Malay steerage passengers, and so I had to give him away, doubtless to be sold again. Birds of the loveliest hues and the sweetest plumage were for sale, also; and leopard skins, and tiger skins, and almost every other tropical thing, on the grand bazaar. We had some young Siamese passengers, on their way from Siam to be educated in England, with more money than brains, who bought a little of most every thing, until their hands became as thickly covered with rings as if the rings were a shield.

Every new country we go to seems to have its peculiarities in boats, and carriages, or other modes of conveyances. Galle is an open port, but feebly protected from the winds, and upon its rocky sides the surf furiously beats. The boatmen have here, arranged for this sea and this surf, long canoes, like our log dugouts, which they steady in the seas with a heavy outrigger, hanging over and into the water, beyond the reach of their oars. If the gale is heavy in full sail, they put out a man or two to sit on the outrigger, and as the breeze demands one man, or two, they call it a *one-man*, or a *two-man* breeze. These canoes ride over and through the surf with very little difficulty.

Another peculiarity of this island is, that the men wear shell-combs in their hair, and the women do not, while the dress of both is so much alike, that, in consequence of the combs, the traveller is ever mistaking the man for the woman, and the woman for the man. But the race, be it man or woman, seems bright. Their climate needs but little food, save what grows on the cocoa, the bread, or the orange tree, little or no clothes; and the consequence is, that the main work done is to be done by coolies from India, or Chinamen from China. The British Government here have regiments of native Ceylon "rifles," who, with a few European troops, keep all in order. The climate seems healthy on the seacoast and hills; and, judging by a drive into the country, with a view from a hill, the scenery must all be beautiful.

. . . . .

MADRAS, *October* 21, 1871.

In the British P. & O. steamer, the Golconda, from Suez and Aden, *via* Galle, we embarked on the 19th for Calcutta, *via* Madras, where we tarry some hours, only to let out British goods in bales. Madras is the seat of government of the Madras (British) Presidency, over which Lord Napier, some fifteen or twenty years ago the British Minister in Washington, now reigns. His lordship is reported to be as great a beau here as he was in Washington, when a younger man—a great favorite with the ladies, and, of course, not so great a favorite with the men. The Government House, or Palace, here, and the public gardens around, are sumptuously kept up; but there is nothing in the place to see, except the European residences on the coast. There are a quarter of a million of people in the city, and it is as hot just now as hot can be, and the fashionable people have not yet come down from " the hills," to their houses on the coast. This coast, by the way, is bad, very bad, and, in this cyclonic season, perilous. The roadstead is all open to the sea, and the winds pour in a surge and surf that only native boats, manned by some twenty or twenty-five native men, can manage to ride over—and this, too, in boats not nailed, but sewed together, so that their seams accommodate their motions to the surf!

This part of India—the Bay of Bengal side, and the other, the Arabian, or Indian sea side—is the first part the Europeans got hold of, after the Arabs led the way from the Red Sea. First, came the Portuguese, with their settlements; then, the Spanish; then, the Dutch, French, and English—all now lost to the Continental nations, except Pondicherry (French), on this side, and Goa (Portuguese), on the other. One asks, and keeps asking, Why have the great Portuguese and the yet greater Spanish, been almost extinguished in the East, while the British flag rules and reigns, here, there, and everywhere? Many say, " because of the Roman Catholic religion!" Nonsense. The Dutch have not been Roman Catholics, and they have nothing left but Java and Sumatra. The English here are, in religion, Roman Catholics, Hindoos, Mohammedans, Buddhists, Parsees, any thing and every thing, to keep power. They patronize, uphold, and vindicate gods of all sorts, from Vishnu to Buddha, for the sake of mammon. The Veda and Shastras are as good as the Bible to them, if as well bound in gold. In my judgment, the true secret of British power here is the Anglo-Saxon inveterate, incurable, indomitable conviction that the white man is the intellectual superior of the red man, or black man, and was created by God to be his superior. This is not Exeter-Hall preaching, I know, which has been transferred to the conventicles of the United States, but it *is* the conviction of the Englishman here, and the CONVICTION and ACTION on which he governs with a rod of iron, though a very malleable and tender rod, his 200,000,000 of Eastern subjects. The Portuguese, and the Spanish, and the French, and the Dutch, to some, though a lesser extent, attempted government in India upon the different principle of equality and fraternity, and consequent amalgamation, while the Englishman has preserved his caste and his race. Just what is the story in Mexico and other Spanish American states, is the story here—half breeds, quarter breeds, all sorts of breeds of Portuguese, Spanish, and French, and hence, consequent degradation of the race, and loss of empire—while the Briton inflexibly maintains the superiority and mastery of his race, and hence has extended his empire, almost in the lifetime of many, from Madras and the Malabar coast, far, far beyond the Ganges and the Indus,—to the Himalaya Mountains on one side, and to the Persian Empire on the other—from Australia and New Zealand—from the equator, south, to thirty-five or forty degrees north. The merest handful of Englishmen here are governing a world, far, far beyond the wildest dreams of Alexander the Great, or of Julius, or Augustus Cæsar.

But, how one wanders off! I forget I am on board ship, buying new Indian native puzzles for a few cents, to take home to puzzle Americans, or looking at native jugglers, who bring snakes (the poisonous cobra) on board ship, to hug and to kiss, and to tease to make them swell up and look terrible! I forget I am seeing sticks and swords thrust down men's throats, and mango-trees made to grow—*lo presto!*—on board ship, as a little water is sprinkled upon the dry sand in a basket, where we see the seed put in. What a world of brains must have been wasted upon these magpie jugglers, to enable them to cheat us so! And then they are nearly naked. An *anna* (three cents) abundantly pays them for swallowing a sword, or spouting out fire and smoke from their nostrils. And such is the greed to earn the *annas*, or to make the sales of puzzles, and baskets, and embroideries, and tiger slippers for men, that the quartermaster of the steamer has to stand with a huge lash, laying it on the backs of these magpies and monkeys, to thump them off the chains and rigging of the ship, that, otherwise, they would cover like flies.

The "Golconda" is soon to go by the poetic mines of Golconda (all over now), and by the land of the car of the Juggernaut—the car yet going, but no more fools going under its crushing wheels, there to be ground into glory. English government has got rid of some crimes in India—such as the victimization of this Juggernaut car, such as the *suttee*, the self-burning of the widows to follow their fresh dead husbands to the hereafter,—the awful Thugs, and the filling of the Ganges with corpses. We have a pleasant set of passengers on board this Golconda, the most of whom, now, are Calcuttians, merchants and officials, some with their families who have been down to Galle to breathe the sea air, or to the Neilgerry hills, in Madras. We read all the histories and novels we can get —the latter, especially—and they dance (the Virginia reel, even, here), and they have concerts, and sing John Brown, away off here—(with a *gusto*, too, and as if in compliment to me)—whose (Brown's) poor, dead "soul," if it was " to march on " in British India as it "marched on," for five or six years, in America, would not leave a Briton alive to sing or to dance at all. And we have service on the Sabbath, from a clergyman on his way, with his new wife, to be settled somewhere, he knows not where, in India. Thus, on a threatening sea, as we are now, and on a coast, this month very perilous from the cyclone, a hymn like this, sung by many voices, touched all our hearts:

> Eternal Father, strong to save,
> Whose arm hath bound the restless wave,
> Who bidst the mighty ocean deep
> Its own appointed limits keep,
>     O hear us, when we cry to Thee
>     For those in peril on the sea.
>
> O Christ, whose voice the waters heard,
> And hushed their raging at Thy word,
> Who walkest on the foaming deep,
> And calm amidst its rage did sleep,
>     O hear us, when we cry to Thee
>     For those in peril on the sea.
>
> Most Holy Spirit, who didst brood
> Upon the chaos dark and rude,
> And bidst the angry tumult cease,
> And give, for wild confusion, peace,
>     O hear us when we cry to Thee
>     For those in peril on the sea.
>
> O Trinity of love and power,
> Our brethren shield in danger's hour
> From rock and tempest, fire and foe,
> Protect them wheresoe'er they go,
>     Thus evermore shall rise to Thee
>     Glad hymns of praise from land and sea.
>                     Amen.

## LETTER XXXII.

### *BRITISH INDIA.*

England Forever and Ever—200,000,000 British Subjects—Standing Army of 320,000 Soldiers.—Vast Imports and Exports.—East Indians.—Monkeys or Men.—Trade and Commerce of India.—The Holy Ganges.—English Water-Works on it.—Calcutta no longer the " Black Hole "—Hot, not Unhealthy.—The Punkah Fan the Great Institution of India.—The Punkah Everywhere.—Tudor and His Ice the Great Things of the East.—The Hancocks, the Websters, Nothing.—The Tudor Every Thing.—Wenham Something.—Boston Nothing.—The Hoogley River and the Cyclones.—Enchanting Approach to Calcutta.—The King of Oude.—A Seventeen Days' Hindoo Holiday in Calcutta.—Polygamy and Polyandry.—Hindooism, Buddhism, Brahminism and Mohammedanism.—The 320,000 Standing Army Government of India not a Bad One.

CALCUTTA, *October* 27, 1871

ENGLAND, once more, one everlasting England! That little sea-girt island has not only girdled the great isles of the world, and put its stamp upon them, but, here am I, in the portals of a British East India Empire, the very magnitude of which is astounding. Think of it, over 200,000,000 of people, native and British in this Indian Government proper, under the British flag! Satiated with the very vastness of dominion here, the British Crown declines more land, and farther or fresher conquests! It has got all the land, and all the population it wants—nay, more, too, and refuses, actually, to be bothered with yet more! Think of the revenues and expenditures of this British Indian Empire, $260,000,000 of our money, incoming and outgoing, each. Think of its immense army,

320,000 soldiers in all, of whom 70,000 are European, the others, Indians, under British officers, all! Think of a Christian government over 110,000,000 of Hindoos, 25,000,000 of Mussulmans, 12,000,000 of Aboriginal Nothingarians, 3,000,000 of Buddhists, etc., etc. What a medley of humanity to rule! What a mixture of laws, as well as of creeds, and of tongues, and languages! (There are sixteen, or more, languages here, that a British ruler ought to learn.) What a vast trade, some $250,000,000 of imports, and over $500,000,000 of exports! The little England at home, which governs all this vast territory, and these millions of people, dwindles, herself, into insignificance, when contrasted with this, her mighty Empire of the East.

But what a population! When I first began to hear and see the Indians of the East, in Singapore, or in Ceylon, as well as here, rushing about like madmen, in boats, around our ship, I could not but cry out, "How like monkeys! What monkeys! Have they immortal souls?" "Yes," said a good English lady by me, "all of them, souls to be saved, or lost, as well as yours!" Doubtless, it is so; but, nevertheless, as first seen on the shore, "What monkeys!" "What wild monkeys!" How different from the sober, sedate, grand, dignified Chinese, and how like monkeys! Rapid conclusions are, however, always perilous; and no nation should be judged by its boatmen or watercraft men; and, therefore, already I begin to see India is not a nation of monkeys, but of men, real live men, and men with souls, too, if they do believe in any thing and every thing, in religion, that we laugh at, only, or pity.

The British Indian Government is in Presidencies, with a governor in each, and a governor-general and council over all. This governor-general has a salary of over $100,000 per annum, and lives and moves in royal style, to astonish and astound the Indians, if not the Britons. Calcutta is the seat of government in coolish weather, from November to March, and Simla, on the Himalaya range of mountains, the headquarters of the government, during the rest of the year. Some of the sources of revenue to support this government are from—

| | |
|---|---|
| Opium | $40,000,000 |
| Salt (a monopoly) | 30,000,000 |
| Land | 108,000,000 |
| Customs | 12,000,000 |

EXPENDITURES.

| | |
|---|---|
| Interest on Debt | $14,000,000 |
| Army | 64,000,000 |
| Public Works (1870) | 33,000,000 |

The government has over 5,000 miles of railroads in operation, on which it guarantees five per cent. interest to the corporators; and the huge army of 320,000 is supported by only sixty-four millions, because the native soldiers receive only $3 50 or $4 00 per month, *feeding themselves and their families* out of that miserable pay, and almost altogether on rice.

Well, I am on the waters of the Ganges, the holy

Ganges (the Jordan of the Hindoos), to be buried in which is a sure passport to glory! If glory is yellow like gold, the Ganges, then, is glorious—that is, yellow, muddy, dirty. The heathen English here (think of it) pump this holy water into reservoirs (some miles above this city), and draw it off in pipes, and filter, and drink it, and use it for all sorts of unholy, as well as holy purposes. They have issued terrible paper edicts against throwing Hindoo dead or dying bodies into it, on their way to glory; but, nevertheless, the dying as well as the dead Hindoo is yet dumped into it, and a police corps has to be kept, especially, to sink the dead Hindoo, when his corpse pops up above the water. There was a terrible commotion, at first, among the Hindoos, when the English first began these water-works, and not a Hindoo then would touch, taste, or handle the desecrated waters; but some high and lofty priest was tempted to say, the Hindoo god would overlook the desecration, and now the Hindoos use it just like other people. Of course, the city is made far healthier by this use of good water, and the sewers carry off the impurities that once fostered and created the terrible cholera, and yet alarming diarrhœa. Calcutta is no longer the "black hole." Caucasians live in it, the whole year round, jolly and hearty; and, though their livers do suffer occasionally, they say, nevertheless, they live, eat, and drink here as elsewhere—though, in the drinking of claret, soda-water, Bass's beer, etc., the population, in proportion, consume more, probably, than any other people.

Every country or state has its "institutions." We have ours in the United States—*peculiar* institutions; but *the* institution here is the punkah. What is the punkah? you ask, perhaps. Well, it is the great blower of India—the institution of the blow-out. *We* fan in America. *They* fan in Japan and China; but here, the punkah, the everlasting punkah, the spread-out, oblong, parallelogram fan, moved by coolie power only, fans you, night and day. You wake up under the fan; you rise under the fan; you breakfast and dine under the fan, and you go to sleep under the fan. There is an everlasting breeze kept up over you by some invisible coolie, hid away, in some hole, somewhere. The coolie pulls the fan for two or three dollars per month, and finds himself, and clothes himself—that is, in a clout, which costs him about twenty-five cents the year. I thought, here, of suggesting to some acute Yankee the invention of some pendulum, or self-moving artificial power, to pull the punkah, that would do away with the coolie, and send him to the country to raise indigo, or linseed, or jute; but the coolie here is cheaper than wood, and no pendulum clock invention, even from Connecticut, could compete with this cheap coolie power. Nevertheless, the punkah here is an indispensable institution. I am writing now under a glorious breeze—the artificial zephyr of the punkah, but for which I should be on the sofa, puffing, panting, and struggling for breath.

There is another "institution" here — a great American institution—that is, ICE. It is not so cheap as the punkah, for it comes all the way from Boston; but, to a Caucasian, here, it is about as indispensable. The Tudor Ice Company supplies nearly the whole East with ice "from Wenham Lake," here, they say; and Wenham Lake, therefore, is better known in India than Lake Michigan or Lake Ontario. While Winnipiseogee is unknown, Wenham, dear Wenham, is cherished, and blessed, and embraced, and kissed with a fervor, here, no woman's lips ever felt, frigid as is ice. Nearly all that is known in many parts of the East, is Wenham, dear Wenham. The Quincys, the Otises, the Websters, the Everetts of Massachusetts, are all unknown; but Wenham is illustrious—such is fame! Tudor, too, towers on turrets far loftier than Bunker Hill; and where Warren never was dreamed of, Tudor stands out as the bright Northern Star! Great is Tudor in the East.

We Americans meet with some rough misconceptions of us now and then, among ignorant Europeans —not many, however, for our flag, in days gone by (not now), spread our name and fame far and wide in the East. Once American ships "did" one-half or three-fourths of the freighting of the commerce of Calcutta; but, alas! not now, did I see an American flag on the Hoogley. Once we carried cotton, and rice, and indigo to England. At one time, this Eastern coasting trade was largely in our hands. Alas, not now! The misconceptions I allude to come of our "ice," and because we hail from a once copper-colored Indian country, supposed to be like this.

Some few, very few, yet think we are red, like these East Indians. More are sure, we are come from a Greenland, or a Norway, or Spitzbergen, because of our ice. Ice could now be had as cheap from the Himalaya ranges, by rail, as from Boston, or, from Hakodadi, in Japan, or, from the Peiho River, China —save the return freights to America, which here are profitable. Our only exports for India now are ice and petroleum, while once the fabrics of our looms came into competition with those of England.

But, before I run on much further, I ought to introduce you to Calcutta, the metropolis of the 200,000,000 British-governed people, I have written of. We did not enter the portals of Calcutta with first impressions very captivating. A cyclone, or something like it, kept us in the lower waters of the Hoogley River, a branch of the Ganges, and nearly one hundred miles from Calcutta, from a Monday till a Friday. The pilot did not dare take our steamer up the Hoogley—*ugly*, we then pronounced the stream. The rain poured down as if all the heavens were let loose, and the winds blew, as if they really would crack their cheeks. This is customary weather, this time of year, when the Southern monsoon has a fight with the Northern monsoon for the mastery of the winds, in which, of course, just now, the Southerner was whipped. But, thanks to our good fortune, we had no cyclone. I have dodged both typhoons and cyclones thus far, in the East, and feel now quite secure of not being tossed up in the air, or swashed over in a mountain wave, by either of them. The season for such freaks, out here, is now about over. An interesting island, called Saugor, with only a lighthouse on it, and *that* stockaded to keep out the tigers, was all, for four days, that we had to look at! It is an island of jungle, so inhospitable, and so full of wild beasts, that not even an Indian will live on it. Several British vessels, and some craft from the Maldive Islands, were anchored near us, and steam-tugs from Calcutta were inviting them, in the calmer hours, to be towed up. Saugor, however, and the tigers of Saugor, and the rain and gale ended at last, and the sun broke forth, if in all its splendor, in all its fury, too. Thick sea clothes were laid aside, and felt hats, and out came the pith-head umbrella coverings, called hats, and linen and grass cloth. As the steamer ascended the river, fishermen's villages and scattered huts began to appear, embosomed in stately *purlieus*, amid trees of shapes unknown before, fields of sugar-cane, wide levels of paddy ground, with a verdure universal, and as bewitching as in spring time. As we neared Calcutta, on a bend of the river called Garden Reach, the *coup d'œil* was enchanting. Palatial-like houses studded the banks of the river. There, is the palace of the King of Oude, who has only four wives, but as many concubines as Solomon, whom the British government support here (after stripping him of his kingdom of Oude), at the expense of a quarter of a million a year. There, is the Bishop's college, where Episcopalians, native as well as Europeans, are trained up to preach Episcopalianism to Hindoo, and Mohammedan, and Buddhist, and Parsee, with but a very poor success, I am sorry to say. And then, there are the mansions of the rich merchants, the British nabobs, who have hoarded gold, and destroyed their livers, but who, while living, live here luxuriously. Beyond here is the river, covered with boats of every conceivable form, and multitudes of vessels and steam-engines, while palanquins, buggies, phaetons, ghares, hackeries, and other odd modes of conveyance, line the shore, and tempt you to land, to be carried off into the city. Calcutta has no walls. You enter it without portcullis, or any other threatening fortification. Fort William, nearly in the heart of the city, is strong, well filled with soldiers, and, in the event of an Indian insurrection, the whole European population could be huddled into its circumvallation.

I have got here, I see now, just in the wrong time; and I cannot get any money to get out till the right time comes. This is the Doorga Poohjah holiday week—seventeen days, the Hindoos make of it—and no bank or banker opens, and the custom-house is shut, till the Doorga Poohjah holidays are over! This is consoling, in a city you get into to get out of as soon as you can raise the wind, and from which, almost everybody, you would like to see, is gone to pass the holidays. If it were not for some ten or twelve Christian churches here, of almost all the great denominations, I should call this altogether, not almost altogether, a Hindoo country. Every thing is closed up. There is nothing to get at or into, only the exterior to see. But, on Monday next, Christianity revives, and the banks and the custom-house open.

Pondering upon this topic, I tumble upon another, and that is, what an odd, extraordinarily odd, Christian country John Bull has made of this vast India! Polygamy, here, is just as prevalent as with Brigham Young, in Utah; but here, not as in Utah, it is yielded to, and sanctioned by law! A Frenchman living here, the other day, did not love his own French wife enough, not to want another. To win that other, a French captivating milliner, he shuffled off his Christianity, and put on Mohammedanism. The *to-be* wife and the double husband both became Mohammedans. Then, under this British government, it became lawful for him to have two, nay, four wives, while, as a Christian, it would have been polygamy to have more than one. The British press laughs at us, because of Indiana divorces; but all a Christian Briton has to do, to be rid of one wife, and to have another, is to come to India, turn Mohammedan, and then, if he pleases, he can marry four. In the Madras presidency, where Lord Napier reigns, there is a sect called Nayers, who observe the Marumak-Kaytam doctrine, where polyandry is no offence. A woman may have as many husbands as she likes. I only suggest this to John Bull, when his press is rather hard upon our dark spot, Utah, or, the divorce courts of Indiana. The fact is, the British government, in order to keep quiet possession in India, not only keep up an army of 320,000 men, but keep up, too, Hindooism, Buddhism, Brahminism, Mohammedanism, and all the other *isms*. The British government rules over such a variety of races, languages, manners, laws, and religions, that, in order to live in peace, it caters to all.—Curious government, is it not? The Governor-General, or Viceroy, from England—and a council, here, created by him—the two legislating for all, without any elections, or the bother of them, enforce all edicts by an army of 320,000 men. Nevertheless, the British government has been, in the main, a good government for India, for it snatched her from the perdition of civil commotions, and secured for the governed, equity and justice, though the land robberies perpetrated in so doing have been prodigious. There are native as well as English-born magistrates in the lower magistracies. There are native policemen, and native juries, in some cases; but the jury system does not work well, magistrates tell me, among the natives here. There are some few natives in the high council of state. But in almost all cases the officers, civil as well as military, come from England. I do not suppose there are 200,000,000 of Indians anywhere so well governed; and yet, were it not for the 320,000 soldiers, ever in arms, the British flag would not wave a year in India. It hangs over a volcano, ever ready for an eruption. But good-by for to-day.

# LETTER XXXIII.

### THINGS AND THOUGHTS IN CALCUTTA

The Impudent Crows of Calcutta.—How they chatter.—A Drove of Elephants embarking for War.—The "Central Park" and "Hyde Park" of Calcutta.—Funny Liveries.—The Trade of the Metropolis of India.—Exports, Cutch, Coir, Jute, Indigo, and so on.—The Cocoa-nut Tree.—American Trade.—Assam Tea.—The Opium Trade, a Government Monopoly.—The Flocks of Servants in Calcutta.—No Women Servants.—All Men.—Men as Washerwomen.—The Woman invisible.—English Women going to India.—The Chit and the Coolie.—The Ladies' Chit.—Charming Social Life in Calcutta.

CALCUTTA, *October* 29, 1871.

THE morning music of Calcutta is not very bewitching. After the loud morning gun from the fort, about 5 A. M., which startles, now, before daylight, all from their slumbers, comes the "caw," "caw," "caw," of great droves of crows, which fill, and at times almost darken, the sky. They not only keep up a frightful clatter, but they pop into your windows, and if you are not watchful while breakfasting on the veranda, they will steal your bread and toast from the table. Crows are respected in Calcutta as scavengers, as are dogs in Constantinople. Crows and vultures pick up the offal in all directions, and do much toward maintaining good air and good smells in Calcutta. Hence, the noise and thieving of the rascals are borne with, and they are not shot, as they ought to be.

I have been to see a drove of elephants hoisted on board of a steamer, to be taken somewhere into Burmah. Some Indian tribe there has been raiding upon British territory, and a little army of natives, and a lesser force of Europeans, are to be sent out to teach them better manners. The elephants belong to the commissariat, and are to carry the provisions and the burdens—each elephant being able to walk off with at least eight hundred pounds on his back, besides his driver. There were some forty to be hoisted upon this steamer, and, naturally enough, the novelty of the derrick that lifted them from their feet high into the air, was not very agreeable; but these war elephants are under good discipline, and do what is bidden. They were fed on sugar-cane, to make them sweeter tempered, perhaps, and bathed in the river, and washed by their masters, to cool off their temper, it may be.

And I have been to the evening drive—the Central Park and Hyde Park evening show of Calcutta—where turn out the fashion, the glow, and the glitter, and the horses, and the equipages, of this metropolitan India. A band of music regales the visitors in a garden near by; and this night, the full moon, mingled with the showy gas-light, and the good music of a great band, with the novelty of Indian carriages in livery, and Indian nurses with European children, the scene was not only novel but charming. The Indian liveries of "the swells" of the city are quite startling. There are two men behind the coach, with the driver before—all in a groundwork of white, generally with flaming turbans and sashes on, but with bare legs and naked feet. There are Indian native "swells," with their liveries, as well as European and Parsee "swells." I have not seen, however, the full glow and glitter of this evening drive. This is not the fashionable season. "The Court" —that is, the Viceroy—is hundreds of miles off, among the Himalayas, hunting tigers and leopards and other wild beasts; and all that is left here is what could not run away.

Calcutta is a city of great business, as well as the metropolis of India. The Ganges and its tributaries roll down their wealth here, as well as their waters. But the Ganges is not navigable the whole year round, like the Mississippi or Missouri (the lower parts). Sands and silt fill up its currents, and in the dry season, forbid steamboat navigation. There go from here rice, cotton, linseed, and almost all sorts of seeds, cutch, coir, indigo, dyeing materials of most kinds, and many materials for manufactures, among which jute has become a great article of export, mainly to Dundee, in Scotland, and largely to America. Of jute, now—and an article of commerce scarcely known ten years ago—even excellent colored shirts are made, as well as paper. What was worth nothing in India but yesterday, is now of great value! The Dundee jute manufactures abound in America. Jute, like coir, is a vegetable good for rope; and like the cocoa-nut tree, from the fibre of which coir rope is made, jute is good for every thing. There are only five or six American houses in Calcutta now, and the Greek merchants are crowding them out with their immense ready capital, while we, here as everywhere else in the East, do business "on tick," *via* London, or through the Oriental Bank and its branches in every Eastern city of any size. Our freighting ships have been crowded off; our exports of Lowell and Lawrence goods have been killed; and hence, we must "tick," "tick," "tick," *via* London, as we have not the *wherewith* here to pay. Tea, Assam tea, especially, is becoming here a large article of export to England. It is stronger than the Chinese teas, and is mixed with them in Liverpool and London. There are thirty-one tea companies in Calcutta, and the Assam, the oldest, divides over fifteen per cent. Poor China will be in a bad way with British India, if Assam teas ever crowd off Chinese teas in the marts of the world—for, now, India sends thirty or forty millions of dollars' worth of opium to China every year, deriving a revenue therefrom of from thirty to forty millions of dollars a year. But India is not to have, in this respect, all her own way. The Chinese now are increasing their growth of opium, and preparing to supply themselves. But what a melancholy trade all this is! What death to the Chinese, thus to support the nabob governments of India! There is no topic on which Britons more dispute, here in the East, than on this opium trade. Many merchants will have nothing to do with it; but there are enough left who will. Many denounce their own Government for the Chinese opium war; others pronounce the trade immoral and wicked; but, nevertheless, rich argosies of opium are ever going from Calcutta and Bombay to China.

Opium in India is a Government monopoly. Nobody can raise, buy, or sell opium but under Government sanction or authority. The Government fixes the price it will pay the planter—a pretty liberal price, too—buys all he has to sell, and then sells all that to the highest bidder at public auction, when the merchant becomes possessed of it, and when he sends it in opium ships to the markets of the world. To regulate prices, the Government names the number of opium bales it will sell every year, and thus guarantees the merchant from any supply beyond his calculations. From thirty to forty millions of dollars per annum are raised by the Government in this way; and, "how can we do without this revenue?" they ask. "What can we substitute for it?" "We have stamp-taxes, income-taxes, and a salt monopoly, now." "What can we pile on, if we take opium off?" And thus poor China pays the piper, who plays "God save the Queen," in India, from Burmah and Ceylon on to the Indus and the Himalayas. Thus, in strong money-links the British now have the whole Eastern world, Japan alone excepted, and that with a perhaps.

What, among other things, excites the astonishment of visitors here, are the flocks of servants, yes flocks—swarms, too, I might add—in every house. The castes are so strong, and such is the religious determination of one caste not to be degraded by another—so many are the superstitions touching food, and even clothes, that a separate servant must be had to do almost every class of labor that is servile. A bachelor acquaintance of mine, whose income as a civil officer of the Government cannot be great, not such as the income of a merchant, numbers twenty-two in his little bachelor establishment! Every horse has to have *a* man for that particular horse—certainly one, and two, probably—one, to cut the grass for the horse to eat, and another to take care of the beast; then the driver or coachman, and then the livery-men, two, if not three, in cheap, barefooted liveries, to be sure, and not costly, though very showy in colors at times; then, men to pull the punkah night and day; then, his personal man, to stand by him at all times. These servants, to be sure, have only six or nine cents wages per day, finding themselves, and they sleep, by choice, on the verandas, in the open air, with no cost, therefore, for room or beds; but, nevertheless, there are so many of them, for almost every thing, that they must be costly as well as troublesome. Some head butler, however, better paid than his subordinates, saves his master from all trouble and care; and when once a household is well trained, all move like clock-work, though the machinery of the work, it must be confessed, is far more imperfect than among the superior, and far more intelligent Chinese. Trust these servants, masters say here, and then they may be safely trusted in their respective vocations; but doubt them, and lock up from them, so as to enable them to shuffle off responsibility from the one to the other, then, they become thieves of a hard kind. They have little or no character at bottom, we are told—no *fond*—and the machinery must ever be well handled, and well oiled, to work well in an establishment.

There are no women chambermaids, or other female servants, anywhere in the East, except a very few nurses (Ayahs) for children. Men are very often children's nurses, in one sense—of course, not in all. Men surround American or European ladies, and do all their servile work, from that of chambermaid to washerwoman. They wash and they iron to perfection, even ladies' most complicated ruffles and plaits (three cents each is the average price for every thing); but as they thrash the soiled clothes on the rocks, to thrash out the dirt, clothes, under such hard treatment, of course, will not last long. The wash-board, the destructive rubbing machine of our country, is unknown here, and the turn-crank washing-machine, even if steam-driven, could never compete with the paws and claws of "the heathen Chinee," or these more heathen Indians. Women, therefore, are scarce luxuries to be seen in these Eastern countries, except the very common class, for a true Mussulman would almost as lief die as have Christian or Hindoo eyes light upon his first, or, forty-first, wife. I have just seen one muffled-up "better half" (or better one-fortieth, perhaps), on a chair, covered all over with " copper plate," " dumped into " the ladies' department of the ladies' railroad car, invisible to mortal eyes, even to mine, with a double pair of glasses on. These dear Eastern creatures never see daylight when men are about, and the Hindoo women of high caste are as scarce as these Moslem women. What a country, then, for men to live in, with no women to see! More especially for European men, whose eyes, long lost to the blessing, brighten and glisten, therefore, whenever that dazzling article of creation comes along. They do say—it must be scandal, though—that English women come out here to India, for this very reason, to tempt forlorn, deserted bachelors into being husbands; and it is hard, very hard, for the forlorn bachelor, not to take, for better or for worse, even the spinster who has run out her career in London or Brighton, and who opens, or hopes to open, a new career, if not in Calcutta, in some hill station among men, where there is not even one woman, except the invisible Moslem, or Hindoo. Five or six very pretty and unmarried ladies came up with us in the Galle steamer, direct from England, with fresh English-looking cheeks, and bouncing ringlets. One of them was going out "engaged," and to be married the day or two after she landed in Burmah. But how her red cheeks will soon " wash out," pallid and pale, in this hot climate, and her ringlets bother her, as the perspiration trickles down them! The fact is, though,

Englishmen, unless they are rich merchants, cannot afford to marry here, heavenly as the luxury of a good wife must be in this hapless land. Their salaries, though big in our estimation, are not big enough to support a wife in India; and children, when born, cannot live here, after four or five years of age, being certain to die, or to dwindle down into cream-cheese, idiotic sort of anatomies, with little life, and less intelligence, in them. All, therefore, must be sent home to England in their childhood.

Calcutta (or rather, Bengal and Burmah) is the mother of many other institutions than "the punkah," to fan and blow, for—despite what Cowper wrote—

"I would not have a slave to fan me while I sleep," etc.,

every Englishman in India turns the Indian into a sort of slave—not chattel slave, not marketable, but none the less, the slave, who not only fans him while he sleeps, but does all other sorts of like kind things for him to keep him alive and cool. Among these other institutions is "the Chit," which has been freely adopted from India into both Japan and China. In a country where it is so hot that you cannot run out to talk, or trade, or send a messenger to talk for you, because none of them well enough understand the English language, writing is always resorted to—that is, "Chits"—and the Indian takes "the Chit" from white man to white man, awaiting the formal acceptance in a book he carries with him, or the reply, in another "Chit." Every thing, thus, is done in writing. Messages are often recorded in a common book, which everybody sees, as that book passes from one to another. This is well enough, ordinarily, and in business life, but when ladies enter upon the Chit business, they often make "a muss" of it, especially if the "Chits" be of affection or love, or, between man and woman. "Yours, lovingly," does not read well in public record, even, if ever so innocently, between lady and lady's man. Nor do rouge, or powder, or cologne, or false hair, if thus sent for, read as well as if not read at all. "I am dying to see you," writes one, and another reader wonders if the death has taken place, or if the visit was made to save the life. Chits in ladies' hands, it is easy to come to the conclusion, are a perilous Indian institution, however necessary among men. A telegram here is called "a telechit." A wearied Chit writer says, "I have been *chitting* all day." Chits pour in upon you at all times, before breakfast, in bed, in the bath, at "tiffin," at dinner, in the theatre, at the ballroom. There is no end of Chits. Elsewhere in the world you may escape a bore, but in India there is no escaping a Chit. Nevertheless, the institution is indispensable in a climate like this, where, for some hours in the day, it is as much as a man's life is worth to face the sun, unless he has a two-storied pith hat or helmet on his head, and colored goggles to save his eyes.

But, hot as it is, I am sorry to leave Calcutta—

for, socially, it seems to me a charming place. I came without a single letter of introduction; but, through passengers on board the steamer, many doors have been open to me, and I have been as hospitably welcomed as if I were an Englishman in high position, and all the more welcome for being an American.

# LETTER XXXIV.

## *THE RUN ACROSS INDIA.*

Things in India.—Rail from Calcutta to Bombay.—The Raging Sun of India.—The Parsees of Bombay.—Fire Worshippers.—Sunday Evening's Work in Calcutta.—India Railroad Cars.—How they are cooled, and how they are converting the Pagans.—The Telegraphs of India.—Journalism in India.—Coal in India.—The Way Coolies work.—Indian Muslins and Cashmere Shawls.—The Plains of the Ganges.—The Pagan Temples of India.—Hindoos more intelligent than Mohammedans.—Allahabad.—Jubbalpore.—The Passage of the Ghauts.—Entrance into Bombay.

BOMBAY, *October* 31, 1871.

INDIA "done" up! One week in it!—from Calcutta to Bombay, 1,420 miles, in sixty-two hours! Who can beat that? And I have seen so much, and slept through so much, that quite a book might be filled thereon. The fact is, I am in a hurry to get home, have seen enough, and don't want to see any more. My eyes are weary, and all my senses surfeited with the glories of Buddhism, Hindooism, Mohammedanism, Parseeism, and the dominion of England over them all. No man ought ever to travel for instruction, or pleasure, over three months at one time, for, after that, all the senses become intoxicated, as it were, and then so blunted that the eyes decline to see, or the ears to hear. Rest, long interludes of rest, become as indispensable to the traveller—rest, for all his senses—as day and night; and hence, six continuous months of sight-seeing have blunted curiosity, and all the faculties connected therewith. But, 1,420 miles "done" in India, in sixty-two hours, from the Bay of Bengal and the Ganges, to the Sea of Arabia—think of that! And we slept by the way a good deal. We wasted much time at many, many stations; but our speed, while going, was thirty miles, and sometimes forty miles the hour, over first-class railroads, better built than any we have in America, costing three dollars per mile to our one; over frightfully flooding rivers; through terrible mountain passes—but then again on long level plains, as smooth as our prairies, and with cultivation more beautiful, if possible, than many parts on the Connecticut River.

And it is so hot here yet, when the raging sun roasts and burns us; but, happily, cool and consoling, when that fiery monster goes down at night! The sun, here, though creating and vivifying all the elements of life, is Caucasian man's mortal enemy. The very look at it, in the daytime, runs a poor fellow half wild with fever. An ice-house is paradise, and ice is manna, or whatever you like best, be it roast beef and plum-pudding (the English manna), or mint julep, or sherry cobbler. Heaven bless Tudor again, the immortal Tudor, who is here, as well as everywhere else, in the East. I hear from New York, September 22, that a Bombay Parsee (a Mr. Wadiah) was suffering from the climate, and compelled to wear three overcoats to keep him warm there! I could lend him, to-day, my skin, the epidermis and cuticle, at least, if he were here, to keep him warm; for, just now, there is no need of clothes, nay, no need of a skin, as even bones might melt in the noonday sun. The great Creator has made these Indians, as well as the Chinese, our superiors in one thing, at least, and that is, in standing bareheaded, if necessary, the full blaze of the sun's noonday rays. Nevertheless, many Englishmen do live and thrive here, in good health, and with sound livers; but they eat little, and drink less. Great feeders and drinkers here die early, or go home without a liver.

The first thing that arrests an American traveller's attention here, is the hard Parsee names—(Parsees do a large portion of the business of Bombay)—such as Badabhoy Durshaw Gandy, or, Cursetjee Nesserwanjee Cama, or, Hajee Zanel Abardin Sheerazee. One great man of Bombay was Sir Jamsetjee Jeheebhoy, and another, Cowasjee Jehanghir, who both did much for charity, and thus left names to future fame. The Parsees are said to be fire worshippers, but this is doubtful, in the sense outgiven—for who could worship fire or sun, here, or any idol but ice? They are European in look, build, and style, but tawny. They have all the skill and quickness in business that Europeans have, and the same faculty for making money. The Mohammedans, they say, drove them out of Persia some centuries gone by, and they came here, as the Puritans did to Plymouth, for religious peace; but they agreed to do what the Puritans would never do, live quietly and like other people; and hence, they (the Parsees) eat no pork, and speak the native language of the country. Hence, they have had for centuries safety and peace, and are now most loyal subjects of Queen Victoria. During our civil war, on the rise of cotton, they made immense fortunes, and rolled in wealth; but, when our war went down, their cotton went down, and many of them with it. I have been introduced to some of these Parsees—but think of remembering their names, or of even saying, "How do you do, Mr. Dhungeebhoy Framgee Bhandarkar," or, any thing like it—more especially now, fresh, as I am, from the monosyllabic names, the Changs, Engs, and Wangs of China.

But, come now, go back with me to Calcutta. I "lunched out" a Sunday, there, and drove out on the fashionable drive, which begins Sunday, at 5 P. M., and ends at church, at 6 or 6½ P. M.,—in the English church in Fort William, the fashionable Sunday evening church, where sixteen Hindoos pull the punkah for a thousand Christians, or more, during divine service, and thus play hide-and-go-seek with the clergyman's eyes and gestures, or, fast-and-loose with the notes of the organists and boy chanters—then, went home to the hotel, the service being over—packed up —out to dine at 8½ P. M., and off in the cars for Calcutta, over the Hoogley, at 12 (midnight). I enter into all this *minutiæ* to show you how hard it was "to do Calcutta," in the brief space of time given me there. I have lost Delhi, and Agra, and Cawnpore, and Lucknow—and Agra is a real loss, because of the wonderful tomb, an Indian prince erected there in memory of his wife. And I have lost Mohammedan mosques and Hindoo temples innumerable; but this world is big, even when you go round it by steam, and life is not long enough to see everything. That unfortunate threat of the cyclone, delaying the steamer nearly four days in the mouth of the Hoogley, lost me India, in detail, after all the sacrifice of time, and the risk of health run to see the detail, and compelled me to rush on to Bombay for the weekly steamer to Egypt, as if I had been shot off on a cannon-ball.

The Calcutta-Bombay first-class through sleeping-car is a luxury—(fare, about $70, with baggage)—but not quite equal to our "silver palaces," though with some few advantages over them. The air is cooled a little, when the cars are in motion, by air forced through water from the bottom of the car. There is a punkah, which the motion of the car moves a little to fan you—a very uncertain sort of fanning, though. The windows of the car do not slide up and down, as ours do, but swing on hinges, every alternate window, from the right to the left, and *vice versa;* and you arrange them, on their hinges, to the reverse motion of the car, so as to keep out the dust, and then enjoy the air. The windows are of colored glass, to shut out the terrible glare of the sun. The water to wash with is forced up from below by a force pump, as you need it. Over the windows, one and all, is a wooden projecting shade to keep off the sun, and to forbid the windows from opening too far. These are advantages over our cars; but there are no sheets provided for beds, no pillow-cases or pillows, no towels, no soap, no ice, no attendance inside. Outside, at stopping places, are coolies by the score, and policemen; and the coolies, from skins slung over their backs, filled with water, supply it to you, for drink or washing, if you need it, or, pull the punkah fan to cool you, if you desire it. There is a great retinue about every station—a retinue in uniform—and the stations are often very costly, as at Jubbalpore and Allahabad.

The railroads of India are doing more, it seems to me, for the conversion of Hindoos, if not Mohammedans, than all the missionaries; and if the English government here would give a little bit of preference to the Holy Bible over the Shastras, and Vedas, and the Korans (only a little bit), I should have some hope that the railroads would do what the missionaries have, for now two centuries, *not* done—that is, turn the people from the error of their ways. The railroad is breaking down slowly the Hindoo castes. The proud, and lofty, and blue-blooded Brahmin must now go into the same car with the poor, despised Pariah, or not go at all. The hard-hearted English conductor pushes in, or tumbles in, Pariah on top of Brahmin, and Mohammedans among them too. Each wraps up his garments around him, and preserves himself, as much as possible, from the horrible contamination; but, when once holy Brahmin is in the car with polluted Pariah, go he must, or jump out and die. The railroad, now, has become here the great vein of life, the heart, as it were, of the geographical anatomy of the country; and hence, this mixed circulation of all these various religious sects and bloods in it, is amalgamating, slowly, despite religion, caste, and creed. And this is happening in a land, too, where, if even the shadow of a Christian, or a Mohammedan, or Pariah, should pass over the food of a Brahmin, he would not eat it, or over his body, he would feel himself polluted. Railroads are great levellers everywhere; but railroads in India are levelling heathenism, and may, by-and-by, bring it up to Christianity. What conquers caste here, equalizes. What equalizes heathenism here, strips it of its pride, selfishness, exclusiveness, etc., and thus prepares it for something better than itself. By the way, we live well and fare well on the rails of India. The conductor asks us miles ahead, "if we breakfast, or dine," here or there, and the telegraph is used to have the meal all ready for us, the prices being about the same as in the United States. There are miles and miles of telegraph, now, all over India, from the seas to the mountains, on to every inland military station, and the rates are very cheap. I can thus reach New York, from Delhi or the Punjaub, in less than a day; and from Bombay there are three distinct lines to Europe. I read scraps of New York and U. S. news every day, in the Bombay journals, which are about as good as ours in New York. Indeed, there are British journals, and journals in the native tongue, all over India. The press is as free, as keen, as sharp, as critical here, over public men, and on public measures, as in London or New York. The only real restraint here, on the absolute government, is this free press—save and except those deep-rooted and widespread free foundations of English law, viz., the *Habeas Corpus* and *Magna Charta*.

What I *saw* at night, in my flight across the Indias, is a "bull" you will not expect me to make, but I have no doubt that, as I slept, I slept by many holy, as well as, business places—some British and Dutch battlefields, and many of the historical sacred spots of Warren Hastings and Lord Clive; but, as I have written before, one can't see every thing, and one must sleep—what a pity!—to live. The Portuguese Catholic priests were all about this country as long ago as A. D. 1540. When, in 1632, the great Mogul came to Hugly—a place I passed in the night—there were 2,000 souls crowded for safety on board one Portuguese ship, the captain of which blew it up, with all on board, rather than fall into the hands of the Mohammedans. We passed Burdwan, too, the rajah of which pays two millions of dollars rental, for his estates, to the British government. We waked up at daybreak, off the flat-land, and amid hills, if not mountains, in the coal regions—for the supplies of coal are as abundant here as in Pennsylvania (U. S.), and so cheap, that in Calcutta it is sold for about five dollars a ton. Two annas per day (six cents) is the price of labor in the coal mines, and on the railroads, in this part of India—the coolie finding himself, in clothes (little or none), and in food, rice and vegetables. But there is little or no work in him, unless driven. Every thing is carried in baskets—on the head—coal, dirt, etc. The wheelbarrow was tried in railroad building, and the scoop; but the native did not take to these novelties, and would try to carry the wheelbarrow on his head, and no artificial scoop or dredging power was so cheap as the power of perpendicular bone and muscle. Man was cheaper than steam, or cheaper than machine. There is no patent right so cheap in India as the God-made machine, called man. Nevertheless, there is no slavery here. It is a free country. Every man owns his own bones and brains. But, in contradiction to all this, some of you will remember—nay, not longer than 1830—when even muslins for our shirts came from India, while now, the far costlier labor, but powerful loom machinery of England, has nearly destroyed the manufacture here, and substituted in its stead immense importations of all sorts of drygoods therefor. The cashmere and India shawls, and some few objects of art manufactured now, alone survive the competition of dearer labor and cheaper machinery in England and America. Reconcile this logic, so contradictory. I can't stop to do it now.

Then, we came down from the hills into the level, beautiful, alluvial, broad-spread plains of the Ganges, where for miles and miles there is little to see but highly-cultivated patches of the rich soil, and myriads of bullocks, and tropical vegetation of all kinds fascinating to the eye. The land seems full of people, and capable of supporting any number of them. But the eye soon wearies with vegetable wealth and flowers everlasting. One covets a mountain, or a waterfall, and soon feels, in this hot climate, that a poor life on the hills is better than a rich life on the everlasting plains. The people on these plains have no need of clothes, no real need of work, for it is ever hot enough to run naked, and the plantain and other tropical food would feed them, even if the country were a jungle. Nevertheless, the cultivation of the country shows great industry. The farmers, just now, are putting in some new crop, and the plough—the earth-scraper, I had better call it—with the bullocks pulling it, covers, more or less, all parts of the now living country. The Ganges, which but the other day covered every thing with its waters, has now gone to rest, and left behind its fat treasures of deposits to enrich the land. . . .

But up, and on, or I shall never get to Bombay! What a pity I could not stop at that holy Hindoo city of Benares, with her one thousand temples "wholly given to idolatry." A half a million of gods are said to be worshipped here! Thousands of monkeys there are, in, and about one temple—fine, fat, well-bred monkeys, from the venerable patriarch to the babe in its mother's arms—all holy, holy, holy, and not to be desecrated by unholy Christian hands!

The Hindoo venerates the ape, because of some services, somewhere, some smart monkey did the Hindoos in their wars with the Mohammedans, before their surrender to the Great Mogul. In the shades of the second evening we passed Mirzapoor, where, once was the great temple of the Thugs of India, at which they worshipped, before they went to waylay, rob, and murder the traveller. The Thugs are extirpated, now, everywhere, and travelling is safer in India than in any other Eastern country. It was midnight when we reached Allahabad (the city of Allah, it means), where join the Jumna and the Ganges, and another great river, the Hindoos say, that flows direct from heaven, which, however, is allowed to be invisible to mortal eye. Certain, there is no railroad bridge over it. When a Hindoo pilgrim arrives at Allahabad, he sits down at the bank of the river, and has his head and body shaved, so that each hair may fall into the water, the sacred writers promising him one million of years' residence in heaven for every hair thus deposited! I did not drop a hair, but thought of it, in the moonlight, though many a Christian does, as he passes, so I am told, in order to be on the sure side.

These Hindoos, nevertheless, are not such fools as these superstitions would seem to indicate them to be. The English, here, pronounce them to be far the superiors of the Mohammedans, who *do* believe in God, though in Mohammed as his prophet. They have more intelligence than the Mohammedans; often educate themselves to a high standard of learning; often hold offices under the British, and oftener, are employed as bright men in practical business life. It is noted in history that when the Mohammedans, the better soldiers in their day, conquered the Hindoos, the Mohammedan chiefs had ever to employ the Hindoos, in large numbers, successfully to govern the country. The Mohammedans were only soldiers, while the Hindoos were the better civilians. They growl and grumble, now, under British rule, as the British prefer the Hindoos in official employ; and, just at this moment, a fanatical sect among them, the Wahabees, are suspected of having employed the fanatic who recently assassinated the Chief Justice at Calcutta.

From Allahabad to Jubbalpore is the line of rail—228 miles—recently opened, connecting Calcutta and Bombay, without the intervention of bullock carts, or any other like unearthly conveyance. Darkness came over us on the Ganges plains; but daylight opens on us in a rude, rough country, among hills and mountains, with a sharp, biting air, where two overcoats were not uncomfortable to sleep under. We have been going through, we are told, a land of tigers, leopards, bears, sambuk, spotted deer, antelopes, etc., etc. None of them jumped into the cars, or disturbed our slumbers. Hills are on each side of us, and now, we are winding at their base, and then, through many a sharp curve and steep incline, we climb and wind our way through scenery nearly as picturesque as seen on the Pacific road in Utah. Bold headlands often strut out like mighty bastions, the red strata laid bare at the top, and looking like a bluff point crowned by a fortress.

Jubbalpore, the end of the Great East India Railway, and the beginning of the Great Peninsular and Oriental rail, we reached in season for quite a sumptuous breakfast. A thousand feet up in the air, it is not hot at early morning. It is a pretty-looking place, full of English, with an English church. We enter here the valley of the Nerbudda, wild, woody, and uncultivated. Then we go on, miles and miles, crossing three rivers on costly bridges, before we are done with the tributaries of the Nerbudda. We pass Burhampur, where they manufacture muslins, flowered silks, and brocades. Then, on, and on, through parts of Scindia—not far from spacious Buddhist cavern temples, hewn in the solid rock of amygdaloid, and thus indestructible by Mohammedan iconoclasts. The great Aurungzebe figured here, and about here. Then we come to the Western Ghauts — not our Spanish-American cañons, but passes, over hills, or mountains. Shady forests, rippling streams, lofty hills, and smiling dells, all make the country pretty. The passage of the Ghauts is one of the magnificent works of modern engineering. The rail line passes through 13 tunnels, over 6 viaducts, one, 250 yards long and 288 feet high, solid work of rock and iron. There are 15 bridges and 62 culverts in three Ghaut passes here. The road winds and curves around precipices like the worm of a screw. We were an hour going 10 miles; but, when we began to descend down the sea face toward the Indian Ocean, we flew at the rate of 40 or 50 miles the hour, through wooded gorges, by streams, cascades, forests of palms, tall teak trees, groves, and flowers, till we reached the swamp level of the sea, on which we go into Bombay, and again snuff the salt ocean air.

Enter Byculla, the chief station, near most of the hotels—but I go farther on, into the heart of the city, where, on the old Fort ground, is the Esplanade Hotel—a hotel built on purpose for a hotel, not sprung from patched-up houses, as are most hotels —a hotel of iron sent out from England, five or six of the loftiest stories high, over every room in which runs a current of air, with this disadvantage, that what you say or do in one room, is certain to be known in its neighbor room. The depot scenes of travellers' exit are nearly alike the whole world over (New York city excepted). There, surround you, cry for you, under discipline, though, the drivers of bullock carts (two bullocks drawing at times rather a pretty vehicle on springs), shigrams (a sort of rockaway, closely shutting up, to keep off the sun), and buggies; and there are palanquins (a sort of shut-up bed to stretch out on), with four hamals, or six (coolies), to carry you on their shoulders, if you wish. Never was a hotel, with baths, etc., more welcome. All the waters of the Indian Ocean can scarcely wash one off after such a flight, as mine, overland; but, I am up, " redeemed, regenerated, disenthralled," from dirt, high up in the air, in a balconied room, overlooking the city, its suburbs and its seas, and never in better health, though in India, and hot as it is in India.

# LETTER XXXV.

### SIGHTS IN AND ABOUT BOMBAY.

Bombay.—What it is as a City.—Calcutta the Court; Bombay the Mart.—New Influences of the Suez Canal.—The Treasures of India here.—Cashmere Shawls.—The Bombay Fashionables on a Drive.—The Parsees.—The way they don't bury their Dead.—India Gods.—Where manufactured.—The Temples of India.—The Wonderful "Elephanta."—Dining Out in the East.—The Route to Persia and Aden.—The Census and Exports of Bombay.—Extent of Railroads in India.—Sound Banks and a good Currency.

BOMBAY, *November* 4, 1871.

BOMBAY is a very respectable city, with over 800,000 inhabitants. Where they are put, though, I cannot see; but it is a stretched-out city, with long arms, and very. long legs, and "considerable of a body." It is as flat as a prairie, excepting Malabar Hill, or a promontory where the Quality live and drive, and two other little places of no great note, unless the Government House makes the Parell Hill a notability, and, of course, out here it does. A Governor in the East is, everywhere, the great "swell." Isn't he the representative of the Queen's majesty? Of course he is; and hence, Sir Edward Fitzgerald, the Governor of the great Bombay Presidency, makes Parell Hill a great notability—for he is the light set on that hill. Bombay has a fresh, lively, clean look, that reminds one of some of our rich mushroom Western cities. The merchant princes do not generally do business under their household establishments, as, often, elsewhere in the East, but live out in villas, amid the cooling breezes of Malabar. Calcutta is courtly; Bombay is mercantile. There is great rivalry between the two cities. One is the Court, the *ton*, as well as *the* town, while the other is gathering up, and taking away, the trade and commerce of Calcutta, because here is the nearest outlet, by the rail, of India to England, and for all the ships on the seas. The French canal through the Isthmus of Suez, too, that the British merchants so long bitterly opposed, in the fear that the French would thus monopolize the commerce of India, is becoming the greatest boon to Bombay; for here now, without bulk breaking, or sailing around the Cape, come steamers from all parts of England, and from Trieste and Brindisi, and from Genoa, Naples, Marseilles, and the whole Mediterranean. Bombay is thus brought into close contiguity with all Europe, while Calcutta is all the way around the Island of Ceylon, and up the Bay of Bengal. Bombay says, too, she is "healthier than Calcutta." Calcuttians deny that. "Our pure rivers, now, from the rectified Ganges, and our sewers," they say, "make Calcutta one of the healthiest cities in the world." (The world, however, will not believe that for many years to come; for the most that is known of Calcutta in the world is, "the Black Hole" of history, there.) Bombay says, "Look at our magnificent harbor, where whole navies can ride in safety; the entrance to, and the exit from, which is easy, while the Hoogley River, the entrance to Calcutta, is dangerous and costly in pilotage, and ever giving trouble to all the ships that go in there." Calcutta is silent on that theme. The Suez Canal navigation is concentrating here, directly, the steamships of Austria—Russia (from Odessa), and Italy, as well as France—nay, perhaps more and more, the direct trade from London and Liverpool (and scattering it all over Europe); but, nevertheless, all are to be to the profit of Bombay.

Bombay is the mart of India manufactures, from the far up-country of the Indus down to Madras; and hence, one has to shop here, of course—but shopping is easier in India than in New York, for the things come to you, not you to the shops. On the front of our hotel veranda, were spread out the treasures of India — boxes of sandal-wood, ivory, shell, teak, carved and lacquered—work in wool, in muslin, in silver and gold, embroideries, etc.; but the Indian is no match, now, as a manufacturer, with the Chinese or Japanese, while the European has stolen almost all his arts from him—all, perhaps, except the Cashmere and Indian shawls. The Indian embroiders yet cheaply, on European fabrics, more cheaply than the European can, and, hence, commands a market for some of his fabrics. The wealth of shawls here, however, rather startles the European or American, even one accustomed to the high prices of New York or Paris. There was one pair of shawls noted, for which the Indian dealer wanted 5,000 rupees, each

—that is, $2,500. They were very long, very, *very* fine, but would not quite go through a finger-ring, as, some say, some of the very finest will. Prices of the good cashmere vary from $150 to $500 and $1,000; but few, or none, of the latter are sold, except to royalty. Months and months of labor are spent upon some of these cashmeres, more than upon the laces of Belgium; and the work upon them is immense. The "wool" of which they are made is the under wool, or hair, of the goat, as of the under hair of the seal, and of the very finest quality. Moore, the poet, has given the world his fancy views of the vale of Cashmere; but his fancy is very near the fact in his poetic description of that beautiful region, which is not yet British, though under the influence and sway of Britons.

There are many things to see in Bombay, but all cannot now be seen, lively as I have been. I went to the evening drive on Malabar Hill, but, in dash and crash here, there is no comparison with the Calcutta fashionable drive. The red and yellow of the turbans, and of the liveries, arrest one's attention. Sometimes it would seem as if all the scarlet in the country was afloat in Bombay. There are fellows, with golden turbans, swelling out a foot, almost, on either side the head—but bare-legged, and barefooted, with all that. Bare legs is a part of the fashionable livery of India. We see on this drive rich Parsees, out with their equipages; and some rich Hindoos, too. There is a Parsee theatre here, in

Bombay, but it is too hot to shut one's-self up in hot walls, these hot nights. The Hindoos have not yet reached theatrical refinements; but their festivals, and show festivals, too, are innumerable. There is a dreadful sight, at times, here in Bombay, even to an old traveller like myself, who has reached the *nil admirari* of Horace almost to perfection—and that is, a Parsee funeral—a Parsee—interment? No!—a burial? No!—a Hindoo incremation, burning up of the body? No! But—I do not know what to call it, and hence, must describe it. Parsees die, of course, and are never buried, like Christians, or Mohammedans, or burnt like the Hindoos, but taken to a high tower, on Malabar Hill, soon after death, and there, naked, on an open grate, left to be eaten up by the vultures; and their bones, when the flesh is gone, drop through the grate into a vault below! The vultures have learned to snuff a Parsee funeral in the distance, and hover over it, and croak about it; and no sooner is the corpse left on the grating, than they enter upon the scramble for the flesh that is on it! They tell me—I don't vouch for this, though—that at times, in the fashionable quarters of Malabar Hill, on a veranda, is dropped a stray finger, or toe, that the vulture has found rather indigestible. The Bombayans don't seem to think much of all this. It strikes me as the strangest, most startling of things I have yet to record in all my ramblings.

Long ago have I given up seeing heathen temples.

One wearies, after a while, in Europe, even, of cathedrals, to say nothing of churches; but in the East I have seen here so many gods (they make them, by the way, in Manchester, now, for export to India), that I had resolved never again to enter Buddhist or Hindoo temple. But, on an island about six miles from Bombay, is one which has so great a name— that is, is so famous—that I went with a pleasant party in a sail-boat, to have a luncheon in it, and a good time generally. The temple is called the Cave Temple of Elephanta. The Hindoos picked out a romantic island for their great temple, and in a solid rock, under two hills, cut out a temple—with what instruments, who knows?—and *how long* ago, who can tell? The work *is* a wonder, almost as much of a wonder as the Pyramids, and more than the Sphynx. We go up to it from the water about half a mile on stone steps, a stone-ascending pavement, the avenue walled with stone on both sides. Two ponderous pillars and two pilasters, forming three openings under a steep rock, overhung by brushwood, first meet one's eyes. The great temple is one hundred and thirty-three feet broad, one hundred and thirty and a half feet long, and twenty feet high, the roof being supported by ranges of massive pillars, with ornamental capitals of varied designs, all hewn out of the solid rock. Opposite the entrance is a gigantic bust with three heads, supposed to represent the Hindoo Trinity. There are two smaller temples, one on each side of the principal one. There are now no priests in this temple, no worship. It is given up to Bombay *pic-nic* parties, and visitors eat, drink, and make merry in it. We planted our table in the opening, with a lake-like view of the water before us, that reminded me of West Point; and the feast the coolies brought down to us from the city, we enjoyed with a zest, in the cool air of the temple cave, with an appetite inspired by the little boat voyage. If any reader of mine should ever go there, let him remember he must mount on coolies' backs, to be carried to and from his boat, so shallow are the waters on the shore. I would like to tell you of the purposes of two of the altars in this temple, but I can only tell verbally, never on paper.

Were you ever invited out to dinner, accepting the invitation, and not knowing where to go, and not knowing enough of Hindostanee to ask anybody? Well, that was my condition the day of the *pic-nic* —dinner, 8½ P. M., place three miles off—and how was I to get there? Pantomime did the job. Fingers are about as good to talk with as tongues, if you have only one word to work on, and *that*, I had—excellent Hindostanee. The Tower of Babel—plague on it—has been the cause of more trouble than any thing in this world, except Mother Eve's defalcation. I *pantomimed* into my dinner party at 9 P. M.—a hungry, half-angry, but very polite company awaiting. Europeans live here, as in China and Japan, like princes. If they don't soon check their extravagance, the cheaper-living Germans, and the cheaper-yet Parsees and Chinese, will root them out of the trade of the country. To go to a dinner-party, in woollens—in a fashionable bob-tailed woollen coat, with a well-lined vest and pantaloons, made for the winter in New York, the thermometer there often in the neighborhood of zero—is not exactly comfortable in Bombay, where the thermometer wanders in the nineties; but such is the *dictum* of Fashion in Calcutta and Bombay;—and in woollen, and white choker, you have to stand it, if you will dine out with other people. They do say, but I did not see it, that in pity the master of the feast sometimes offers you a linen jacket in exchange for your woollen coat, which said jacket, by previous arrangement, you bring from home with you; but this was not our case, as we ate, drank, and made merry only in the woollens — calmed, however, if not cooled, by the blessed punkah.

But I am off this evening to Aden, Suez, Alexandria, Brindisi—twenty-one days, though, yet from London, in one continuous, everlasting steamer motion. I *don't* want to go home, and I *do* want to go home; and in this verbal, there is no mental, contradiction. The more a traveller goes, the more he pants to go. My mouth is watering for a nice little run on the Persian Gulf, in a steamer, from Bombay to Bussora, and thence, by steamer, on to Bagdad, in Persia, where close by, I could see what is left of Babylon and Nineveh, and go then up the Euphrates, to Aleppo and Alexandretta, on the Mediterranean, where the French steamers touch. If I were a free man, I would go home that way.

| DISTANCES. | MILES. |
|---|---|
| Bombay to Bussora (by steam) | 1,915 |
| Bussora to Bagdad (by steam) | 500 |
| Bagdad to Alexandretta | 900 |

—on which latter route there is steam on the Euphrates to Mescany, which is fifteen hours' ride from Aleppo, and Aleppo is eighty-four miles from Alexandretta.

Before I leave Bombay, however, let me add on more statistics.

The census of Bombay, in 1864, showed the following population:

| Hindoos | 585,968 |
|---|---|
| Mohammedans | 145,800 |
| Parsees | 49,201 |
| Europeans | 8,415 |
| Jews | 2,872 |
| All other races | 24,226 |
| Exports the last year from Bombay | $126,454,000 |
| Imports | 81,729,000 |

These exports are increasing, in consequence of Bombay's being made the railroad, as well as steamboat centre. Cotton is the chief article, and our prices current of that article in America are daily telegraphed here. There are thirteen lines of steamers connected with this port—four from Europe, the great P. & O. (English), once a week; the Austrian Lloyds, from Trieste; the Italian, from Venice; and the Messagerie, from Marseilles—the three last running through the Suez Canal, where the P. & O. (English) will soon have to go, or else lose most of the freight and passenger trade.

There have been four hundred million dollars expended upon the India railroads, now over five thousand miles in extent, and increasing. They reach the Indus now, and are soon going up to Cashmere and Caubul.

The currency of India is excellent. The banks are now in high credit, and their notes circulate all over the land at par, being receivable for Government dues. The rupee (fifty cents) is the silver coin. There is a gold coin, but it is hoarded as soon as issued.

Doubtless, you will smile when you read these letters from India, naturally enough wondering how, in a single week in India, I could pick up so much material, all the while being, as I have been, on the wing. When a traveller reads every thing he can lay his hands on in a country, and is surrounded by intelligent men who can answer all his questions, he learns a great deal in a very little while. I have been thinking, since I came here, that one might stay at home, and thus travel, with photographic views only of the countries he would visit; but the difficulty there is the geography. One can get the geography of a country in his head only by running into it, or over it. This I have done in India; and hence, have gathered up so much in so little time. The world is too big, and life is too short, to go and stay everywhere. Skim, fly, read, study, hear, question, keep eyes and ears all wide open, and, with the geography of a country well in your head, you can understand its commerce, and trade, and life, pretty well afterward.

# LETTER XXXVI.

### ON THE ARABIAN AND RED SEAS.

Lascars, Africans, Chinese, Portuguese, and Englishmen, managing a Steamer.—The Infernal Sun of India.—The Reservoir of Surplus Englishmen.—How India exhausts European Life.—The British Soldier's Luxurious Life in Peace.—The Native Troops of India.—The Grip of England upon India.—Effect of Christianity upon Hindoos and Mohammedans.—The Hindoo Pantheon and 333,000,000 Gods.—The Brahmin Castes.—Bankers below Barbers.—Arabs and their Ocean Craft.—Railroad from London to Bombay.—Time, Five Days.—England encore, toujours, forever and ever.—The Red-Hot Red Sea.—This Unfinished Part of the Earth.—Aden the Fag End of Creation.—The Divers of Aden.—Strings of Camels Led by their Noses.—The Proper Time to Travel in the East.—Fares and Distances.

ON THE ARABIAN SEA, *November* 7, 1871.

I AM on board the steamer Sumatra, bound to Aden (1,664 miles from Bombay), and to Suez (1,308 from Aden, distance in all, 2,972 miles). I have two weeks (the time of the voyage) to read, write, and think in. The steamer is one of the first-class of the P. & O. line, and nearly all the passengers we have, about thirty, are used-up Englishmen, on their way home to recruit, or, English women, faded in India, and white and pale, and going home to get red and rosy again, with some dozen children, the palest, sickliest, puniest little doll babies, that Indian nurses, men nurses as well as women nurses, ever had to care for. There are about one hundred and thirty in all of the crew; Lascars for sailors (it takes three of them, at least, to do one Englishman's work), negroes, from the coast of Africa as firemen, red-hot black fellows, who, born under Africa's fiery sun, now stand England's red-hot coal, even down in the third story of a ship, where no air ever gets, except through the windsail; Portuguese (mixed breeds) for servants in the cabin; Chinamen for carpenters and other like smart work; and a few Europeans, for brains, as captain, quartermaster, engineers, clerks, doctor, etc., etc. Take us all in all, we are a very motley set; and considering that the most of us have been *fried out* during the summer, in India, or Ceylon, or China, the wonder is, that there is stamina enough in any of us to eat and to drink; but there is, for all, save the pale, washed-out ladies, do duty regularly at table three times per day, if not four, or more. The sea is as smooth as a lake—this is not the raging monsoon season—and we make our 230, 240, 250, or 260 miles per day, without trouble, but able to do more, if consistent with the time regulations of the company, that has so to manage as to bring in a China steamer at the same time with a Bombay, and Australian steamer, too, and to meet those coming from Southampton (Eng.), and Brindisi (Italy), to Alexandria. But, though we eat and drink freely, there is scarcely life enough left in the passengers to talk. All are as solemn as owls. The starch is out of most of us. There is no singing, dancing, and making merry, as among the Galle-Calcutta passengers, fresh from England—while now, the chatter is of the infernal sun of India, the fevers, the jungles, the bungalows (houses), only kept cool by the punkahs, and with grass doors, ever kept wet by a constant throw of water on them from the coolies. What a life Englishmen thus lead in India, for gold, or glory, or what is more likely, from inability to live at home, and, therefore, under the necessity of earning a livelihood abroad!

India now, I see, is what our great West is—the reservoir of the surplus life of the old country. What England would do, but for this reservoir, into which to empty its gentry, I cannot well see. Perhaps Englishmen revolutionize, as the French do, for the want of some such reservoir to empty their surplus life into. India is England's great office *placer*, where, mine the educated youth of England, who can find nothing to do at home (save work, and *that* is not fashionable there); or, where are banished officers of the army (legion in number), in command of the native troops of India. India rescues England from the proud and educated, the idle, but not hard-working, Englishmen. Much of the best blood of England is in India, no more idle, though, than it is at home; for, when it finds no vent in wars, it hunts tigers, or leopards, or panthers, or deer, or any thing, even elephants, that the jungles hide. It is no sinecure, certainly, to command in a country where you have to use punkahs and grass-covered doors, ever wet with water, to be able to live at all. Nevertheless, life is so judiciously economized in India by the government, that the European lives, and recovers, often, even from a lost liver. When sickness, or threatened sickness, assails him, he is sent home. Even when well, he is allowed to go to England every five or six years, and to stay a year to recruit in. The laws of health have been so well studied, that when illness threatens in the plains, the highlands are resorted to, and every thing that can be done in dress, barracks, and provisions, for the British soldier, to save his life, is here done. In person, all he has to do is to drill in early morning, or at sunset in the evening. Coolies wait upon him. All his cooking is done by others, and baths are provided for him. The sanitary regulations are now the best human ingenuity can devise to save life, and they are generally successful.

All British officers acknowledge that England has a very frail hold on India, and that it could not hold it a day without an army over 200,000 strong. Nevertheless, its *grip* is greater and closer now than ever before. To say nothing of the reaction in favor of British power since it quelled the terrible mutiny, its railroad and telegraph systems are worth to it 100,-000 soldiers, or more. There is no confidence between Englishmen, and Hindoos, and Mohammedans. There is no bond of unity in any way, except that of force. The races are in all respects repugnant, the one to the other. To increase its security, the Government makes up the native regiments about one-half from Hindoos, and the other Mohammedans; and it relies more upon the Sikh soldier for protection than upon any other—the Sikh from the up-country, who has great contempt for the men of the plains—the Sikh, who, in the last mutiny, stood faithful, when every thing else was dropping away. Education is doing something to soften the mistrust of race; but Christian missions, as yet, seem to be doing little or nothing. Education, however, at first, only makes Deists of Hindoos and Mohammedans. It takes away from them all respect for their own customs, while it cannot sever them from the associations of their brethren and kindred. They lose their respect for the Koran and the Vedas, and yet they have no more respect for the Bible. But, doubtless, this is a process through which the heathen mind has to go, before it can comprehend the sublime truths of Christianity. According to the best authorities, the Hindoo Pantheon is peopled by precisely 333,000,000 gods—and such a lot of divinities, of course, are not to be got rid of in a hurry! Then, the castes are not to be broken down without tremendous social struggles. The Brahmins, even, count 2,000 separate, distinct families of their order alone! Then, the abominable castes in some parts of India—that is, the outcasts—outnumber these Brahmins in the proportion of three to one, exclusive of the other impure and very low tribes! Bankers in Bengal rank below barbers! But I shall not write a book on castes. Nor shall I dwell more upon the Indian, as contrasted with the European—for what can I know in my flight over, and through the land? All I can give is impressions;

and one of the most vivid of my impressions is, that the Indian is far inferior to the Chinese or the Japanese, in almost every quality that goes to make up the man.

This Arabian Sea I am coasting along has all sorts of a history, from the days when Alexander's fleet was off the Persian Gulf, to the victorious eras of the Arabs, who led the way to the coast of Malabar. But the Arab fleets do not amount to much now. They *do* bring down coffee from Mocha, and little things from Muscat; but their ocean craft cannot have improved much for a thousand years. Despite the English gunboats, they keep up the slave trade from Zanguebar, and run the gauntlet to Turkish ports, here and there, in order to find a market for the chattel. It is not creditable to the spirit and spunk of the African—is it?—that even the Indian and the Arab can kidnap and sell him? But let us not undervalue this Arab, as once, if not now, he was a mighty man, not only of the East, but of parts of the West; for he gave us our algebra, our numerals, and other arts and sciences too numerous to number here. Just now, the Turk has got him under foot; but he is fighting in Arabia this very day, as I go by, to recover his lost prestige, and Turkish fleets and Turkish armies float all about here, in order to keep the Arab down.

Shall we always have to go to Aden, and roast in the Red Sea, in order to get to, or from Europe? No! A railroad, to run from London to Bombay in five days, is earnestly talked of even now, to do away with the twenty-one days by sea; and some such rail, within twenty years, will be laid, the way the world hurries on. *That* road will run through Constantinople to Bombay—in the Valley of the Tigris, by the ruins of Nineveh, and where once were Seleucia, Ctesiphon, Ophir, etc. All sorts of plans, however, are now laid out to connect India by rail with Europe. The Russians have their plan, as well as the English; but the English, since the opening of the Suez Canal to commerce, ought, as a measure of power, if not of speed, to be pretty well content with the waters that, in a month or less, will float a British steamer from Southampton to Bombay.

• • • • • •

ADEN, *November* 12.

*Encore*, Anglais! *Toujours*, Anglais! England forever, and ever, and ever! There, is the British flag once more, on top of these volcanic crags of Aden! There, is a British (white) regiment, and there, is another, coffee-colored, regiment; and there, is a battalion of British artillery, a fort, etc., etc. Is there no end of England? There, is a British steam engine, condensing ocean salt water for these poor, exiled soldiers to drink, and there, is a British steam-machine, making ice to cool off the wretches, whom the volcanic sun is roasting. A few hours' steam beyond this is the little (British) Island of Perim, in the mouth of the Straits of Babelmandel, seized by the English, and covered with British guns, to command the entrance to, and exit from the Red Sea. Aden, and this whole country round about here, certainly, as we read in Bible history, were among the first places the Lord made on earth—if not Aden, the Red Sea, and Mount Sinai—and all bear marks, in the dry rocks, on which the rain seldom or never pours, and on the sandy deserts, of the very earliest of the arts of world-making. Certain, it has never been finished, never covered with grass, never adorned with trees, but left, as laid out, for the sun to roast and bake, with all who would venture to dwell thereon. Nevertheless, the British have made Aden habitable. They have laid out excellent roads. They have remade the ancient tanks, where once water was, but not a drop now. They have tempted over the Somauli—bright sort of darkies, without woolly heads—from the African coast, to work for them, and they have tempted the Arabs from the interior to come in on their camels, and sell them notions of many kinds. One can now live in Aden. One need not necessarily die during the year; but the officer of a life insurance company who should issue a policy longer than that on a dweller in Aden, ought to be dismissed for incompetency of judgment, to say nothing more.

But Aden *is* the fag-end of creation—the jumping-off place of Ishmael, nevertheless. The population live (no Europeans among them, except the officials), I should say, from my first introduction, by *div-*

*ing*—that is, by jumping into the water, and diving down deep for the sixpences and the coppers travellers throw there to tempt them. Swarms of youngsters hovered around our steamer, swam all day, and twenty, thirty, or forty would dive for a copper, if you threw it into the water, some one always getting it, or under the steamer, for a sixpence, coming out safe and sound, under twenty feet of water. But all, of course, do not live by diving. There are hosts of coalers for the steamers passing by. There are four steamers in the harbor to-day, all coaling. Then, there are strings and strings of camels, with the nose of one tied to the tail of another, stretching into town and stretching out. The curiosity trade of this place for strangers is ostrich feathers; but this being the Jews' Sabbath, who have the monopoly of the business, few or none were offering, and the trade was hard to drive—(cost, 150 to 200 cents, or less, for first-rates, price demanded, $5 to $10). I rode out three or four miles to the cantonments of the soldiers, and to see the tanks, which ought to hold the water that won't now run down from the mountains into them. The tanks are a grand work; and the cantonments do credit to the care the British take of their soldiers.

. . . . . . . .

THE RED SEA, *November* 15.

I am passing by where Mount Sinai, if not Mount Horeb, ought to be seen among the high-towering mounts upon my right. I have taken out Genesis, and Exodus, and Leviticus, to read the whole story of Pharaoh and his host, and of Moses, and the stiffnecked Israelites, the forty years' wandering in the not very big wilderness, and the promised land. The Bedouin Arabs now have possession of all this land, and it is unsafe to go upon it—so unsafe, that the Egyptians and the British have built their lighthouses for the Red Sea on the opposite (African) coast, not daring to trust the keepers to the tender mercies of these Arabs, whose hands are yet against every man. We have just passed Abyssinia, where, a few years ago, a great British host, both from England and from India, were mustered to punish the king for some disrespect to the British authorities; and we have passed Nubia, and Yeddah, where the Mohammedans land, by the thousands, from all parts of the East, to make their pilgrimage to Mecca; and we are now off Egypt, in a cooler air, fuller of oxygen, with some vitality in it, so that we can breathe with a will once more.

All sorts of tales are told of the Red Sea navigation, some of which are true, among them, one—that at times it is so hot here, passengers on board the ships drop down dead from heat, apoplexy, or exhaustion. Now and then it is so hot, that steamers running down the sea with the wind are obliged to change their course, and go backward, to catch some puffs of air, both to preserve the lives of their firemen and passengers. The hot air of the deserts—the simoon, it may be—actually melts people, when shut up in this Red Sea furnace. But, just now, as we are entering the Gulf of Suez, the air from the north is exhilarating and charming. For the first time since I have been in the East, save the few weeks I was in or near Pekin and the Great Wall, I begin to breathe an air such as I have been accustomed to in Europe and at home. The sun, in this dry atmosphere, is no longer man's terrible enemy. It is a dreadful thing to feel, as one does all the while in India and China, that the sun, which gives life and verdure to the earth, is European man's greatest enemy—as fatal to him, without pith-protecting hat, or thick umbrella, as bullet or cannon-ball.

But I have taken the wrong season to travel in the East. What an American ought to do, is to leave San Francisco in August, see Japan a month or less, and then, dodging Shanghai, make his way, in September or October, to Pekin; then, returning by the way of Shanghai, see that place; then, coast off China; then, to Hong Kong and Canton; thence sail for Singapore and Calcutta, to reach there in December, tarrying not over two months, and being sure that he is out of India in February. The voyage, then, to Egypt and the Holy Land will be pleasant in March, and one has all Europe before him for the summer. I nearly reversed this order of the months, because it is only in the summer, just now, that I can travel. I would not advise any other traveller to follow my months and my course here, in the East—for the sun *may* send him to his long home, before he would wish to go there.

* * * * *

Suez, *November* 18.

Before I part with the Red Sea, as a guide to future travellers, I will add, the cost of fares from Southampton (Eng.) to Shanghai (China), which has been much reduced of late, in consequence of competition with the French *Messagerie* line, the American (San Francisco) line, and the Holt's line, which runs from Liverpool through the Suez Canal without change of steamer. These rates do not include wines, or the £3 railroad fare over the Egyptian road, from Suez to Alexandria (224 miles' run, at night, in 10 hours).

*Rates of Passage from Brindisi (Italy) to Southampton (Eng.) to—*

| | | | |
|---|---|---|---|
| Aden | £40 | Batavia | £85 |
| Bombay | 60 | Hong Kong | 85 |
| Ceylon | 60 | Shanghai | 95 |
| Calcutta | 65 | Yokohama | 95 |
| Singapore | 75 | Melbourne & Sidney | 80 |

The fare from Brindisi to London, by rail, is about 306 francs.

The distances are, from Brindisi to—

|  | Miles. |
|---|---|
| Alexandria | 825 |
| Suez | 224 |
| Aden | 1,308 |
| Bombay | 1,664 |
|  | 4,021 |

|  | Miles. |
|---|---|
| From Bombay to Galle (Ceylon) | 911 |
| "         "       Penang | 2,124 |
| "         "       Singapore | 2,505 |
| "         "       Hong Kong | 3,942 |
| "         "       Shanghai | 4,812 |
| "         "       Yokohama | 6,432 |

Passengers on the P. & O. line can stop as they please, or go, *via* Madras, Calcutta, and overland by rail, to Bombay, paying their own rail and hotel expenses.

# LETTER XXXVII.

*SUDDEN FLIGHT FROM ASIA AND AFRICA INTO EUROPE.*

Among the Alps.—The Isthmus of Suez.—Suez Canal.—Will it pay?—Egypt and Alexandria.—Confederate Officers in the Pasha's Army.—Horrid (English) Railroad Cars.—Boreas and the Egyptian Sands.—Across the Mediterranean to Brindisi.—Things in Brindisi and Turin.—How cold it is.—Mt. Cenis and the Great Tunnel.—Glorious Scenery.

TURIN (ITALY), *November* 23, 1871.

ANOTHER Hegira. Mohammed, the inventor of Hegiras, didn't fly so fast as I have been flying some time back. I was roasting in Suez, on the Red Sea, on the 18th, at night, and now I am freezing here, in the Alps, among snow and snow-storms. I have been hot so long, roasted so often, in China, Ceylon, and India, and the tropics, that I had forgotten there was need of thick clothing; and here I am stopping to buy wool and woollens, and furs, and comforters, to keep even tolerably warm. The hills are all white with snow. Muffs, boas, etc., protect the women from the blasts, and the men, wrapped up in furs, chatter their teeth, and shiver and shake. What a sudden change from the gauzes and linens of India, and the Arabian and Red Seas!

Well—but how did you get here so quick? What

did you see? I shot through Egypt in a night (my excuse is, that I had seen the Pyramids and the Nile before). A whole day was given us at Suez, to see the Suez Canal, and to see, if we could see, where Moses led the Israelites over that Red Sea, and where Pharaoh and his chariots and his hosts went under. Now that I have seen the borders of the desert, where for forty years the Israelites wandered, I marvel no more, as I once did, that they looked upon the rocks of Jerusalem and its surroundings as the promised land—for rocks and crags, even, are preferable to interminable sands. No wonder the Israelites were happy when they got into grass and vegetables, and had something better to eat than sands and manna. What, however, more interests the Present than even the Biblical history, is the better turn, the moderns have made of the Red Sea waters in the great Suez Canal. There were five steamers coming through the day we were there. The canal is a perfect success for the commerce of Europe and Asia, and the world owes a great debt to M. Lesseps for forcing it through, despite all English ministerial opposition. It hardly pays, however, and probably never will pay, until it passes into English hands, which, sooner or later, will have a majority of the stock, and then, at low prices, make that stock profitable.

Alexandria is a great city for commerce now, but the canal is already making a hole in its trade, and will soon make a greater hole. Vessels of all nations, but ours, are now in its port. We are *minus* almost everywhere, I am sorry to say. Our American Confederate officers are numerous, I am told, in the Pasha's army, and are making good artillerists and soldiers of the Egyptians; but American vessels on the Mediterranean, this part of it, at least, are scarce, very scarce. We got out of the railroad cars early in the morning, miserable and worn. The English compartment car is here, and a miserable thing it is, in a night ride, for India-worn travellers. Such a sorry, forlorn set of us, as turned up in the ferry-boat in the morning, from all parts of Asia and Australia (two steamers, pretty full, had disembarked their passengers at Suez, and met here)—the lame, the halt, the blind, some on litters, others in arms—the travelling world seldom sees. There are no sleeping-cars. We had to sit bolt upright, all night, and study Egyptian astrology, as we peeped through the windows, or lamp-ology, if we looked at the lamp streaming in our eyes. One set of the miserables departed forthwith for Southampton, direct; another set, I among them, for the old Roman port of Brundusium, once the great exit of the Cæsars, for Greece and the East. A sand wind blew from the coast, and littered every thing on deck with atoms of sand. I was glad to be out of Alexandria that day, therefore, as fast as steam could carry us.

Our steamer was the Candia, a wretched concern, ever so old, and half a century behind the age; but it was commanded by a handsome fellow, a little over sixty, whom the English call "Gentleman George." I thought he was the Lord High Admiral of all the East, the first squint I had of him. The P. & O. line of steamers have, almost everywhere, superb officers, first-rate sailors, as well as well-bred men; but such "a swell" as Gentleman George of the Candia, I never met before. It is a mistake, though, to waste so much talent upon the sea. He ought to be the Lord High Chamberlain at St. James's or Windsor Castle. We should have been in Brindisi in about seventy hours from Alexandria, but we brought it, in seventy-five hours—for, though Boreas blew dead against us, our Gentleman George counteracted him by blowing on board. We lost our way at night, and, in the morning, got in only by tracking the colored water on the coast; but I never felt any alarm, nay, should not have felt any, if Vulcan had given out in steam, or Boreas in wind—for there were enough of both in Gentleman George to drive any ship ahead.

Brindisi, that Horace and many other classics wrote of, more or less, died when Rome died, but is reviving fast, now, as the shortest railroad terminus to Egypt and the East. We stopped there two or three hours, full long enough to see all now worth seeing in Brindisi, unless one is an antiquarian, or archæologist, or a student of classical lore. The telegraph runs from here all over the world; and the railroads all over the European part of it. The port is re-made, and a very good port it is, now, with water enough for any ship that comes along. We left at noon on the 22d, and were in Turin at 10 A. M., on the 23d—distance, about 575 miles, but that is the time. Bologna and several other famous places were passed in the night; but nothing tempts me to stop now. My head is full of sights, and all I crave is to see no more—which only proves what I have written before, that three months' continuous travel and sight-seeing is about as much as the human mind can stand, on one stretch, after which all is labor, labor.

In Turin there is a good deal to see, if one is not travel-blinded, as I am now. Its shops are pretty. There are many beautiful buildings. Its streets are all in fine order. The hotels are many, and all seem excellent. The King of Italy no longer lives here, and the Court is gone; but Turin is worth a tourist's day, and the bazaars are very tempting. All I want, or crave, however, is to be warm, warm. I begin to wish I was back in Bombay or Calcutta. The snow, that at first looked so bewitching on the Appenines and the Adriatic Sea, as we flew along the railroad track, amid miles and miles of olive plantations, is no more bewitching now. An icicle, which four or five days ago I would have given at least a rupee to look at, is a hateful sight to-day.

Don't talk to me of Italy, any part of it, as a retreat to spend the winter in. I have tried all parts of it, in winter—half-frozen in all. I am pencilling now with an overcoat on, and a woollen glove on the unwriting hand, to keep it warm, while a costly wood-fire, bought by the pound, is blazing before me —all the heat going up chimney, though. Don't talk to me of Pisa, where once doctors sent consumptive victims, to be sure to die; or, of Florence, or Rome, or Naples. The sun is hot enough, when, at noonday, you are in it; but indoors, on marble or wooden floors, or even on carpeted floors, you shake and shiver, and your teeth chatter, and you long for the coal fires of home. The only place in Europe to spend a winter in is St. Petersburg, or, possibly, England, where the fires are good, and the comforts are great; or, to use a solecism, in Cairo, in Africa. There is not a winter's comfort for an American, or an Englishman, in winter, south of the British Channel.

. . . . . .

Mr. Cenis, or the Great Alpine Tunnel, *November* 24.

But, there *is* something new to see, travel-blinded as I am, and *that* is this tunnel, and the approach to it on the Italian side. Wonderful work! I crossed, and re-crossed, Mt. Cenis and other Alps, years ago, on foot, with a pack on my back; but then there was no pleasure like this, now, amid snow, and ice, and glaciers, little, if not big. Two or three locomotives are taking us up the ascent, and we seem to be transferred from the plains of Italy to Alpine cottages, as if on wings. The sun is illuminating every mountain crag, and the ice is reflecting, and respreading, his rays. We are all in a high state of excitement as we enter the tunnel, which is eight miles long, and which we are to be twenty-five minutes in passing. The cars are lit by gas, and well heated with long hot-water metal foot-warmers. The thermometer must be in the neighborhood of zero.

• • • • • • •

IN FRANCE.

Wonderful work, indeed! We are now on the French side, and the sun is hid, and there is but little to see, save mist and snow. The gas-light of our car-compartment was jostled out by some jerking motion of the car, and we were left in total darkness in the heart of the Mount. Then it was that a Frenchman's economy and love of smoking turned to use for us all. Out of his carpet-bag came the relics of his candle, that he had paid a franc for, the night before, in his Italian hotel (the Frenchmen always carry their candle bits away; we, less prudent, leave them behind)—and out of his cigar match-box came his match, and with the two we soon replaced the lost gas-light, and re-lit the gas.

The Indies and the East are made a day nearer by the opening of this Mt. Cenis tunnel, and Italy and France are brought close together. The British India mail is now going this way, instead of going through Germany.

The soft, soothing tongue of Italy is heard no more, and we are hearing the short, sharp, curt syllables of the French. The nuisance of passports begins here—here, in this now Republican France—while Italy, a monarchy, is freed from them. I have passed through all Asia, and a part of Africa, and never heard of a passport; but here the French officials huddle us up in a coop and demand one. I happened to have one, describing me years and years ago, which is no more a description of me now, than Senex would be of Juventus; but what matters? It is in English, and the French officials cannot read a line of it. There were venerable French *visas* enough on it to suit either the Republic or the Empire—for I was in France when there was a commotion once before. There were some Australians with us, on their way to England, who, like us, had not stopped long enough any where, since they left Melbourne, to have a passport made out; but we coaxed them through, and the French officials were yielding, and very polite—as grave as owls, however, in warning them never thus to venture through France again without the inevitable passport. My American *vouching* for them, I think, had more influence with the officials than the half-dozen Englishmen who were helping them along; for the French officials must have felt sure an American was not conspiring for the re-instalment of the empire, whatever monarchical Englishman might be thinking of doing.

You will hear from me next in Paris, where I am bound for a rest, and a refit, and for repairs in general, after this long and hasty flight.

## LETTER XXXVIII.

*THINGS IN PARIS AND LONDON.*

Things in Paris and in London.—Shopping in both Cities.—Paris sad just now.—
An American almost Home in England.—Liverpool.—Rough Rocking on the
Atlantic.—Put into Newfoundland for Coal.—St. John's.—Fishermen there.—
Home again, Sweet Home, etc.

PARIS, *December* 10, 1871.

FROM the great capitals of Yedo, Pekin, and the great cities of Canton, Calcutta, and Bombay, coming as rapidly as I have, it seems like a dream to be here, in what deems itself the very focus of civilization, and in what is (or has been), in many respects, the most attractive city of the world. But, of Paris I can scribble nothing new, unless I tell you, I am here repairing, refitting, just as you repair and refit a hulk that has been knocking around the world, and has lost much of its rigging. One's wardrobe melts away in the heats of the tropics, and I am scraping up the relics of my India-rubber overcoat and galoches, that have melted under the heats of Singapore and Penang. I find my woollens well spotted and inclined to be rotten. More experienced travellers take this voyage of mine in tin trunks, whereas I have used only my American coverings. Gloves look like leopard skins. Razors are so rusty that they remind one of shaving in the Barber of Seville. My companion in travel has but little left, save shreds; and hence, before we can reappear in civilization, we must refit for it.

Paris is the greatest place for shopping on earth. If any member of Congress had half the eloquence of a Parisian shopwoman, his fame would be made as the greatest orator of the age. I have read Isocrates, studied Quintilian in days gone by, read and re-read Cicero *de Oratore;* but I never have so realized Demosthenes's idea of eloquence—*action*, ACTION, as in the action of these Parisian shopwomen. The dear creatures—if they only wore trousers, and would come over to the United States—not a man could stand up against them in stump-speaking. But, oh, how they will fib! What marvellous tales they will tell! and how they will swear to them—and you could not help believing them all, if you had not been standing such batteries of eloquent action, a long lifetime. The East India shopkeepers are eloquent, and the Chinese have but little regard for truth; but the French shopwoman will fib with such grace and gentleness, that she insinuates herself into your pocket, despite your head, while all is done with such dignified suavity, that you could not contradict, if you would. If you order a garment to be made, you have not the least certainty that it will be done within a week after the day promised. You make all your arrangements to depart on a certain day, bid adieu to your banker, and settle up accounts with him, but the promised articles do not begin to appear. In rage you rush to the shop to scold. . . .

"Madam, you solemnly promised me to have it ready on Saturday."
"*C'est vrai*, monsieur, and it shall be ready on Saturday."
"And why is it not ready?"
"Ah, monsieur, you did not say this Saturday; if you had, it should have been all ready. But you said 'Saturday week.'"

The dodge was irresistible. I gave up in despair, happy to have a fresh promise that it would be done the *Wednesday* before " the Saturday week."

I lectured another breaker of promises. There was no dodging the point I made with her; and I ended with saying:

"I am willing to stay in Paris all winter, madame, waiting for your things, if you will only pay my hotel bills."
*Madame* (in reply)—"I should be too happy to do that, and thus have the pleasure of seeing you every day."

What could be done with such French politeness as that? I gave up, and pay my own hotel bills, of course.

### ANOTHER SCENE.

*Monsieur* (speaking)—" And they are not ready?" (with a sigh, and the most plaintive look of appeal).
*Madame*—"No, monsieur. Such a taille; such a figure (throwing up both hands in most eloquent enthusiasm). We are creating the most ravishing robe that ever went from our fingers, and we have put our best artists upon it—and do give us time. You would not hurry up a Raphael, or a Guido, would you? And we shall do something worthy of them!"

The humbug was irresistible. The only way to be sure of any thing in Paris, in a given time, is to get part of it, and then threaten to go off with that part unpaid for, and a promise to pay for the rest when it is all sent, with express expenses paid, in addition. This generally produces a result.

#### ANOTHER SCENE.

*A plump and jovial American at the door*—" Is the jacket of my wife ready ?"

*Madame* (in reply)—" Ah, *mon Dieu*, monsieur, I cannot say. I will inquire. It is a most beautiful jacket."

Passing by me in the room, into another room, *sotto voce*, she says:

"I know it is not (with an indescribable shrug), but what fib shall I tell him now, *le malheureux !* "

The plump American, of course, did not get his wife's jacket.

The fact is, a week or two is not wasted in Paris, to hear the eloquence of French shopwomen. It is more touching than that in the Assembly, now, at Versailles.

And the art with which a French woman makes you buy what you don't want, and pay her own price for it, is wonderful.

"It is ravishing," she exclaims. "It exactly fits your figure and complexion." "It is the last great *chef d'œuvre* of—somebody." "I have sold just such a one to M. ——, your countryman, whose taste, you know, is perfect," etc., etc.

But Paris is sad, sad enough, just now. There are few or no strangers here. The shops have but few, very few, customers. Paper money has made the expenses of living almost as great as in the United States; and paper money is increasing in quantity, and prices are rising. There is snow on the streets, and the cabs with difficulty work their way through. The little wood fires in the hotels but make one shiver, and force upon one the contrasts of the red-hot anthracite at home. (*Mem.*—Never spend a winter in Paris, unless you can have a coal fire.) There seems to be a new revolution impending, and the *feeling* of it in the air affrights strangers off. The hotels, therefore, are as empty as the shops, and the Parisians all look blue.

* * * * * * *

LONDON, *December* 20.

It is refreshing, after a voyage around the world, to be again in an English-speaking country, and to be able to comprehend all you see and hear. An American exile from his own land for months, feels, when here, with all these English surroundings, as if he were home again. And what a wonderful city this is—these millions in it—on so little an island as Great Britain is! No part of our Western country, not even Chicago before its extinction by fire, has grown faster than this London has, within the twenty-five years past. The fields I saw here but a few years ago are now streets, built with palatial houses. No wonder, after all, as I see now, in coming around the world, that London is the heart of the millions of India, as well as the focus of Chinese commerce and trade. This London stretches its arms now all over the earth, and its ships and its capital are in every port where a keel can float.

Think of a man's being thankful that he has not seen the sun here for ten days, save through clouds of coal-smoke and fog, that makes the sun, when shining even, seem as if seen through a smoked glass. I am thus thankful, now. The burning, blazing sun of the East, that I have just escaped from, makes me feel as if I never wished to see the full-orbed sun again; and hence, England in December is not to me the miserable climate it would be to most Americans just now.

The shops of London are the representative shops of the whole earth, in which they differ from Paris, or any other great capitals. The Japanese, the Chinese, the Indians, the Ceylonese, the Borneans, the Moors, the Arabs, the Africans, all have representative shops in London, and there is no place now on earth like London for shopping and shops. The French *modistes* eclipse the English in the arts of creating a beautiful woman, despite nature, too; but the English tailors now are among the first in the world, unless there be exceptions in some of the New York shops. The free trade of England has made every thing here about as cheap as at the place of production, save the necessary expenses of transportation; and hence, the wares of the whole earth can be had almost as cheap as in the places of their creation.

Americans can learn a great many things in London; but Englishmen, it seems to me just now, can learn more in the United States. The English car-travelling is yet almost barbaric; but what is unfortunate, the English have modelled the car-travelling of the greater part of Europe. This is not felt so much on the little isle, where distances are short, as on the Continent, where distances are long, and where our sleeping-cars would be real blessings to the traveller. The imprisonment of an English car is a species of incarceration, that fevers and enrages an American; and no soft cushions or luxuries seem to atone for it. The underground car-travelling in London, and the cab locomotion there, are far superior to any thing we have in the United States. There are no hotels in London to be compared with ours in New York and elsewhere in the States; and prices are practically higher, with fewer luxuries, though the expenses of hotel keeping in London must be far less than in New York.

· · · · · · ·

LIVERPOOL, *December* 23.

Last evening, as I came down from London, exhausted by the kind hospitalities of numerous friends there, I dropped to sleep, and waking up, wondered whether I was in, or had passed, Liverpool, or was shot on to Manchester. There was no way of finding out whether I had overslept or not. The conductor could not be approached. There was no neighbor in my compartment to inquire of. There was no one accessible to answer any question respecting any place, or any thing. The isolation, or incarceration, rather, was like solitary confinement—at least for that part of one's life. When the locomotive halted to coal or water, I popped my head out of the car, screamed to a neighbor in the car in the rear, and learnt that Liverpool had not been reached, and that the rail I was on, could not take me to Manchester. Think of what *profitable* travelling that must be for a stranger in such solitary confinement as this! But we did go fast!—full forty miles an hour, and with ease and safety, too.

. . . . . .

CHRISTMAS and NEW YEAR'S on the rough winter North Atlantic, with furious gales of wind! Never go westward in winter, if you can help it, for the furies of Greenland will be poured out upon you. We have had eleven days of continuous gales, gaining, one day, only forty miles upon the storm!

. . . . . .

ST. JOHN'S (NEWFOUNDLAND), *January* 7, 1872.

The Algeria (our steamer), a sturdy, but not rapid, Cunarder, has put in here for coal. Boreas and Vulcan have had a terrible tuzzle for two weeks, or more, on board the steamer, and Vulcan, exhausted, knocks under, and makes for Newfoundland, to recruit in fuel and steam.

One does not feel exactly comfortable in approaching a rock-bound coast, in the thickest sort of a fog, where the entrance to the harbor, as that of St. John's, is hardly wider than the length of the steamer. No lighthouse or beacon could be seen—nothing, indeed, save fog, fog, fog; but by the help of our guns, responded to by guns at the mouth of the harbor, we felt our way safely in—and *felt* much better when we found coal enough for us in store from the Nova Scotia mines.

*The* Saint, John, has his name affixed to many places over the world, but to none other, I believe, in so cold and inhospitable a climate as this. It is a very religious place, too, judging by the throngs going to church, and returning therefrom, in the furious snow-storm to-day. The Catholic Church here, as I judge by the numbers attending, is, numerically, the most powerful. Immense crowds, morning, noon, and afternoon, thronged into the capacious cathedral, all responding with feeling and fervor to the services of the priest of that church. The most of the great crowd — nearly all, well dressed — must have been fishermen, as were the Apostles of old, for the odor of fish rose above the odor of incense. The seal-oil trade is great here, and much of it once went to the United States, where it is now excluded by a high tariff. The seals are now hunted by steamers, several of which are now in the harbor, to start as the spring opens, in order to chase down the seals on the floating cakes of ice. Agriculture amounts to but little, very little, in Newfoundland. The ocean is the great *placer* to be worked for wealth. A wild story is now travelling here of a Labradorian mail-carrier, who started from St. John's this winter, in his snowshoes, and whom the wolves devoured, on his way to the interior, leaving nothing of him and his charge but his gun and a portion of the uneaten mail, while several slain wolves were about, shot by the mail-carrier before he was devoured.

· · · · ·

NEW YORK, *January* 12, 1872.

Once more at home! "Sweet home!" I feel like re-singing the song of Catullus, when apostrophizing his Peninsular home of Sirmio.

[From Catullus, Car. 28.]
O quid solutis est beatius curis?
Cum mens onus reponit ac peregrino
Labore fessi venimus larem ad nostrum
Desideratoque acquiescimus lecto.

My own, my chosen home, oh, what more blest
   Than that sweet pause of troubles when the mind
Flings off its burden, and when, long oppressed
   By cares abroad and foreign toil, we find
Our native home again, and rest our head
Once more upon our long lost, long wished-for bed.

# HOME FROM A FOREIGN SHORE.

ARRIVAL OF HON. JAMES BROOKS IN THE ALGERIA.—A LONG VOYAGE, AND A HEARTY WELCOME HOME.

[*From the New York World, January* 13, 1872.]

A numerous party of the private and professional friends of the Hon. James Brooks yesterday proceeded down the bay to accord a welcome to that gentleman on his arrival home after a long and perilous journey. It having been ascertained that Mr. Brooks would arrive by the Cunard steamer Algeria, the Henry Smith, Captain Baulsier, with the band from Governor's Island on board, had on the previous day gone in search of this long over-due vessel, but, as she failed to put in an appearance before sun-down, it had been arranged that the trip should be repeated early on the morrow. Accordingly, Colonel Ingalls having again placed the Henry Smith at the disposal of the reception committee, the welcoming party left Whitehall yesterday morning, at the rather unreasonable hour of 7 o'clock. The steamer was gaily decorated with flags, and on the pilot-house was displayed a white banner, bearing the words : "The friends of the Hon. James Brooks. Welcome !" The military band was again in attendance, and discoursed pleasant music on the trip down. Arriving at the quarantine pier at about 9 o'clock, it was found that a telegram had just been received from Sandy Hook, stating that the Algeria had that moment crossed the bar. The reception party, therefore, quickly pinned on their badges of white silk, each of which bore the word "welcome," and proceeded slowly down the bay. On reaching Fort Tompkins the long-expected steamer was discovered in the distance, with her fore and main top-mast housed. Steam was therefore shut off, and the Henry Smith lay to, only waiting to run alongside the Algeria directly that vessel would be abreast the fort. Meanwhile, the final preparations for the reception were completed, it being arranged that ex-Mayor Gunther should make a short welcoming address, to which Mr. Brooks would necessarily reply. At about 10 o'clock, therefore, the Henry Smith, with band playing "Home, Sweet Home," gave three tremendous shrieks with her whistle, dipping, at the same time, the flag at her bow out of respect to the English steamer. This was followed by a hawser being cast from the Algeria when the smaller steamer drew alongside. Then came the congratulations of Mr. Brooks's friends, who were, however, unable to grasp him by the hand, but contented themselves with handkerchief-waving, cheering, and entertainments of a similar character. This welcome met with a hearty response from both the cabin and steerage passengers on the Algeria, the latter, who seemed to be pretty well worn out with their long voyage, being particularly demonstrative in their joy. Then, as the two steamers proceeded alongside each other, all manner of inquiries were exchanged between the welcomers and the welcomed.

When off quarantine, the anchor was dropped, and Drs. Carnochan and Mosher immediately appeared in the Fletcher and commenced to pass the passengers. On a second hawser being thrown to the Henry Smith, the two vessels were drawn near each other, when Mr. Gavit sprang off the paddle-box where he had been standing, cleared the bulwarks of the Algeria with a bound, and in less than a second had thrown his arms around Mr. Brooks's neck and was hugging and kissing him. So suddenly had the attack been made that the recipient of this outburst of affection had had no time to place himself in an attitude of defence, but was compelled to receive and bear all with a smiling countenance. As soon as he could conveniently do so, Mr. Brooks quickly and in a dignified manner unlocked himself from Mr. Gavit's passionate embrace, and forthwith saluted his son, who had followed closely on the heels of the demonstrative committeeman. Then the other members of the committee poured over the side of the vessel, and one general round of embracing and saluting went on for some minutes. Miss Brooks, who had accompanied her father on his grand tour, was also the recipient of many welcomes. Both the voyagers appeared in excellent health, and seemed to have benefited by their protracted journey. Mr. Brooks having changed his seal-skin travelling cap for a more official-looking silk hat, was fully prepared for the inevitable address, which was forthwith spoken by Mr. Gunther on the deck of the Algeria. After extending a hearty welcome to Mr. Brooks the ex-Mayor proceeded to state that he hailed him as a representative man, and as such was always proud to welcome him. Many days had occurred since Mr. Brooks's departure for the Old World, and they were therefore doubly pleased to have Mr. Brooks again in their midst. In behalf of the city, his constitutents, and the country generally, he gave him a hearty welcome. Mr. Brooks replied that he felt extremely proud for the reception which they had accorded him; in fact, it had been quite an ovation, and totally unexpected by him. He was proud to be a representative man, and would speedily set about using his utmost endeavors to set right any principles that might have suffered by his absence. As his career had been in the past, so it would be in the future. Since May last, when he left this country, he had travelled more than thirty thousand miles, and felt very glad to be again in the midst of his friends, and he could assure them that to him there was no place like home.

A great waving of handkerchiefs and much cheering followed at the conclusion of these remarks, and the band appropriately began to play " Home Again." Mr. Brooks was then taken on board the Henry Smith, his daughter accompanying him, and immediately conducted to the saloon, where a repast had been prepared. Miss Brooks, being the only lady on board, retired to the after-cabin, where she passed the time in her brother's company. At the lunch the customary toasts were given and responded to, the only noticeable feature in the proceedings being a tendency among the guests to pledge Mr. Brooks's health in champagne about every thirty seconds. Having landed the young lady at the Battery, the Henry Smith proceeded to the Cunard Dock in Jersey City, where Mr. Brooks obtained his luggage. Four carriages were in waiting, and into them the private friends of Mr. Brooks entered, the whole party proceeding to his residence in Fifth Avenue—not before, however, the old editor had paid a visit to the office of his journal on Park Row. At the private residence the guests were received by Mr. and Mrs. Brooks, who, after exhibiting the various trophies that the travellers had brought and sent from abroad, conducted them to the dining-room, where an elegant luncheon was provided. After partaking of refreshment it suddenly appeared to the guests that the host and hostess had been sufficiently worried for one day, so, beating a hasty retreat, the whole party left and came down town.

THE END.

# THE DESCENT OF MAN,

### AND

## SELECTION IN RELATION TO SEX.

### BY
### CHAS. DARWIN, M. A., F. R. S.

Two Vols., 12mo.

## WITH ILLUSTRATIONS.

PRICE, . . . . . $4.00

In these volumes Mr. Darwin has brought forward all the facts and arguments which science has to offer in favor of the doctrine that man has arisen by gradual development from the lowest point of animal life. He had originally intended this work as a posthumous publication, but the extensive acceptance of the views unfolded in his book on the "Origin of Species" induced him to believe that the public were ripe for the most advanced deductions from his theory of "Natural Selection." Aside from the logical purpose which Mr. Darwin had in view, his work is an original and fascinating contribution to the most interesting portion of natural history.

### From the *London Spectator*.

"For our part, we find Dr. Darwin's vindication of the origin of man a far more wonderful vindication of Theism than Paley's 'Natural Theology,' though we do not know, so reticent is his style, whether or not he conceives it himself."

### From the *Citizen and Round Table*.

"Even the charge of atheism, which was so violently urged against Mr. Darwin, is now rarely heard, and theologians, whose orthodoxy is unquestioned, have ventured to admit that it is possible to believe both in Christianity and the Darwinian theory at the same time."

### From the *Charleston Courier*.

"No one can rise from an ordinarily attentive consideration of Mr. Darwin's treatise, without being impressed, not only with the extent and depth of the knowledge which he has attained upon the subject under treatment, and his long, unwearied labor in collecting *facts*, but also with his possession of qualities equally rare—the true scientific temper, the transparent candor, and the truth-seeking soberness, with which he expresses to you his conclusions, and the processes by which he reaches them.

"Whether you like his discourse or not—though you may refuse to acquiesce in his conclusions—still you are compelled to bear your witness, that this man has *not* been laboring to find facts to support a preconceived theory, but *that the theory is the irrepressible outgrowth of his accumulated facts*."

### From the *Evening Bulletin*.

"This theory is now indorsed by many eminent scientists, who at first combated it, including Sir Charles Lyell, probably the most learned of living geologists, and even by a class of Christian divines like Dr. McCosh, who think that certain theories of cosmogony, like the nebular hypothesis and the law of evolution, may be accepted without doing violence to faith."

Sent *free, by mail*, to any address in the U. S., on receipt of the price.

## D. APPLETON & CO., Publishers.

# COOPER'S
# LEATHER-STOCKING NOVELS.

"THE ENDURING MONUMENTS OF FENIMORE COOPER ARE HIS WORKS. WHILE THE LOVE OF COUNTRY CONTINUES TO PREVAIL, HIS MEMORY WILL EXIST IN THE HEARTS OF THE PEOPLE. SO TRULY PATRIOTIC AND AMERICAN THROUGHOUT, THEY SHOULD FIND A PLACE IN EVERY AMERICAN'S LIBRARY."—*Daniel Webster.*

## A NEW AND
## SPLENDIDLY-ILLUSTRATED POPULAR EDITION
### OF
### FENIMORE COOPER'S
#### WORLD-FAMOUS
## LEATHER-STOCKING ROMANCES.

D. APPLETON & Co. announce that they have commenced the publication of J. Fenimore Cooper's Novels, in a form designed for general popular circulation. The series begins with the famous "Leather-Stocking Tales," five in number, and will be published in the following order, at intervals of about a month:

        I. The Last of the Mohicans.
   II. The Deerslayer.       IV. The Pioneers.
  III. The Pathfinder.      V. The Prairie.

This edition of the "Leather-Stocking Tales" will be printed in handsome octavo volumes, from new stereotype plates, each volume superbly and fully illustrated with entirely new designs by the distinguished artist, F. O. C. Darley, and bound in an attractive paper cover. *Price,* 75 *cents per volume.*

Heretofore there has been no edition of the acknowledged head of American romancists suitable for general popular circulation, and hence the new issue of these famous novels will be welcomed by the generation of readers that have sprung up since Cooper departed from us. As time progresses, the character, genius, and value of the Cooper Romances become more widely recognized; he is now accepted as the great classic of our American literature, and his books as the prose epics of our early history.

**D. APPLETON & CO., Publishers, New York.**